J.K. LASSER'S

THE NEW BANKRUPTCY LAW AND YOU

Look for these and other titles from J.K. Lasser—Practical Guides for All Your Financial Needs

J.K. Lasser's Year-Round Tax Strategies by David S. De Jong and Ann Gray Jakabin

J.K. Lasser's Pick Winning Mutual Funds by Jerry Tweddell with Jack Pierce

J.K. Lasser's Investor's Tax Guide by Elaine Floyd

J.K. Lasser's Pick Stocks Like Warren Buffett by Warren Boroson

J.K. Lasser's Your Winning Retirement Plan by Henry K. Hebeler

J.K. Lasser's Strategic Investing After 50 by Julie Jason

J.K. Lasser's Small Business Taxes by Barbara Weltman

J.K. Lasser's 1001 Deductions by Barbara Weltman

J.K. Lasser's Homeowner's Tax Breaks by Gerald Robinson

J.K. Lasser's New Rules for Estate Planning and Tax by Harold Apolinsky and Stewart Welch III

J.K. Lasser's From Ebay to Mary Kay: Taxes Made Easy for Your Home Based Business by Gary Carter

J.K. Lasser's The New Bankruptcy Law and You by Nathalie Martin with Stewart Paley

J.K. LASSER'S

THE NEW BANKRUPTCY LAW AND YOU

Nathalie Martin
with
Stewart Paley

WILEY

John Wiley & Sons, Inc.

Published by John Wiley & Sons, Inc., Hoboken, New Jersey.
Published simultaneously in Canada.

Limit of Liability/Disclaimer of Warranty: While the publisher and author have used their best efforts in
preparing this book, they make no representations or warranties with respect to the accuracy or
completeness of the contents of this book and specifically disclaim any implied warranties of
merchantability or fitness for a particular purpose. No warranty may be created or extended by sales
representatives or written sales materials. The advice and strategies contained herein may not be suitable
for your situation. You should consult with a professional where appropriate. Neither the publisher nor
author shall be liable for any loss of profit or any other commercial damages, including but not limited to
special, incidental, consequential, or other damages.

For general information on our other products and services or for technical support, please contact
our Customer Care Department within the United States at (800) 762-2974, outside the United States
at (317) 572-3993, or fax (317) 572-4002.

Wiley also publishes its books in a variety of electronic formats. Some content that appears in print may
not be available in electronic books. For more information about Wiley products, visit our web site
at www.wiley.com.

Designations used by companies to distinguish their products are often claimed by trademarks. In all
instances where the author or publisher is aware of a claim, the product names appear in Initial Capital
letters. Readers, however, should contact the appropriate companies for more complete information
regarding trademarks and registration.

Library of Congress Cataloging-in-Publication Data:
Martin, Nathalie, 1961–
   J.K. Lasser's the new bankruptcy law and you / Nathalie Martin with Stewart Paley.
      p.   cm. — (J.K. Lasser—practical guides for all your financial needs)
   "Published simultaneously in Canada."
   ISBN-13: 978-0-471-75369-8 (pbk.)
   ISBN-10: 0-471-75369-6 (pbk.)
   1. Bankruptcy—United States—Popular works.   2. Debtor and creditor—United
States—Popular works.   I. Title: New bankruptcy law and you.   II. Title: J.K. Lasser's
the new bankruptcy law and you.   III. Paley, Stewart.   IV. Title.   V. Series.
   KF1524.6.M37   2005
   346.7303'8—dc22
                                                                2005020239
Printed in the United States of America.

10 9 8 7 6 5 4 3 2 1

We dedicate this book to our parents
Hyime,
Reva,
Don,
JoAnn,
and
Saul

Acknowledgments

We thank Carmela Starace, Frederick Hart, Jason Kilborn, Reva Paley, Gloria Ortiz, Leigh Haynes, Simone Seiler, and Matthew Garcia for help with early drafts of this book.

Contents

Foreword   xi

Introduction   xiii

1. How Did I Get into This Mess? A Story about Proliferating Credit, Volatile Job Markets, Rising Health Care Costs, and You   1

2. Psychology of Debt 101: It's Not All Your Fault So You Needn't Feel Guilty   9

3. Happiness Through Saving   12

4. The Economics of Consumer Credit   21

5. The Basics of Debtor–Creditor Law: A Quick Vocabulary Lesson   26

6. Do I Need a Bankruptcy at All?: Assessing Your Situation   38

7. The New Law versus the Old Law: If I Need to File, Should I File Now or Later?   51

8. Preparing to File for Bankruptcy: Don't File without Reading This!   57

9. Basics of Bankruptcy Law That Apply to All Bankruptcies 62

10. The Treatment of Secured Creditors in Bankruptcy 82

11. Basic Bankruptcy Procedures 85

12. The Chapter 7 Discharge and Its Limitations 101

13. Keeping Secured Property in a Chapter 7 Case 115

14. Dismissal of a Chapter 7 Case: The New Issue in
    Consumer Bankruptcy 119

15. Chapter 13 Payment Plan Cases 126

16. Business and Bankruptcy Law 146

17. Investing and Your Future 148

Appendix—Chart of State Law Exemptions 151

Glossary 209

References 219

Index 221

Foreword

Bankruptcy filings in the United States doubled between 1994 and 2004, rising from about 833,000 to more than 1.6 million new cases. Nonbusiness (consumer) filings represent over 95 percent of all cases filed. Nationally, there is one bankruptcy for about every 73 households. In some states, there are as few as 35 households per consumer bankruptcy. The causes of consumer bankruptcies are many, including high debt loads, an interruption in income due to a job loss, family breakup, or sustained high medical costs. Personal bankruptcies tend to rise even during a growing, expanding economy, fueled by the same consumer spending that now accounts for two-thirds of the domestic U.S. economy.

Against this backdrop of unprecedented bankruptcy activity, Congress in 2005 enacted the most sweeping reform of the laws in the past 25 years. The Bankruptcy Abuse Prevention and Consumer Protection Act makes significant changes to bankruptcy law and procedure for both individuals and businesses. The new rules restrict access to the bankruptcy courts, limit the scope of relief, cabin judicial discretion, change time limits, and make many other substantive and procedural changes to the 1978 Bankruptcy Code.

In this timely new book, Professor Nathalie Martin, the Robert M. Zinman Resident Scholar at the American Bankruptcy Institute, provides a highly readable path out of the wilderness for consumers who are facing their financial demons. She and Stewart Paley guide the reader through the options of whether to file for bankruptcy and when, while charting a more pleasant route for life after debt.

Samuel J. Gerdano
Executive Director
American Bankruptcy Institute

Introduction

We hope you enjoy this book, which was written to help you understand your current financial woes and avoid getting into the same mess in the future. It was undoubtedly written to help you understand the new bankruptcy laws and the changes that have recently taken place in these laws. This book was also designed to make you become a financial winner, not a loser, to turn you into someone who is earning interest rather than paying interest, and who has enough savings to ward off financial disaster in the future.

We are a husband and wife team, one of whom is a spender and the other a saver. In this book, we walk you through steps to help you decide whether you need a bankruptcy and if so, when to file. We also help you spend less, save more, and begin to amass wealth.

This book is not just about *The New Bankruptcy Code and You*. It is about *the new you*, and your new financial life and freedom. Through it we hope to take you, step-by-step, from financial failure to financial fitness.

The beginning of this book contains material on household financial matters. These chapters are important!! If you decide to file a petition in bankruptcy, the discharge you receive will not help you unless you avoid the causes of your bankruptcy, start to follow practices designed to keep your spending within your means, and, hopefully, even save some money on a regular basis. If you don't do that, the bankruptcy discharge will be just another event in your financial life. It will not solve anything long-term.

Freedom from debt is power in our society, power to spend money as one chooses and to *not* spend one's paycheck paying off events that have already happened. Although this takes some discipline and planning, it is enjoyable to read investment statements and watch your money grow. In fact, because of the way interest compounds, a 22-year-old person who invests just $20,000 at 10 percent over the long haul (and does not ever touch the money) will have $1,280,000 when she retires 42 years later at age 64. That's not a typo; it says $1,280,000, all flowing from the same $20,000 in savings. If she invests it over the same period at 8 percent (a rate considered very feasible for a balanced portfolio), she'll still have $1,280,000 if she retires at age 72 (52 years later) or have $640,000 if she retires at age 65. We tell you all this right up front so you see that all the interest and fees you have been paying out for consumer credit are stealing your future financial success by allowing those same principles of compounding to work for your creditors rather than for you. This is the trend you need to reverse, and we can help you do that by following the suggestions in this book. First, of course, you need to wipe out your debt, either through paying it down or through bankruptcy. Then you can start watching your own money grow.

While we are interested in teaching you about the New Bankruptcy Code (which we'll just call "the new law" from now on) and its options and alternatives, we are also interested in helping you bankruptcy-proof yourself. We mean that we'd like to help you put yourself in the situation where you will never again have to think about something like bankruptcy. We try to do this in bits and pieces throughout this book but want to say a few things about this at the outset.

1. You will *never* do well financially while carrying a balance on credit cards. If you carry a balance on even one credit card, you pay exorbitantly for the items you charge, and you transfer all the power and privilege in your money to others. You give up what is rightfully yours. You give away your hard-earned money to make other people rich. Part of what you'll learn here is how to make your money work for you, not for other people.

2. You can create your own incentives to save money and then learn to enjoy watching your savings grow. This will be your safety net if you lose your job or get sick or divorced. Power over money is so much more pleasurable than owning lots of things.

3. You should try to think of another way to make money on the side. This money you should sock away, thus making your future brighter.

4. You should try to cut back on what you need to make you happy. We try to help with this by encouraging you to create a list of the most important things in your life. When you see how few of these are material, you can cut out the things that don't count. You should keep track of everything you spend so you know where it all goes. Starbucks won't taste as good when you see how much you spend on it.

5. Stop feeling guilty about your financial condition. Just learn to let go but also to learn from your mistakes.

This book is no substitute for good legal advice. If after reading this, you decide you need a bankruptcy, please find a qualified attorney to help you. You'll need it! The new law makes filing for bankruptcy more complicated than ever.

CHAPTER 1

How Did I Get into This Mess?

A Story about Proliferating Credit, Volatile Job Markets, Rising Health Care Costs, and You

The Consumer Credit Boom

*A Short but Interesting History Lesson**

The United States was pulled out of the Great Depression by World War II, which created jobs for virtually everyone else who was not in the armed forces. Due to rationing of most consumer products and stopped production for others, most people saved their wages. After the war, we experienced a period of inflation, after which consumer demand for various household goods and services increased dramatically. Three things fueled these increases in demand: (1) a pent-up desire for things that had been unavailable during the war, (2) large savings accounts, and (3) the baby boom.

U.S. policy at the time promoted spending to the fullest extent possible. As one consultant announced shortly after the war, "The greatest challenge facing American business was convincing consumers that the hedonistic approach to life is a moral, not an immoral one." This strategy apparently worked well, as Americans began purchasing to be happy, and building social experiences around the act of acquiring.

---

*A different but similar version of this story is told at Nathalie Martin, "The Role of History and Culture in Developing Bankruptcy and Insolvency Systems: The Perils of Legal Transplantation," *B.C. Int'l & Comp. L. J.* 1 (2005):28.

As inflation subsided, the housing and auto industries expanded, and the United States began exporting a huge variety of goods, including farm products. Money was plentiful, and consumer goods appeared everywhere in record numbers. Chains like Sears and Montgomery Ward sold products cheaply, and more and more household electronic goods were being manufactured.

U.S. citizens with ready cash on hand began to believe that they needed these gadgets, that they were a sign of modernity and prosperity, and that buying them would fuel the economy. Thus, a consumer class was born.

Over time we have learned to consume too well. While we can manufacture and produce many products and services worthy of export, our voracious desire to consume makes it unlikely that we will ever produce as much as we use. As a culture, we love to spend and are even encouraged to do so when the economy flags, despite record household credit and record low savings rates.

Another historical event that drastically changed the debtor–creditor system in the United States was the home ownership program introduced by President Franklin D. Roosevelt in the New Deal legislation. Before 1930, home loans had short terms and were used primarily by the wealthy, because one was required to put down 50 percent of the purchase price in order to get a home loan. As a result of these conditions, only about 45 percent of the homes in the United States were owner occupied. Roosevelt sought to foster stability and security during the Depression by making it much easier for the average person to buy and keep a home.

Owning a home became a nearly universal dream for U.S. citizens after World War II. And for many, the dream became reality. As late as 1940, half of all young adults between the ages of 20 and 24 lived with their parents. In the 15 years following the war, home ownership shot up to 62 percent. No one individual was more responsible for this change than William Levitt, who built new identical homes and sold them for $7,990 in the late 1940s, with little or no money down and a $4^{1}/_{2}$ percent interest rate.

These events forever changed the face of U.S. consumerism and consumer credit. They ultimately revolutionized the home finance industry, by making 20 percent down payments the norm, rather than the previous 50 percent required, by stretching home loans out over 25 or 30 years, as compared to the 3 years at which commercial banks were lending, and finally, by amortizing the loans rather than having them end with balloon payments. Under New Deal legislation, houses could be bought with only 10 percent down. All that amortizing means is that the borrower paid some of the principal as he or she went along and did not just pay interest during the loan and pay all the principal at the end. This meant the loans were permanent financing rather than something a debtor would have to worry about replacing with another loan in the future.

As a result of these and other more recent changes, 68.6 percent of U.S. citizens now own their homes, a percentage higher than most other countries in the world. The New Deal legislation unquestionably led to this result, and, along with the advent of private mortgage insurance, now allows U.S. citizens to buy a home with only 5 percent down. These conditions led to a generally higher disposable income for U.S. citizens than for most other citizens in the world.

Low down-payment loans in the United States have led to another uniquely U.S. phenomenon, the home equity loan. Home equity loan indebtedness has substantially increased in a short period of time, from $60 billion in 1981 to $357 billion in 1991. These types of loans are pushed nonstop through the media in the United States, yet are virtually unheard of in Europe.

In fact, European concepts of land ownership are completely different from U.S. concepts. The ownership of land and tenant rights in England had their origin in the feudal system imposed by William I with far more land owned publicly and far more people owning homes and businesses on leased land. Thus, there are far fewer home equity loans in Europe and the rest of the world and thus less overall indebtedness.

Lending found its true cornucopia in the United States, however, with the introduction of the charge card in the 1960s, followed by the credit card in the 1970s and 1980s. Since then, there has been no turning back. Consumer spending is considered one of the most important indicators of economic health in the U.S. economy. Despite the credit industry's claims that consumers are abusing credit, credit industry advertising encourages people to use as much credit as they can get, for every use imaginable or no particular use at all. Some advertisers rely on nostalgia to get people to borrow as much money as possible. For example, in a mailer for a home equity loan, United Pan Am Mortgage writes:

> [r]emember the days when dad worked, mom managed the home, and there was still enough money for a house, cars, vacations . . . even college? It's sure not like that anymore. Today, with single parents or even with both parents working, it's hard to make ends meet, let alone have some of the good things life offers. We think you deserve more and we can help. . . . A friendly phone call will get the ball rolling on putting a lump sum in your pocket. That's right—have the extra cash to make those home improvements you've been putting off, take that vacation you've been dreaming about, give yourself peace of mind, knowing your son or daughter's tuition is covered.

The advertisement goes on to tell the recipient whom to call to get a home equity loan to solve all of life's problems, demonstrating that despite popular belief, you can buy both happiness and peace of mind.

U.S. popular culture oozes with references of spending and happiness. In the tongue-in-cheek novel *Shopaholic Ties the Knot*, Becky Bloomwood notes how her whole life will change when she and her beau own the vintage cocktail cabinet she spots in an antique shop:

> Just think, if we had one of these in the apartment it would change our lives. Every night Luke and I would mix martinis, and dance to old-fashioned songs, and watch the sun go down. It'd be so atmospheric! We'd have to buy one of those old-fashioned record players with the big horns, and start collecting 78s, and I'd start wearing gorgeous, vintage tea dresses.

As a result of relentless and unyielding admonitions to spend, as well as other cultural factors, U.S. citizens have more debt of all kinds than all persons of all other parts of the world. Consumer debt, second mortgages, foreclosures, and personal bankruptcies are all at an all-time high. The average household carries more than $9,000 in credit card debt, and record numbers of U.S. citizens now carry more than one mortgage.

Between 1979 and 1997, personal bankruptcies increased by more than 400 percent. The upsurge in the mid-1990s was particularly shocking because this was a period of widespread economic recovery. History partially explains why this debt picture looks so different from that of the rest of the world. Add a volatile economy and job market, and the credit industry's voracious appetite for more lending, and the statistics are not surprising.

The Birth of the Credit Card

The credit card was invented in 1949 by the Diners Club so executives could keep track of their expenses. In 1958, American Express and Carte Blanche joined, and in the 1960s MasterCard and Visa set up their extensive credit card networks. In 1986, Sears entered the all-purpose card market with its Discover Card. By the end of the 1990s, U.S. citizens carried more than $500 billion in outstanding credit card debt. Soon thereafter, consumer credit interest rates were deregulated, which is why it is now possible to carry cards with interest rates of 30 percent or more.

This means consumers carry this amount, on average, on their cards rather than paying the balance off each month. Interest rates on credit cards range from 0 percent to 39 percent, and people who will have trouble paying off the debt they have accumulated are naturally charged the highest rates.

Prior to these incredible and interesting historical events, people used to pay for things with cash. While some people began regularly paying for cars over time, meaning making car payments, many people still saved for cars at this time. Houses and other real estate have always been financed (bought using someone else's money, like a bank's or a relative's), but some people even believed that one should pay for a house with cash and not buy a house until one had saved enough to do that. This is particularly true of people who had survived the Depression and knew what carrying any debt could do to a person. When really hard times hit, so the theory went, people who owed money to others would be wiped out, and those who did not would survive, especially if they also had money saved for those hard times.

Think about how far we have come from the concept of saving up for something as big as a car or a house. Today, the philosophy is completely different. If we can borrow more against the assets we do own, we as Americans tend to do that. A free asset is a wasted asset, according to current debt philosophy in the United States. We have heard a radio advertisement telling Americans not to throw away all that equity they've built in their homes. The ad goes on to say that trillions of dollars in home equity are being wasted because Americans could take out new home equity loans and use all this equity. Never does the ad mention that these loans would have to be paid back or that the loans could cause the homeowner to lose his or her home.

We receive several calls a week from creditors who'd love to lend on our home. Yet this is one of the worst financial decisions a person can make, period, because your goal over time is to build assets and equity and not to give it away, in other words, to guard home equity and all of your other assets jealously.

Home equity lines of credit are very popular, but are generally not a great idea because they turn unsecured debt into secured debt and could cause you to lose your home. Be *very careful* before you agree to take out a home equity loan. Americans think nothing of refinancing their home and regularly removing all equity from it, without being sure they can even make the new payments. Many home equity lenders charge huge fees and late charges and target certain people (like the elderly and others), who again will have trouble paying off the loan. Once you have given away all the available equity in your home, you cannot give it again. You've lost a huge safety net. People don't know this, and all these factors conspire together to create a society where credit is available at every turn.

Credit card companies target people who will be long-time users, including teenagers. A recent Junior Achievement poll found that more than 11 percent of teens carry credit cards, that some of these teens are as young as 13 years old, and that a surprising 18 percent already carry a balance. This means they are setting themselves up for failure, since they won't have a good job for a long time. Saddled with debt, their future looks less than bright. Plus they are learning financial habits that could be with them for the rest of their lives. The industry claims that parents can educate kids about the financial terms of credit cards, but judging by how adults are using and understanding the cards, it's not clear that they have the knowledge to educate their kids.

Robert Manning, in *Credit Card Nation*, also chronicles the proliferation of credit cards on college campuses as well as in the elderly. Many students apply for the card to get a free T-shirt or gym bag.

The rate on a card can change just because you are one day late with one payment. This rate change can be permanent. Thus, one can buy a sweater on sale for $30 but end up paying hundreds of dollars for it if you don't pay the debt off but instead pay interest on it for a long time into the future.

Credit is unregulated and is given to people who the credit card companies know will never be able to pay the actual balances. These companies do not check to see if you can afford the payments you might ultimately incur, though they have full access to all your credit information if you authorize them to look in your application for credit. This completely unregulated offering of credit to almost all members of society is touted by the consumer credit industry as the *democratization of credit*. The consumer credit industry brags that it is so unbelievably beneficial that now even people of limited means can get large amounts of credit.

What they do not tell the public is that these people, who at one time were considered poor credit risks and who still make less money and have less experience managing money, are charged the highest interest rates for their credit. They are also less likely to understand the interest terms and other consequences of taking on credit.

It is not just the *availability* of credit that is deregulated, but also the amounts of rates and fees that can be charged. There is no cap on the rate of interest that can be charged in most states, meaning no usury laws. While some states do limit the highest interest rate that a creditor can charge the public, the recent trend is not to do so, and thus payday lenders often charged 2,500 percent per year or more, which is all legal in most states. That means that a $500 loan that is carried for one year will cost 208 percent per month or a total of $12,980 a year ($500 in original principal and $1,040 a month in interest).

In Europe, as a point of reference, credit has traditionally been regulated and creditors have not been permitted to lend to people beyond their ability to pay. Historically, if a creditor did lend beyond a person's ability to pay in Europe, then the creditor could not collect these debts. These countries across the pond did not have as liberal a bankruptcy system as we do here in the United States, but in a sense they also did not need it. They had little chance of seeing citizens in the kind of financial condition that many Americans find themselves in: too much debt to ever repay and creditors still offering more. More. More. More.

While the credit structure is now changing in Europe, and many countries are now emulating our own bankruptcy systems, Europeans have traditionally dealt with debt by regulating it, not encouraging it and then discharging it.

Credit cards also work differently from how most people realize. The payment requirements are often set up so that minimum payments do not even cover the interest due, meaning that without ever charging another dime on the cards, the amount due continues to grow even if you never miss a minimum payment. Credit card companies make their money off interest and late fees and do not mind if you carry a huge balance.

Today, the total amount of consumer credit (which includes credit card debt, car payments, and furniture payments, but not mortgage payments) is a record $1.8 trillion. The average amount is $18,700 per household. This would make our ancestors roll over in their graves.

Add to this available credit tremendous societal influences encouraging consumerism, and you have a recipe for financial disaster. Nowhere else in the world are people encouraged to buy more. It is almost un-American not to do your duty and spend, spend, spend.

Who Are the Bankruptcy Debtors?

People who file for bankruptcy are most likely to be from the middle classes, not from the lower economic classes. Middle class debtors are more likely to amass debt, to have assets to protect through a bankruptcy, and to have access to the legal services needed to do a bankruptcy.

Studies also show that bankruptcy debtors are more likely to have attended college than the average American, and more likely to own a home than the average American. Finally, studies show that the leading causes of personal bankruptcy are job loss, health problems, and divorce.

Job Market Volatility

It hardly seems necessary to say that the American job market is volatile and that downsizing and outsourcing continue. The genesis of the downsizing movement was the growing threat of hostile takeovers of publicly traded companies in the 1970s and 1980s. Under attack by raiders, businesses searched for quick and easy ways to cut costs. They discovered that layoffs of workers and managers could boost short-term profits, make the company appear more efficient, and stave off takeover attempts.

This was the original use of the massive company layoff, but no more. Once considered an admission of business decline or defeat, layoffs are now viewed in a new light, as a legitimate multipurpose tool to preserve and advance corporate interests. Current names for layoffs, which include downsizing and the incredibly euphemistic "rightsizing," attempt to legitimize this now-common practice.

The bottom line then? American downsizing and outsourcing continues even when the economy is doing well, leaving most Americans with no job security and an ongoing risk of job loss. If you have been laid off, you need not blame yourself. If this is how you got into financial trouble, you are not alone. Not by a long shot. Job loss is a major contributing factor in bankruptcy cases.

Rising Health Care Costs

In a recent five-state study of the relationship between medical costs and bankruptcy, Harvard scholars found that medical bills, coupled with a low savings rate for most American families, caused about 1 million people to file for bankruptcy each year in recent years.

As one author of the study noted, "Families are paying more and more for health insurance that covers them less and less." According to Elizabeth Warren, a Harvard professor and co-author of the study, the cost of health care is a major contributor of bankruptcy filings in the United States. Thus, if health care costs partially caused your own dismal financial condition, you are not alone.

The study shows that three-fifths of the bankruptcies in this country are caused, at least in part, by medical problems. Many families in the study suffered both health problems and a loss in income resulting from being unemployed or on leave.

While gaps in insurance coverage were a common problem, three-quarters of the people in the study *had* health insurance at the time they got sick. Hardly any of the people in the study had just let their insurance lapse. Of those without insurance, only 2.9 percent said they did not think they needed insurance. The majority (55.9%) said they simply could not afford the premiums, and 7.1 percent could not get insurance because of a preexisting medical condition.

The point is that people who file for bankruptcy as a result of health-related costs (or job loss or divorce for that matter), are not irresponsible. Most had done everything in their power to get and stay insured. Most even *had* insurance when they incurred these huge medical costs. In fact, the average out-of-pocket medical debt for those who filed was about $12,000, and 68 percent *still had* health insurance at the time of their bankruptcy filing.

Divorce

The other common cause of bankruptcy is divorce. As divorce rates have increased, this destabilization of the family unit has caused widespread financial problems. As we said, it is far more expensive to live separately than together.

CHAPTER 2

Psychology of Debt 101: It's Not All Your Fault So You Needn't Feel Guilty

I have met hundreds of people in financial difficulty. Almost all of them feel terrible about not being able to pay creditors. Some writers insist that the stigma of bankruptcy is now gone, but I have never found that to be the case. I have seen grown men cry at meetings of creditors and other people flat-out refuse to file for bankruptcy. Some people are just too ashamed to even consider it.

Ditch the Shame and Guilt

Chapter 1 was written to give you some real idea of how and why you may have been induced to overuse credit and also how unfortunate events may have led you into a huge mound of debt. If you take nothing else away from these first two chapters, know that:

- You are not alone in your debt crisis.
- Our society and its structures lead people to take on more debt than they can afford.
- Our society provides relatively few safety nets for people when they face financial crisis.
- Recent downsizing and volatility in the job market have caused financial vulnerability for more Americans than ever before in history.
- Health care costs are now far higher than virtually anyone can afford.

Now don't take us wrong here. We encourage you to take full responsibility for your debts but also ask you to realize that it is not all your fault that you cannot pay back all of your debts.

The key at this point is to decide what to do about the problems you face here and now, and then take immediate, proactive steps to bankruptcy-proof yourself for the future. Everybody makes mistakes, but hopefully you'll learn a few things in this book that will help put you on the other side of financial crisis.

Learn What Is Important to You: A Spending Self-Examination

To get ready to complete your own financial overhaul, you'll need to see what is important to you, what you spend money on, and what permanent changes can be made to improve your overall financial health. Make a list of one or more of the following:

The things that make you happy in life.

The things you get to do when life is going great.

The things you enjoy most in life.

The way you measure a happy life.

Pick one and do your own list now before reading on. . . . Do not read ours, just do your own.

Okay, here is my list:

Spending time with my family, especially my husband and my dad (especially making my dad, a retired Ph.D., intellectually stimulated and making him laugh out loud).

Walking rather than driving.

Walking on dirt paths rather than on pavement.

Going on fancy vacations.

Watching birds.

Doing yoga and being motivated to do it.

Stewart's list:

Good health.

Good food.

Being outside.

Spending time with family.

Making my list makes me aware of all the things I spend valuable time and money on that do not register on the list, things like cleaning out crowded closets, waiting in line to buy things, dusting worthless things I bought, giving stuff away, and so on.

Life is better for me if I have more time. True, I love luxury vacations and good wine, but extra clothes and household goods just rob me of my valuable time. I don't need extra things to take care of, and few of us do. Why waste yourself on things you don't enjoy?

Ditch Shopping as a Pastime

Addicted to shopping? There are plenty of web pages that can help you think of ways to break this cycle of spending. Clip coupons to take up some shopping time and energy. Shop in consignment shops. While you are there bring in some of your own stuff to trade. Shop for a neighbor who can no longer drive. Help a friend pick out a gift. Just do what you need to cut back on your own spending, especially on things that you yourself do not even want or need.

I am not cured of excessive shopping myself. I talk the talk but still buy things I do not need and engage in more than a little retail therapy. In fact, when bankruptcy reform passed (the new law that is the subject of this book), I vowed to go on a shopping fast to show Congress who was boss. My philosophy was that if we all did that, we'd slow down the whole economy, and Congress would have to change the law back. This fast lasted but a few hours, just long enough to e-mail the idea to several listserves.

But soon I was buying shoes, a few pairs at a time. It was like going on a diet and then wanting to eat everything in sight just because you cannot stop thinking about it.

We suggest that when you shop, don't use your credit card. Use cash. Even if you write a check, it's better, because when you enter the check you will see how your balance is going down. Perhaps it will add to your guilt.

If you can, forget about shopping for a while. Find something else to do with yourself. Once your investments start to grow, the something else can be checking your investments online. That can actually be pretty satisfying. I know, saying that this could be as fun as shopping is about as realistic as saying that exercise can be as enjoyable as eating, but truthfully, it is all about developing habits. I bet some readers out there actually agree that exercise and eating are at least equally enjoyable because there is synergy there, meaning a strong connection between the two. You need to do both, in some reasonable proportion, to take care of your body. Otherwise things are out of sync. The same is true of spending and saving. You cannot be healthy financially without doing both of these things, in some reasonable and realistic proportion.

CHAPTER 3

Happiness Through Saving

Saving money can also be a pastime and here we give you just a few small examples of how this might work. Please be patient. We talk about the new bankruptcy laws soon. If you are tired of the minieconomics lessons, you can skip to Chapter 9. But we want to help you become financially healthy so that even if you do a bankruptcy, you will be financially healthy afterward.

The Cash Habit: Getting Off Credit and Saving for Things in Advance

Though we as Americans are encouraged at every turn to buy things on credit, real financial freedom comes when you snub credit, when you can say, "No, thanks. I have the freedom and the capacity to do this, living well, without expensive credit. In fact, I can become the creditor myself because I am the one who earns interest now, rather than the one who pays interest. Oh what a feeling!"

Stop paying interest on credit card debt! You will read in Chapter 4 how much credit card companies make from interest, late fees, and other fees charged to their customers. One goal of any financially savvy consumer is to stop funding these fees and keep more money for yourself and your future. But how will you wean yourself off credit?

It is not that easy. First and foremost, it means buying with cash, and if the items are big ones like furniture or trips, it means *saving up for them* before buying them. Take a deep breath here because this is the key. Of course this is a huge pain in the posterior, but there is a silver lining. If you save for your vacation rather than charging it, you'll enjoy it more. You also pay far, far less for it, so it is a better deal all the way around. This takes planning and determination and we walk you though the process. The first step though is making a vow to *get off the cards now*!! What we mean is vow right now to never carry a balance again!

We use credit cards (I should say "a" card) because we generally have the capacity to pay off the balance in full. If we ever hit a month when we cannot do this, we immediately go off the card. This is truly inconvenient in gas stations, and so on, but for us it must be done or we'll dig a hole.

By the way, we have just *one* card, issued one copy to each of us, in the household. This is an incredible thing to limit, amazingly powerful, and a great bonding experience and pact with a spouse. "It's you and me against the world, everyone offering cards, and our little secret. I don't want it and won't take it. It's our vow to one another." Meanwhile we get the money, and the credit card companies lose the annual fees, late fees, interest, and so on. Moreover, you have total control over at least this aspect of your life. That means *one* bill to pay the end of the month and total knowledge at any given moment of what you owe, by one click of the mouse or one phone call. At times, we obsessively check the balance, something that is both healthy and a bit over the top, I admit. It's just that having freedom over these huge bills is such a natural high!!

If you cannot control your use of credit cards, do not give yourself many chances. Just stop using them altogether. There is no doubt that some people are addicted to spending and if this is you, you should operate on a cash basis only.

For some people, not using credit cards is also a symbolic gesture that they would like to mark with a major life event. My favorite story about celebrating a cash-basis, credit-free life was described in a funky radio show about freeing oneself from debt. People were mounting their credit cards on wood and shooting them with shotguns! Amazing symbolism, and a great use for a shotgun.

Recently my husband wrapped sticky tape around both our cards. We were carrying a balance and needed a month or two to pay it off. Paying any interest at all completely galls each of us, so we get motivated to keep our money rather than giving it to credit card companies. If you are carrying credit card balances, you are out of control and are giving hard-earned money to credit cards companies, which are part of the most profitable industry in the world. *You are robbing from the poor (yourself) and giving to the rich!*

Saving Money

But getting off credit cards will not make you save money. You could still spend all that you earned. You need a method of saving. The best way I know is automatic withdrawal from your paycheck to your savings account. When we made twice as much money as we do now, we lived in a big city and saved some money but not nearly as much as we could have. We went out to eat a lot, had two homes, took taxis, and did not worry about money.

Not long ago, we read an interesting study that found that how much people save has little to do with how much people make. Steven Venti of Dartmouth and David Wise of Harvard found that when they studied the savings rates of 7,700 households in 10 income groups, even 10 percent of the lowest income group had saved an average of $150,000 per household. Yet the middle-income groups saved an average of just $45,000 per household.

While some of the statistics in this study seem to compare apples and oranges on some level, there is no question that some people who make very little save a lot and vice versa. No doubt, it is easier to save money if you make enough to barely notice what you've ferreted away. But everyone can save some money. It just takes a readjustment in attitude. What do you really need, and what is it worth to have extra stuff hanging around? You may not want to shop in thrift shops and go out to eat less, but if you were willing to try it just for a while, you'd be amazed at the results.

Saving Without Noticing It

We had a friend who used a financial advisor whom he thought was just amazing. She had really made him wealthy, so he said. We went to visit her and learned that her customers had to have at least $100,000 for her to manage. Otherwise, she could not help. We certainly did not have that much and were demoralized. She said that was unnecessary and told us how to fix this. She told us to open a Vanguard account, a mutual fund account with no fee for transactions (we chose the STAR fund), and told us to arrange for $1,000 a month to go directly into this account.* Admittedly, this was in the high times of the early to mid-1990s and interest rates were unbelievably high, like 20 percent to 25 percent per year. Still, by taking this advice, we found ourselves at $100,000 in about four years.

I guess the bad news is that we then spent a good deal of this money. The good news is far better, however. We spent the money to go back to school, take more than a year off work, and to totally restructure our lives. We now live

---

*A mutual fund is a collection of stocks and/or bonds. You can think of a mutual fund as a company that brings together a group of people and invests their money in stocks, bonds, and other securities. Each investor owns shares, which represent a portion of the holdings of the fund. If the fund charges no fee for transactions, we call the fund a *no-load* fund.

comfortably and relaxingly, out West, at less stressful jobs. We have far more enjoyable lives; we make less, but love life more. Under no circumstances could we have made this switch (which will probably lengthen our lives) without the initial money we saved.

Automatic withdrawal is also the best way, by far, to save for retirement. The whole retirement thing is far enough away that it does not seem like something worth funding. Believe us though, we've seen enough people trying to live off Social Security to strike the fear of G-d in us and anyone else who will listen to our rantings.

Saving Small

Are there other, smaller ways to save? Sure thing, and those add up, too. Saving change is a good way. We put it all into a bowl and trade it in for about $600 a year. Invested at 10 percent, this could become more than $19,000 in just 35 years, and that is only one year's worth of change. Think if you did this every year!!* Okay, I'm getting carried away here. You could just use this change money to take a trip, plant trees, or do your December shopping.

Saving Big

When you are saving for something big (we once saved $20,000 to spend one year backpacking around the world), you can turn saving into a game. Have it be a competition with your significant other. I admit by the way that saving is like most most things in life, more fun with a partner. If you do not have one, you can play the game against yourself, making bets with yourself about how much you can sock away and trying to beat your own predictions. This is actually fun if there is a house or a trip at the end for you! This type of saving is temporary and has a big reward at the end. Because these bigger rewards are expensive, saving for these things involves a lot of self-deprivation. When saving for our trip around the world, we did not buy anything, or go out to eat once, in six months. Longer-term saving plans must allow more freedom, of course. And more balance.

More Thoughts on Money and Addictions

One silver lining is that if you can be addicted to spending, you can also be addicted to a lot of other things, including saving. Some of the most obsessive people I know are complete tightwads. While this is not healthy over a whole lifetime either, as some balance is needed in every part of one's life, being a bit of a tightwad now and then can bring absolutely amazing rewards.

---

*If you did this every year for 20 years, using the same estimated interest rate, you'd have $200,000, just from saving change!

Writing Down Everything You Spend

A spending diary will help you figure out what you can cut out. Things like Starbucks coffees and lunches out are so easy to replace with equally delicious food from home. Plus it is fun to write down what you saved. When you are saving for something big, writing down every single expense is critical. However, if you are really on a spending hiatus, there will not be much to write down.

I like writing things down, so listing what I have spent is no big spending deterrent for me. For some people, though, who hate to write things down, just knowing they'll need to write down an expense will keep them from spending on the item. That creates a double benefit from a spending diary; you know where you stand and you avoid spending to avoid the task (or, if you have a partner, the wrath of the conversation that follows).

When Stewart and I go on teaching trips abroad, we share a teaching load and get just one professor's salary. This way we can enjoy the destination and not work too hard. It becomes more like a vacation than just a business trip. To do it, though, two must live as cheaply as one, at least compared to other faculty members. To make sure we do not spend more than we make on these trips, we write down every single expense. It is fun beyond words to go back and look at the lists when we are home. Plus, this system ensures that we do not come back to a huge credit card bill in the States. If that were to happen, it would be the end of these trips. For us, this is all about creating incentives and rewards for not spending, so we can bring more pleasure into our lives.

Pick a Few Ways to Save and Watch it Grow

IN GENERAL   Try to be less stressed and busy. Busy people, who are running late, spend more on gas by overaccelerating their cars. They pay for expensive parking, expensive convenience food, and so on.

Insist on a waiting period before major purchases. I find that most of the time, I don't even want what I was about to buy. I was just killing time.

CLOTHES   When it comes to clothes shopping, I like to make a bunch of outfits with a few well-matched items. For women, jackets, slacks, skirts, and blouses can be fixed and matched to create many different outfits. Plus you can change the look of these outfits with accessories such as jewelry or scarves. Men's clothing offers a wide variety of separates that can be coordinated: blazers, slacks, shirts, and ties can all be interchanged to create a versatile wardrobe with a minimum of expense.

Try clothes shopping at stores like Ross, T.J. Maxx, and Marshall's. They carry tons of labels like Tommy Hilfiger, Ralph Lauren, DKNY, and Jones New York for about 50 percent to 80 percent less than you'll pay at the mall.

Keep an organized closet. After cleaning out my closet, I recently noticed I had 10 pairs of black slacks. If my closet was neat, I would have a good idea of what I had. This would keep me from making duplicate purchases.

Before going clothes shopping, try to make an inventory of the key pieces you already have. If you know you have three pairs of black pumps, you are less likely to buy another pair while out.

AT THE BANK   Beware of checking accounts that are advertised as "free." They often require you to maintain a minimum balance, use direct deposit, or are contingent on some other requirement. If you must maintain a minimum balance to get a free checking account, what would you be earning each month if that minimum balance were in a savings account? Is your checking account paying you the same rate of interest that the savings account would? Is the money you save in fees substantially more than what you could be earning in interest? If not, you don't want to keep your money in an account that earns money for the bank but none for you.

Watch out for ATM fees. If you just need an extra $20 or so, rather than using another bank's ATM, which can cost you up to two service fees, try using your card at a supermarket or convenience store. Make a purchase and many stores will let you get extra cash back. Most institutions won't charge you a fee for these so-called point-of-sale transactions, and that helps you beat surcharges and fees. The fees may seem small—a dollar here and a dollar there—but think about how long you have to keep money in the account to earn a dollar's interest.

Keep it simple. Don't sign up for "overdraft protection plans" or insurance. Use the cheapest checks they offer even if they don't have a picture of hummingbirds.

When it comes to starting a savings account, the amount is *not* the issue. The action of doing is! No matter the amount you set aside each week, the fact that you do set something aside begins to form a habit. It is the habit of saving on a regular basis. It is also a great starting point for bigger and better things. If you can save $5 a week this month, what can you save next month or even next year?

AUTOMOBILES   Make certain to get a rate quote (or preapproved loan) from your bank or credit union before seeking dealer financing. You can save as much as $1,000 in finance charges by shopping for the cheapest loan. Your bank or credit union will almost always get you a better rate than the car dealer.

You can save up to 100 gallons of gas a year by keeping your engine tuned and your tires inflated to their proper pressure.

Avoid leasing a car. At first glance it looks like a good deal because the payments are lower than on a traditional auto loan. The leasing payments are lower, however, because you don't actually own the car. When the lease is up, you either have to return the car or agree to extremely high payments to purchase the car.

Shop for auto insurance; don't just take the policy offered by the dealer.

Be very careful about purchasing "extended warranty protection plans." Studies have shown that they are very expensive.

Finance as little as possible and over as short a period of time as possible. Compare the total amount that you will have to pay over three years with what it costs over five years.

ENTERTAINMENT   Quit smoking. Pack-a-day habit? In New Mexico, that's easily $5 a day—or about $1,800 a year—that can go right into your savings, not to mention what it saves you on insurance and health care.

The average American household spends more than $2,200 dining out, according to New Strategist Publications. Theoretically, that means if you stayed home every other time you had the urge to eat out, you could save more than $1,000 a year.

For years I've watched a relative try to keep up with the Joneses. She now has a baby grand piano that no one in her family knows how to play! It helps to ask yourself, "Why am I buying this?" before making a household purchase.

JUNK THE JUNK   Go through your drawers, your basement, your garage, and your closet. I am always amazed at the amount of stuff I accumulate. There is no logic in keeping clothes that no longer fit because I wish I were still that size. There is no logic in having four flat head screwdrivers. Why do we hold on to so much junk? Ultimately, it is just weighing you down. Have a garage sale, and call a local charity ahead of time to set up an appointment for them to arrive just when the garage sale is over and take what doesn't sell. Be sure to get a receipt for what they take. Donations to charity are tax deductible.

BUYING STUFF   Think about whether you *need* something before you buy it. How much happiness will it bring? How much would you use the bread maker that you're looking at? Do you really want the latest deep fryer?

Creating Other Incentives to Save

I know we said it at least once, but it bears repeating. Pay yourself first. Definitely set up automatic withdrawal of some part of your pay, to go into savings or a no-load mutual fund, before you ever get used to the money. Getting a job and packing some savings away go together, timing wise, like a hand and glove. A garden analogy goes like this. You need to move pine needles from the front yard or haul them to the dump. If you gather them the same day that you weed the back yard you can put them down exactly where the weeds grew and use them as mulch. Voila! No more weeds forever. You've saved yourself a trip to the dump and a lifetime of weeding. Timing is everything, and starting to skim money off the top for yourself early —from the beginning, actually—will make you wealthy later. This is because of compounding. Because you earn interest on interest, this can mean many luxurious days and nights at the end of life. Why not? Having a bunch of stuff is not very rewarding anyway.

I (Nathalie) actually enjoy shopping very much. For the sake of our finances, I should do less of it. What I've learned is that having a whole lot of things to take care of is not very rewarding. My list of things I love includes spending as much time as possible outside and as much time as I can with family and friends. All of these activities are inconsistent with having to take care of a lot of material possessions. One thing money cannot buy is time. Even if you can hire people to do things for you (a nice perk of wealth), you still need to supervise that work. The simple things in life often create the most happiness, yet they often cost nothing.

Now don't get me wrong. I like stuff! Very much, in fact! But I am trying to show you the other side of this issue. I'm no Pollyanna and feel the urge to run to the mall just writing about this. Yet I don't like junk. Elaine St. James says it best in her popular book *Simplify Your Life*. "Don't bring new things into the house without getting rid of something you already have." That right there (finding something to give away and then doing it) sounds a bit like cleaning and I'd hate to be a part of that, so I'll just forgo the new item to save the effort of finding a home for it.

One other story might help. We live near a nature preserve in an area of town that has become extremely desirable. It is quiet and somewhat rural in feel, unlike most of the rest of our sprawling town. Space now goes for twice what it would in many other nice neighborhoods in town, and people are tearing down old houses and putting up million dollar homes in their place. One gentleman around the corner lives in a converted school bus. He owns a bike and probably little else. We see him riding his bike on the nature trails two or three times a day, always smiling. This gentleman obviously lives much more simply than I would like to, but I am still amazed at how happy he is with his life. When I face problems, it helps me to focus on the way that he has created his life without much wealth. This man is very happy and I'm sure he has no debt whatsoever. There is a lesson there for all of us.

The thing that motivates me most about saving money is the concept of compounding interest. For example, Associated Press columnist Humberto Cruz told an amazing compounding story in a Sunday paper that ran nationwide on April 17, 2005. According to Mr. Cruz, compounding is so powerful, that believe it or not, if you can save $100,000 for your child by age 65, you can leave him or her $3.5 million in future income, free of federal income taxes. All you need to do is have $100,000 in a Roth IRA by the time you reach age 65. Then you need to live to be 85 without withdrawing any money from it. You arrange that upon your death, your IRA is rolled into the Roth IRA of your surviving spouse, who then passes it on to the child. Assuming an investment return of 8 percent, if the child is 57 when the last parent dies, and assuming the child just withdraws the minimum required each year, he or she would receive $3,515,951 over the next 27 years. Every penny would be income tax-free for the child because Roth IRA distributions do not count as taxable income.

The main reason to relay this somewhat complex story is that it demonstrates the extreme power of compounding. There are numerous other stories like this one, all proving that savings grows exponentially because you earn interest on interest. One writer says it is a bit like leaving 2 bunnies in a room and coming back later and finding 20. Compounding really is remarkable. Try it!

CHAPTER 4

The Economics of Consumer Credit

Deregulation of consumer credit has made credit card lending more profitable than any other form of lending. In fact, the credit card industry is by far the most profitable sector of the American economy with annual earnings of $30 billion or so per year. According to BCS Alliance.com, found at http://bcs alliance.com/creditcard/profits~ns4.html, in 2004, MBNA earned more than 1.5 times the profits of McDonald's, and Citibank earned more profits than Microsoft and Wal-Mart combined.

The Profits of Credit Card Companies

It is not hard to see what makes this industry so profitable when Americans charge $1.5 trillion per year on their cards. Each time this happens, the credit card company receives a fee from the merchant. Of course, that is just the beginning. With more than half the cardholders carrying a balance on their cards, interest rate charges add up quickly. Card companies actually favor consumers who carry a balance, since interest is one of the most profitable parts of the arrangement.

People who pay off their balances each month have been called "deadbeats" by some companies, and some card companies even charge a fee for this type of behavior. People who do not pay off their balances, and who instead pay exorbitant and costly interest on their purchases, are known as "revolvers" in the industry.

Ed Yingling, president of the American Bankers Association, calls revolvers the "sweet spot" of the banking industry. It's no wonder. Your hard-earned dollars are creating a sweet spot indeed for the companies who issue this type of credit.

Practically speaking, deregulation allows card companies to get unlimited amounts of interest and fees from consumers, by reversing laws limiting the amounts of these fees. Card companies argued that the market forces would keep the interest rates from soaring too high because card companies would compete for business.

While this is true to some extent, there are still plenty of cards that charge very high rates, mostly to people in society who cannot get lower-rate cards, and who have the least likelihood of actually paying the balances on the cards. And of course, the more cardholders (customers) a company has, the more money it makes, even if this is accomplished by lowering lending standards.

Lending to the Weak

Subprime lending, meaning lending specifically to people who are living on the edge, is the most profitable niche in lending. A popular long-term strategy is to get college students hooked on credit cards early, giving away free T-shirts and requiring no income. Some 83 percent of undergraduate students have at least one credit card; a 24 percent increase since 1998 and 21 percent of undergraduates who have cards, have high-level balances between $3,000 and $7,000. Actually, even young and preteens now carry credit cards, and more than half of those carry a balance! How is that for ensuring (or destroying) a beautiful financial future?

Late Fees and Other Unpleasant Surprises

If you do have cards, make sure you *never* make a payment late. Late fees are incredibly profitable for card companies. They rose from an average of $5 to $10 prior to deregulation to $39 or more today. See http://bankrate.com, one of my favorite financial web pages. In fact, late fees are the single largest source of revenue for card companies, surpassing even the amounts earned from interest. Just so you know, late fees sometimes vary depending on your balance. These are called "tiered fees."

This month, I cut it too close (the payment was due in four business days) so just in case, I sent the payment by priority mail. By no means should you assume that if your payment due date is a Sunday, you have until Monday to get it there. Late fees are so large and profitable that companies will interpret the rules to increase late fees. In fact, you cannot even be sure that payments are applied on the day they are received. Don't cut it close, ever! Pay early! Some web pages recommend sending a payment at least a week before the due date. Better yet, pay on line.

There also is a deadly connection between interest rates and late payments (by even one day). Many credit card agreements provide that if even one payment is received late, for the rest of the relationship the interest rate on the card increases to 30 percent or more. Many card companies charge up to 10 percent more once one late payment has been received. By now, you should be able to do the math. Carrying credit card balances steals your future, no *if*'s, *and*'s, or *but*'s.

Universal Default Provisions

To add insult to injury, many agreements provide that if a customer is late on even one payment on another card, held by another company, or if the consumer's FICO (credit) score drops at all for any reason, the rate on their card is forever increased as well. Interestingly, almost none of the members in the Winter 2005 Congress were aware of these so-called cross-default or universal default provisions.

How Long Will It Take to Pay Off Your Balances?

Want to know how long it will take you to pay off your present balances? Endless information is available on line for this purpose. Log on to http://bankrate.com/brm/calc/creditcardpay.asp, and do your own math. Interestingly, since Americans carry an average of $9,000, we ran the math on a balance of $9,000, assuming the lender was requiring a payment of just $250 a month and that is all the customer paid, and assuming a rate of 29 percent. Under these conditions, and of course assuming nothing further was ever charged to this account, it would take 85 months to pay off the balance. That is more than 7 years! And of course, the interest paid over this time would far exceed the amount charged. On the $9,000, the cardholder would pay a total of $21,100. That is with no late fees.

I'm sure some readers are thinking that 29 percent is higher than anything they are paying. You might be surprised if you looked closely at your statements and your agreement. Card companies are not required to notify consumers of rate increases and those 0 percent deals are as flimsy as the paper they're printed on. Normally the rate is for a limited period and assumes that even during that period, you'll pay your minimums on time with both this company and all others.

Additionally, even low rates result in heinous amounts of interest, which you yourself could be saving (and investing) rather than spending. I for one could not care less what the rate is on this card or that because I simply hate to pay it!

For example, Table 4.1 shows similar information for a balance of just $3,000, on which the card user will charge nothing else and will pay $100 a month.

TABLE 4.1 Paying Down a $3,000 Balance at $100/Month

APR	Total Interest Paid	# of Monthly Payments
17%	$960	40 (3 years, 4 months)
16%	$881	39 (3 years, 3 months)
15%	$806	39 (3 years, 3 months)
14%	$735	38 (3 years, 2 months)
13%	$666	37 (3 years, 1 month)
12%	$602	37 (3 years, 1 month)
11%	$540	36 (3 years)
10%	$480	35 (2 years, 11 months)
9%	$423	35 (2 years, 10 months)

Source: http://bcsalliance.com/credit.html

I know these do not look too bad, but think about it. You have another option. You can refuse to pay any interest and instead just buy with cash (or pay off your balance each month). You can then invest the money you would have paid for interest. When that happens, you are the one in control, the one earning rather than paying interest.

Most of Us Are in Denial about What We Charge and Pay Interest On

When I say, I refuse to pay interest, I am sure that at least some of you readers are saying, "Me too! I do not pay interest on credit cards." I urge you to call right now and find out if you have paid interest or late fees in the past year on the cards you carry and if so, how much. Then sit and picture this amount in your investment account, growing every day while you sleep and play. Hopefully, that will be you next year, or sometime soon.

Most of us do pay interest on credit cards and lie to ourselves about the fact. Studies suggest that more than 75 percent of card users report in surveys that they would not make a large purchase on a credit card if they could not pay off the balance right away. Yet hard statistics show that well over half of Americans carry a balance on credit cards. This suggests that many of us are in denial about our spending habits. I suppose not knowing the truth is comforting on some level. That way, you don't need to think about how bad things are. This denial is incredibly expensive, though. It robs you of your financial freedom today and into the future.

Moreover, if you are considering a bankruptcy, you have to understand your current financial picture, and also know how to change things for the future. In other words, the denial must stop. It'll hurt but be worth it in the end.

People Spend More on the Cards Than They Do with Cash

If you need one more reason not to use credit cards at all, here it is: Studies show that using credit cards affects the way Americans spend. In a nutshell, we spend more money with the card than we would with cash. We make larger purchases in department stores, leave bigger tips in restaurants, and are more likely to forget or underestimate the amounts spent on recent purchases. In fact, Duncan Simester, a professor at M.I.T.'s Sloan School of Management, found that consumers are even willing to pay more for the same item, up to 100 percent more, if they are paying for it with plastic rather than with cash.

For me, the scary part of this study is that people seemed to continue spending more on the card than with cash, even after being told about the phenomenon. In other words, they didn't seem to be able to stop doing it.

If you think about all the money you could be needlessly spending on your credit card, perhaps under the rationalization of getting a free airline ticket or two, it might well be cheaper to just buy the tickets. You'd have less garbage to take care of, too.

We are not in favor of the new bankruptcy law, which we will begin talking about shortly. In fact, we are quite opposed because it will make it much harder for average Americans to afford and file a bankruptcy.

If we as Americans can get our collective financial acts together, however, the new bankruptcy law could actually bring about some positive changes in our society. Perhaps people will begin to spend a bit less on things they do not need. Perhaps people will become less willing to pay interest and fees to credit card companies. This is truly our hope and one big goal in writing this book. What an amazing feat it would be if a large number of people paying interest and fees stopped doing so. This would reduce profits for credit card companies, a trend I'd love to be part of. Wouldn't you?

Recently, Judge John C. Nifto II, chief bankruptcy judge for the Western District of New York spoke to high school students about the dangers of credit cards. He noted that many young people are solicited by credit card companies early in life, and later end up in bankruptcy. Many admit that if someone had warned them about the pitfalls of credit use, they would have dealt with credit cards differently and would not have needed to file for bankruptcy.

While spending fasts* are not 100 percent realistic, getting off the cards is. While it may not be possible for you to do this just yet, we hope it will be soon!

The National Consumer Law Center has a fantastic workbook that you can use to see how long it will take to pay off your credit cards without a bankruptcy. It is available at www.consumerlaw.org, or by calling 617-542-9595.

---

*A spending "fast" means you do not spend, except as is absolutely necessary. It is like an eating fast.

CHAPTER 5

The Basics of Debtor—Creditor Law: A Quick Vocabulary Lesson

We now move into the more technical parts of this book, the ones that tell you about the current and future bankruptcy systems. This might seem tedious at times, but we do our best to make it as understandable as possible. This area of the law (bankruptcy and creditors' rights) is highly complex. Congress' new law does consumers a huge disservice, by making the law even more complex, and also by encouraging some lawyers to leave this area of the law, thus making it harder for you to find a lawyer.

Before we tell you the details of the different kinds of bankruptcy, and also explore other options for getting out of debt, we need to go over some basic vocabulary. The things you learn here will help you understand the substance of the rest of this book.

Debtor and Creditors

Debt is the amount you or someone else owes to another person. Someone who owes debts is called a "debtor." You do not pronounce the "*b*." *Debtor rhymes with letter*. Sometimes we also call someone who borrows money a "borrower."

A person who is owed a debt has extended credit to a debtor, either voluntarily or involuntarily, and is thus called a "creditor." The term creditor is broad enough to cover banks you have borrowed money from, companies from whom you have taken out car loans or mortgages, utility companies, creditor card companies, and even people whom you may have injured in a car accident. In other words, your creditors (the people you owe money to) include people who have voluntarily lent you money, as well as people who may be owed by you as a result of an involuntary action, like an accident.

In bankruptcy, your creditors include anyone to whom you *could* owe money, for anything that has already happened, even if no one has asked you to pay anything yet. Thus, if you hit someone with your car and you still don't even know if the person got hurt or not, the person is still one of your creditors at least for our purposes in explaining debtor–creditor law. The claim is *contingent* but it is still a possible claim. When thinking about who your creditors are, think very broadly.

Most people have lots of creditors and so they fall into the category "debtor." Of course, most people are also creditors. If you work, and are owned money for which you have not been paid, your employer owes you money and is your debtor. If you recently lent your sister money, or if you put down a deposit for utility services that you have not yet received, these people are also your debtors. They owe you money. As you can see, most people are both debtors and creditors. We tell you this for two reasons. First, so you will understand what we mean by the words *debtor* and *creditor* throughout the rest of this book, and second so that you will not feel badly about being called a debtor yourself. I am a debtor, Stewart is a debtor, your priest, minister, or rabbi is a debtor. It is the American human condition and nothing to worry about or be ashamed of.

Secured Versus Unsecured Debts: Types of Liens

Debts come in two basic flavors, secured and unsecured. Secured creditors have greater rights against their debtors in all contexts, inside bankruptcy, outside bankruptcy, both before bankruptcy and after bankruptcy. That's why we dwell on the distinction between secured creditors and unsecured creditors early and continue to talk about it throughout this book.

Secured creditors are very powerful creditors. So who are they? Secured creditors are those creditors who are holding particular property or *collateral* to secure their debt. Think of a real property mortgage on a home to secure the repayment of the home loan. Secured claims can also be secured or collateralized by personal property, like cars, household furniture, bank accounts, and investment accounts, almost anything. Collateral or *security* for loans can even include things that are intangible (things you cannot see or touch), such as business assets like trademarks, accounts receivable, the goodwill in a business, and other things.

Right now, you are just trying to understand the concept of collateral, which is property that secures a loan. Most people have granted a security interest to at least a few creditors. We mentioned a home mortgage previously. The home mortgage lender is a secured creditor. Another common secured creditor is the automobile lender. If you buy a car on credit, you give a security interest in the car to the lender. You may have bought furniture on credit and given back a security interest in the furniture to the store you bought it from. Or you may have bought things on a store credit card. When you do that, the receipt you sign usually grants a security interest in the goods you bought from the store. In other words, when you buy a sweater or a refrigerator from Sears on your Sears credit card, Sears usually retains a security interest in the items that you bought.

Who cares, you might be asking? You do. If a creditor is secured, meaning the creditor holds a security interest in some of your property, the creditor can repossess the property that is subject to the security interest if you do not pay the loan, precisely as you promised to. Sometimes the creditor can repossess its collateral (the stuff subject to the security interest) just because you paid one of your other debts late.

Repossession is most common with cars. Mobile homes can also be repossessed, though it is pretty hard to do without a court order. Regular houses cannot be repossessed without a court proceeding. Still, if you do not pay for your home mortgage, you will lose your home. Household goods can be repossessed, but it is rare that the creditor will bother. Still, repossession is always a possibility if a creditor holds a security interest.

You should now sit down and make a list of all your creditors whom you think might have a security interest, meaning those who have collateral backing up their loans. If you are not sure who they are, go back and read the prior few paragraphs.

If you decide not to file for bankruptcy, you will still need to make sure that you know who is secured. You'll need to pay those creditors on time. We help you prioritize your debts later, but keep in mind that paying for your car and your house must be done if you'd like to keep them. I know you probably already know this but just in case, we remind you here. We are always amazed at the number of people we meet who have not kept these payments current. We also realize that sometimes you just don't have the money. Still, keeping these secured debts current should be a high priority.

When we start to discuss bankruptcy options, you'll read that secured creditors continue to be treated very favorably in bankruptcy. In the most common form of bankruptcy, Chapter 7 liquidation, a debtor gets very little respite from secured creditors.

In the other common type of consumer bankruptcy, Chapter 13, secured debts can be restructured to some extent. Bankruptcy reform very significantly limits the extent to which this restructuring can occur, as you'll read in Chapter 15. Thus, in Chapter 13 secured debts are still very strongly favored. For the most part, if you do not pay them, they have the right to take back their collateral, sell it, and apply the proceeds toward the loan.

Note

Returning a car you do not want or can no longer pay for will *not* wipe out the car loan. You will still owe that part of the loan that the lender was not able to recover from selling the car. We call this a *deficiency claim*. I've never seen a repossession or return of a car that did not result in some remaining debt due after the car was returned or repossessed. This debt, the deficiency claim, is no longer secured. It is in that other category of debt, unsecured debt. Lots and lots of different kinds of debts are unsecured debts.

Unsecured debts are debts for which a creditor does not have any collateral. Most debts fall into this category. Credit card debts (other than those store credit cards we talked about) are unsecured debts. Doctor and hospital bills are unsecured debts. Utility bills, lawyers bills, bills for services such as lawn care or car repairs, school tuition bills, are all also unsecured, unless you pledged or gave collateral to back them up.

Again, you may be asking why you care. Basically because unsecured creditors (those without collateral) do not have the same collection rights as secured creditors and do not have the same power over you as secured creditors.

Since unsecured creditors do not have any collateral supporting or backing up their debts, they must go to court to reach any of a debtor's property in order to satisfy their debts. As you will see in more detail later, many debtors have no property from which an unsecured creditor can be paid. This is because every state allows debtors to hold and keep some property, free from the claims of creditors who are executing and trying to get paid. You could be one of these people. If you are, you may not need to file for bankruptcy in order to keep all of your property. You'll learn more about this later.

To review, secured creditors have collateral backing up their debt. As a result, the secured creditor usually has the right to simply repossess the collateral, sell it, and get paid on the loan from the proceeds. Courts need not get involved. Therein lies one of the big differences between being secured and being unsecured under state law.

Types of Secured Claims or Liens

There are three basic kinds of secured creditors, and all hold what we call *liens* in particular property:

1. *Voluntary* liens or security interests, which are created by contract. A creditor holds one of these types of liens if you voluntarily give it a security interest or a mortgage. This is typically done when you buy the house, car, household goods, or whatever.

2. *Involuntary* liens, which are created through the state court execution process described later. These liens are not created by contract; the debtor must be forced to pay through the judgment, execution, and sale process. This all occurs against the debtor's will, which is why they are called involuntary liens.

3. *Statutory* or *common law* liens, which are created by state statutes or by courts. They give special property rights to certain creditors, by legislative or judicial creation. Examples include landlords' liens in property left on premises, which can be sold and used to pay past due rent, and mechanics' liens in favor of contractors who have created a benefit on a property owner's land or property but who have not been paid.

All three types of liens, voluntary, involuntary, and statutory, allow the creditor to get the property in which they hold the lien so they can sell it and apply the proceeds to the debt.

State Collection Law and Exemptions

Since unsecured creditors do not have an interest in any particular property of yours, if they are not paid back voluntarily, they generally must go through a long and tortured process to be paid. They must go to court, get an order of the court that asks the sheriff to sell some of your property, give the order to a sheriff, get the sheriff to seize your property, and sell it. This is a long and expensive process.

While a creditor can attempt to exert societal pressure or another form of leverage upon you to get paid, if none of that works, the creditor must go to court, get a judgment against you, and get a sheriff to execute or seize property and sell it in satisfaction of the judgment.

Once the creditor obtains a judgment, which can take quite a while in and of itself, the creditor cannot seize any of your property that it chooses. Rather, the creditor must determine what is exempt from execution, and then get a sheriff to *levy* or *execute* on the judgment.

Every state allows people to keep some things, even if they owe other people money. A typical state exemption statute would allow a debtor to keep some equity in a home, a car, clothing, and so on. There is a chart of the exemptions (Appendix A) in the back of this book. Again, if you owe money to someone who does not have collateral for his or her debt, or whose collateral has already been returned to the creditor, the creditor cannot collect any money from you except from assets that do not fall within the state law exemptions.

This has nothing to do with bankruptcy. Look now and see what assets are exempt in your state in Appendix A in the back of this book. Do you own anything that falls outside the exempt categories and assets? If not, you do not need a bankruptcy to protect your assets. In essence, you are "judgment proof," which does *not* mean you do not have any assets. It just means that you have no nonexempt assets, no assets from which to satisfy unsecured claims.

So why does the law protect your assets from creditors in this way? The theory behind allowing the debtor to keep these things is that it will accomplish very little to force people to become homeless, to take away their transportation to work, and to take away their clothing. These assets are presumably needed to hold down a job, and are virtually worthless to a creditor. People should be able to keep enough to survive, so the theory goes, and to avoid becoming wards of, and charges upon, the state.

If you look at Appendix A, you'll notice that state law exemptions vary incredibly from state to state. For example, in New Mexico, each person can keep $30,000 in equity in a home, and $4,000 equity in a car, free from any executing creditor. In Delaware, however, there is no allowance for a home (meaning no *homestead exemption*) and very little exemption for a car or anything else. In Texas and in Florida, a debtor can keep unlimited equity in a home, even if the home is worth many millions of dollars. Thus, an unpaid creditor, or even the victim of a hit-and-run accident, could not force the sale of even a million dollar home in Texas to pay a judgment that a court held was now due and owing.

Keep in mind that what is considered exempt property is determined based upon the debtor's *equity* in the property, meaning the amount of value in each item over and above any secured loans on the property. To determine the equity in a piece of property, you must value the property, and then subtract the amount of any secured creditor claims.

Example

You own a $70,000 home with a $50,000 mortgage on it as well as a $15,000 second mortgage on it. Your equity in the home is $5,000. In other words, your state law exemptions are calculated based upon the amount of equity you have, not the total value of the house, car, and so on. You just take the value of the assets, subtract the amount of the lien and what is left is the equity, which must fit within the exemptions.

Introduction to the Different Types of Bankruptcy

In the next chapter, we help you assess your situation to see if you need or could benefit from a bankruptcy. Here, we introduce you to the basic forms of consumer bankruptcy so you will know a few things about the process before assessing your own needs.

Federal bankruptcy law is a uniquely American phenomenon. It is an intricate system designed, in part, to fuel and support capitalism. The system has in the past been quite lenient on debtors in many ways and has allowed people to get out from under their debts with few societal repercussions. Some of these rules are now changing. The new Bankruptcy Code, effective October 17, 2005, is unquestionably harder on consumers than the old law. Whether the changes will affect you personally is something we take up in Chapter 6.

For now, we move on with our general introduction to bankruptcy law. Just as we saw under state law, secured creditors have superior rights in bankruptcy when compared to creditors who do not have any collateral. You'll also read that some unsecured debts receive special treatment (which we call *priority* status) because society finds them important. All the rules are designed to reflect what we find important as a society. If you can learn the policy behind a bankruptcy rule, it will help you understand the rule.

In the United States, all the different kinds of bankruptcy are designed to balance two things: the rights of debtors to a fresh start or a second chance, and the rights of creditors to be paid. This tension is present in all aspects of the system, and all types of bankruptcy send off the same general vibe: Get in trouble with your creditors and the bankruptcy system will help you find a way out. This is far less true under the new law, however.

Bankruptcy cases in the United States fall into two models or categories. They are either "sell out" or liquidation-style cases (also sometimes called "straight bankruptcy" cases), in which the assets available for creditors are sold and distributed to creditors, quickly ending the case, *or* they are "pay out" cases in which the debtor promises in a plan of repayment to pay some or all creditors from future income over time. Both the phrases "sell out" and "pay out" can be misnomers, but these are quick generalizations that should help you learn the basics.

Chapter 7

In the past, about 70 percent of all personal bankruptcy cases filed in the United States have been Chapter 7 cases. These are called liquidation cases, or sell out cases, and are quickly resolved. In each Chapter 7 case, a trustee is appointed to gather all assets available to pay creditors, sell them, and distribute the proceeds according to a priority scheme that favors some types of creditors over others. The trustee is a fiduciary for all creditors (he or she must work for the benefit of creditors) and is charged with maximizing value for estate creditors, usually by rooting around for nonexempt assets to be used to pay creditors' claims. At the end of the case, the debtor receives a discharge, meaning the debtor does not have to pay the old debts.

Just so you know, just as under state law, some property is exempt in a bankruptcy as well. As a result, in 96 percent of Chapter 7 liquidation cases, none of the debtor's property is liquidated. The debtor loses none of his or her property. Instead, in exchange for a complete and full disclosure of all financial information to the general public records, the debtor receives a discharge of most of his or her debts within 90 days of filing the Chapter 7 case. Secured debts are not discharged, nor are certain other debts such as student loans, most taxes, alimony and support, and certain others described more fully later in this book.*

Most Chapter 7 cases are simple and uneventful. What issues might come up in an individual's Chapter 7 case? First, if the debtor's disclosures are not complete, the case could be a total disaster and the debtor could even end up in jail. We don't mean to scare you, but telling the whole truth is critical in a bankruptcy case. If you can't do that, skip to Chapter 6 and we discuss some other options.

What else? The trustee could disagree with the debtor about which property is exempt and may challenge the values of the debtor's property as too low, thus arguing that there would be assets available to creditors if the property (or some part of it) were sold. The trustee or an individual creditor might object to the debtor's discharge due to wrongdoing on the part of the debtor right before or during the bankruptcy case (if the debtor hid assets, for example). Perhaps a creditor will object to the dischargeability of its particular debt, or perhaps the United States Trustee's office or the court might object to the case because the debtor has income over and above his expenses and thus could afford a Chapter 13 plan.

In most cases, though, the case will be over within 90 days of the filing. There are no court hearings, and after these 90 days are over, the debtor obtains a discharge of most of his or her debts.

Chapter 13

Chapter 13, as compared to Chapter 7, cases are pay out rather than sell out cases. As a general matter, the debtor does not sell its nonexempt assets and instead is allowed to keep all the assets as long as the debtor is paying at least the value of these nonexempt assets to creditors under the plan.

Chapter 13 cases are for individual debtors only. Thus, corporations or partnerships cannot use Chapter 13 although the people who own the partnership or corporation can use it.

The idea behind Chapter 13 is that the debtor will propose a repayment plan for paying creditors and will make the proposed payments for three to five years. During that time, the debtor will pay all secured claims in full (as you'll see, this is not necessarily the whole debt), all priority claims in full, and will pay a distribution to unsecured creditors as well, assuming the debtor has sufficient disposable income to do so.

---

*Chapter 7 is available to both legal entities like corporations and limited liability companies, as well as to individuals. If a corporation or company files a Chapter 7 case, this is the easiest case of all. There are typically no issues. The corporation is entitled to no exemptions because it does not continue in existence. For the same reason, it also does not get a discharge. Thus, the two most litigated issues in a Chapter 7, exemptions and dischargeabilty, are not in issue.

The case is administered by a Chapter 13 trustee, who, like the Chapter 7 trustee, is a fiduciary for creditors and is charged with creating the best possible recoveries for the debtor's creditors. The trustee may do this by trying to get the debtor to contribute more of his income to the plan, by objecting to the debtor's expenses as profligate, or by encouraging the debtor to sell some property if this is the only way the plan will work.

Common issues in cases arising in a Chapter 13 case include: (1) the value of the allowed secured claims, and thus the underlying collateral (because in some cases the debtor can just pay the value of the collateral, rather than the whole loan); (2) the priority treatment of certain claims; (3) whether the debtor has contributed all of his disposable income to the plan, which is required under Chapter 13; and (4) the value of exempt property as that bears on the minimum distributions the debtor must pay under the plan. Under the new law, disposable income is measured under the new *means test*.

The Chapter 13 trustee plays a very large role in the success of Chapter 13 cases and is often the one to object to the plan and otherwise insure that it complies with the Code.

Chapter 13 cases are huge commitments. They require the debtor to contribute all of his or her disposable income to creditors for a period of three to five years.

Right now, the debtor normally gets to choose whether to do a quick and dirty Chapter 7 case and just walk away from his or her debts, or whether to instead do a Chapter 13 payment plan. Those debtors who choose to do a Chapter 13 payment plan, usually in order to pay off arrears on a home mortgage, can choose either a three-year or a five-year plan. Under bankruptcy reform, many debtors will be required to do a Chapter 13 case rather than a Chapter 7, and many will be forced to do five-year plans.

Unless a debtor needs a great deal of help with past-due taxes or support, the home mortgage is in arrears, the debtor has large debts resulting from fraud or an intentional tort (an action taken against another that caused the other person monetary harm), or had a good income and a lot of nonexempt assets he or she wanted to keep, most debtors under the old law chose a Chapter 7 because it created more benefits more quickly than a payment plan.

Chapter 7 will be less available after October 17, 2005. Moreover, Chapter 13 will be less desirable. If you are considering a bankruptcy and this date is approaching, you may want to read fast!

Although most of this book is about the two most common forms of bankruptcy for individuals, Chapter 7 and Chapter 13, here we briefly introduce you to two other forms of bankruptcy, just for your general information.

Chapter 12

Chapter 12 is a bankruptcy scheme for family farmers. After October 17, 2005, it will also cover family fishermen. A family farmer (or fisherman) is a person who receives more than 80 percent of his or her gross income from farming or fishing, and who (with his or her family) owns a large part of the business that generates that income.

Chapter 12 is very similar to Chapter 13 but has slightly easier repayment rules and higher debt limits. The debt limits for a family farmer until October 17, 2005, are $1,500,000. That means a person can file a Chapter 12 if his or her debts are at this level or lower.

Chapter 12 has been changed rather significantly by bankruptcy reform. The new law has created even higher debt limits and also made other changes that make it somewhat easier for family farmers, as well as family fishermen, to restructure their debts. The debt limits are now $3,237,000 for family farmers and $1,500,000 for family fishermen.

Family farmers and fishermen are allowed to pay less on their secured debts, so this type of bankruptcy can be very beneficial for some debtors. The new Chapter 12 also has very favorable tax treatment for farmers.

Chapter 11

Chapter 11 is a pay out style case available to individuals, but almost always used by business entities like corporations. You can read about big Chapter 11 cases that are pending right now by reading the front page of the *Wall Street Journal*. Recent cases include K-Mart, Enron, WorldCom, and so on.

Most individuals file a Chapter 11 case only if they are over the Chapter 13 debt limit, which is $307,675 in unsecured debts and $922,975 in secured debts. Remember that these numbers increase on April 1 every year and these numbers are for 2005. The reason individuals prefer Chapter 13 to restructure their debts, even if they are business debts, is that Chapter 13 is far less complex and far less expensive than Chapter 11.

Chapter 11 cases involve restructuring the debts and other obligations of companies that need help. The general idea, as with Chapter 13, is that the debtor will repay a portion of its debts over time, from its future operations. Its plan will need to pay its allowed secured claims in full, its priority claims in full, and will pay a distribution to its unsecured creditors as well.

Introduction to the Concept of Discharge in Bankruptcy

Most individual debtors file a bankruptcy petition under either Chapter 7 or Chapter 13. For most individual debtors, the whole purpose of the bankruptcy is to obtain a bankruptcy discharge. This frees the debtor from the legal obligation to pay discharged debts, and creditors are forever barred from collecting those discharged debts under a permanent injunction against collection. Though not all debts get discharged, most do, making the discharge the most important and powerful motivation for filing for bankruptcy.

In a famous case called *Local Loan v. Hunt*, 292 U.S. 234 (1934), the U.S. Supreme Court explained the policy behind this incredibly important aspect of bankruptcy law:

> One of the primary purposes of the bankruptcy act is to 'relieve the honest debtor from the weight of oppressive indebtedness, and permit him to start afresh free from the obligations and responsibilities consequent upon business misfortunes.' This purpose of the act has been again and again emphasized by the courts as being of public as well as private interest, in that it gives to the honest but unfortunate debtor . . . a new opportunity in life and a clear field for future effort, unhampered by the pressure and discouragement of preexisting debt.

This policy of a *fresh start* has historically been a uniquely American phenomenon. Ironically, as we are moving toward a more difficult discharge, many countries around the world are moving toward our more lenient system. This is often being done to fuel flagging economies around the world.

Note the emphasis in the *Hunt* case on a "clear field for future effort." The theory is that American capitalism is best served by making sure that people are motivated to make money, and free to spend and fuel the economy in the future.

Discharge in a Chapter 7

If you qualify for a Chapter 7 case and you file one, you will probably be discharged from most of your unsecured debts. More on this in Chapter 12 of this book. You will need to keep current on your secured debts for the most part, or you can return the collateral to the secured creditor and get discharged from any deficiency. *If you fail to disclose all your assets, you will not receive a discharge.*

Even if you *do* get a discharge, it will not discharge debts for alimony and support, most taxes, student loans, fraud, intentional torts, and some cash advances and luxury goods charged to credit cards during the months before your bankruptcy case. The rest, though, should be discharged and this should happen within 90 days of filing your case. This is amazing if you think about it. Once the 90 days is over, the discharged debts are gone forever, and creditors with discharged debts are never again allowed to ask you to pay them. This is the point of filing for bankruptcy for most people.

Important

You can get a Chapter 7 discharge only once every six years under current law and once every eight years under the new law in effect on and after October 17, 2005.

Discharge in a Chapter 13

Chapter 13 involves paying debts off over time with future income. While some Chapter 13 plans pay all creditors in full, even general unsecured creditors, most do not. In most Chapter 13 cases, secured creditors get paid in full (at least up to the value of their collateral but sometimes the whole debt) and claims entitled to priority get paid, but general unsecured claims typically receive just a percentage of the amount they are owed. The rest of their debts are discharged at the end of the Chapter 13 case.

In a Chapter 13, under pre-October 17, 2005, law, you can discharge fraud claims, embezzlement claims, certain tax claims, and claims for intentional torts. Thus, the current (pre-October 17, 2005) Chapter 13 discharge is broader than the Chapter 7 discharge. For that reason, the Chapter 13 discharge is sometimes called a "super-discharge."

Under the new law, these debts (for intentional torts, fraud, and so on) will not be discharged under either a Chapter 7 or a Chapter 13.

Important

In a Chapter 13, you do not get a discharge until you have completed all of your plan payments. This means the discharge occurs (if at all) three or five years after your case is filed. We have seen cases dismissed without a discharge when the debtor paid the whole Chapter 13 payment plan except the last $75.

For this reason, under the new or the old law, if you have a choice about which type of bankruptcy to file (and you may *not* under the new law), we strongly recommend Chapter 7. Most Chapter 13 plans fail. That means that most Chapter 13 debtors do not get a discharge, even after years of making payments.

You need not feel guilty about using Chapter 7 if it is available to you, and just discharging most of your debts. The law allows you to voluntarily pay back whomever you like, so you need not feel like a deadbeat. You can file a Chapter 7 and still pay back whomever you like!

CHAPTER 6

Do I Need a Bankruptcy at All?: Assessing Your Situation

You now have the basic vocabulary to hold a sophisticated conversation about your own finances. Soon, you'll need to pull out the calculator and figure out how you spend money, to determine if you need a bankruptcy.

Tracking Your Expenses

One thing that will help, if you have a couple of weeks, is to keep a spending diary so you can see where every dollar is going. To determine if you need a bankruptcy, you'll need to see how much money you have each month after paying your big bills. Do you have enough to pay down your credit cards and other bills, or is that just fruitless?

Pull out a pen and paper and do your best to spell out where your money goes each day. Your checkbook register or online banking records will also help. Most people can patch it together pretty well, though there are still huge mystery amounts. The spending diary will help with that.

If you can, fill out Table 6.1, and include everything you spend. This will take about two hours. If you cannot do this yet, do a spending diary for two weeks and try again. In the meantime, keep reading.

TABLE 6.1 Budget Worksheet

Category	Monthly Budget Amount	Monthly Actual Amount	Difference between Actual and Budget
INCOME			
Wages Paid			
Bonuses			
Interest Income			
Capital Gains Income			
Dividend Income			
Miscellaneous Income			
INCOME SUBTOTAL			
EXPENSES			
Mortgage or Rent			
Utilities Gas/Water/Electric/Trash			
Cable TV/Internet Service			
Telephone			
Home Repairs/Maintenance			
Car Payments			
Gasoline/Oil			
Auto Repairs/Maintenance/Fees			
Other Transportation (tolls, bus, subway, etc.)			
Child Care			
Auto Insurance			
Home Owners/Renters Insurance			
Computer Expense			
Entertainment/Recreation			
Groceries			
Toiletries, Household Products			
Clothing			
Eating Out			

(Continued)

TABLE 6.1 (Continued)

Category	Monthly Budget Amount	Monthly Actual Amount	Difference between Actual and Budget
Gifts/Donations			
Health Care (medical/dental/vision, inc. insurance)			
Hobbies			
Interest Expense (mortgage, credit cards, fees)			
Magazines/Newspapers			
Federal Income Tax			
State Income Tax			
Social Security/Medicare Tax			
Personal Property tax			
Pets			
Miscellaneous Expense			
EXPENSES SUBTOTAL			
NET INCOME (INCOME LESS EXPENSES)			

Source: http://financialplan.about.com/library/howto/htbudget.htm

PROCEDURE FOR KEEPING A SPENDING DIARY

1. Start with the budget worksheet.

2. Go through your checkbook or bills for the past two to three months and add and delete categories from the worksheet to fit your expenditures.

3. Think about your hobbies and your habits, and be sure to add categories for these expenses.

4. Go through your pay stubs and calculate your average monthly gross pay.

5. Do the same for any interest income, dividends, bonuses, or other miscellaneous income.

6. For each expense category, try to determine a budget amount that realistically reflects your actual expenses while setting targeted spending levels that will enable you to save money.

7. Once you're comfortable with your expense categories and budgeted amounts, enter expenditures from your checkbook from the past month.

8. Keep track of cash expenditures throughout the month and total and categorize these at the end of each month.

9. Subtotal the income and expense categories.

10. Subtract the total expenses from the total income to arrive at your net income.

11. If the number is negative, your expenses are greater than your income. Your situation can probably be greatly improved by changing your spending habits.

12. If you have a positive net income, transfer most of it to a savings or investment account at the end of each month. Extra cash left in a regular checking account has a way of getting spent.

13. After you've tracked your actual spending for a month or two, analyze your spending to identify where you can comfortably make cuts.

14. Once you've got the budgeting process in place, take an in-depth look at your largest spending categories, brainstorm about ways to reduce spending in specific categories, and set realistic goals.

15. Update your budget and expenses monthly.

TIPS

- Don't try to fit your expenses into somebody else's budget categories. Tailor the categories to fit your own situation.
- Make your categories detailed enough to provide useful information, but not so detailed that you become bogged down in trivial details.

Think of your budget as a tool to help you get out of debt and save money, not as a financial diet.

If an expense is incurred more or less often than monthly, convert it to a monthly amount when calculating the monthly budget amount. For instance, auto expense that is billed every six months would be converted to monthly by dividing the six-month premium by six.

The Moran Group law firm recommends the budgeting allocation in Figure 6.1.

Another book called *All Your Worth* by Elizabeth Warren and Amelia Tyagi Warren recommends that you spend 50 percent of your pay on *must-haves* like the mortgage, the car payments, and insurance, 30 percent on *wants* like haircuts and meals out, and 20 percent on savings.

Whatever formula you ultimately choose, we hope the exercise of preparing a budget has caused you to learn a lot. Do you have a little money left over at the end of the month, which you could use to pay down your unsecured debts? If so, you may be a poor candidate for bankruptcy but a good candidate for other options.

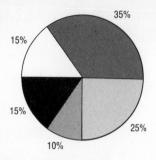

FIGURE 6.1 Household Budget

Alternatives to Bankruptcy

Bankruptcy should be a last resort. In addition to following you around on your credit report for at least 10 years and practically guaranteeing that you will have higher interest rates on new purchases, several types of debt are not discharged in bankruptcy. These include but aren't limited to IRS debt, student loans, and any debt obtained through fraud.

Generally, bankruptcy is better for people who:

- Are older and will have less time to pay off their debts and also save for retirement.
- Are young and have huge debts, but expect a very bright future.
- Have large credit card and other debts relative to their income, so large that they will never be able to pay them off.
- Have few assets outside what is exempt under state or federal law.
- Have reached rock bottom financially, and are starting to see the light at the end of the tunnel. After all, you don't want to blow your rare chance to file for bankruptcy by incurring tons of debts after you have filed. You need to time the case correctly.

Before declaring bankruptcy, consider these alternatives.

Contact Your Creditors

One of the first and easiest things you can do on your own is to call your credit card company. You may be surprised that many creditors are more than willing to cooperate. Explain why you cannot make your payments. Often collectors will suggest an arrangement that could work for both of you. Certain credit card companies are willing to renegotiate the terms of your debt. The credit card company may settle for 70 or 80 cents on the dollar (or less), lower your interest rate or both. You should not feel badly about accepting such an offer. A good negotiation is beneficial for both you and the credit card company. If you declare bankruptcy, they know they could end up with nothing on what you owe. Therefore, they are often willing to renegotiate so that they can get at least part of what they are owed. It helps you because if you are able to work out a payment plan without declaring bankruptcy, your ability to obtain future credit will be greatly enhanced.

Debt Consolidation Loans

If you have many different unsecured loans and credit card balances at high interest rates, debt consolidation can be a big help. This approach relieves you of being saddled with debt from multiple creditors, since you will be making payments only to one lender.

Start by approaching your bank or credit union about combining or consolidating your debts into one loan. Your financial institution will pay off all your debts and, in return, you make a monthly payment to that new creditor. Once this goes through, it is very important to *avoid* new credit purchases on all those zero balance credit cards you just paid off. This could make your debt load too great for you to handle.

Warning

It is usually a bad idea to borrow against your home, for example through a home equity loan, to pay off credit cards. While the lower interest rate and convenience of one monthly bill is tempting, *you'll be trading dischargeable credit card debt for a secured loan and could end up losing your home.*

A similar approach to the debt consolidation loan is to apply for one new low interest credit card to which you can transfer all the balances of your old cards. Often, new cards will reward you for transferring balances by giving an especially low interest rate on those balances—often as low as zero percent for a whole year. Remember to get rid of the old credit cards after the balance transfer. Otherwise, despite great intentions, you could find yourself with double the debt a few months down the road. And do not charge anything else on the new cards! The payments you make could be applied to the old debt, the new purchases will accrue interest, and the interest-free period will be lost.

Consumer Credit Counseling Services

Specialized consumer credit counseling services may be able to negotiate with creditors even after your own efforts have failed. They may be able to achieve results you are unable to get on your own like reducing finance charges, lowering monthly payments, and updating past due accounts with creditors. Often, credit counseling services are nonprofit organizations, and many are run by community service groups.

> ### Note
>
> Beware of counseling services that are actually fronts for profit-making companies. Does the service charge excessive administrative fees? Sometimes, the initial fees go to the counseling company rather than to creditors, which obviously makes the debt situation worse instead of better. A company that is advertising extensively on TV or radio is probably making a profit at the expense of unfortunate consumers. Remember that anyone can set up a Web page advertising a business. Do a little research over the phone to make sure you are not doing business with a faceless P.O. Box in Fargo, North Dakota.

If you do retain the services of a consumer credit counselor, be sure to take full advantage of the counseling services they offer. If you've gotten to this point, it's probably not enough to just eliminate your current debt. Rather, it is just as fundamental that you learn how to avoid debt in the future and manage your finances effectively. Working with a consumer credit counselor gives you the opportunity to school yourself in the best ways to readjust your spending habits to avoid bankruptcy.

We are extremely wary of most nonprofit consumer credit counseling services because so many have been investigated for fraud and even criminal activity. You should take extreme care before allowing anyone else to renegotiate your debt for you. Chances are, you'll get a better deal just doing it yourself.

Keep Some Payments Current No Matter What, While You Are Working Things Out

While you are trying to straighten out your finances, always pay your mortgage or rent and your car payment. At least you will not get evicted or foreclosed upon, or have your car repossessed. Also try to avoid using your IRA or hard-earned 401(k). This is a big no-no because these assets are frequently exempt from creditor execution anyway. Moreover, borrowing from these may cause you to create even *more* debt, in the form of income taxes and penalties for early withdrawal. Whatever you do, you do not want to get less than the full value for your hard-earned savings. You also don't want to simply substitute your current creditors with Uncle Sam as a tax creditor.

Finally, never ever pay someone else to fix your credit report. This is different from consumer counseling and just involves correcting mistakes on the report. The credit reporting agencies give you detailed instructions on how to do

this. Agencies that charge you to do the same thing are rip-offs under any scenario. These outfits don't do anything for you that you cannot do yourself.

Some People Are Not Good Candidates for Bankruptcy

Some people really cannot file for bankruptcy. Others will benefit so little from
a bankruptcy that there is no point in doing one.

People Who Are Judgment-Proof and Will Never Make Much Money or Have Many Assets

In Chapter 4, we briefly discussed how some assets are exempt or free from all
unsecured creditor's claims, even if you never file for bankruptcy. Someone in
this position is referred to as *judgment-proof* because they have no assets that
can be reached by a person with a judgment.

The theory about being judgment-proof is that people who are judgment-
proof do not need a bankruptcy. As the theory goes, such a person does not
need a bankruptcy because he or she has no assets over and above the property that is exempt under state law. He or she does not need a bankruptcy to
protect what they have. Under state law, without a bankruptcy, they can keep
everything they have. In others words, creditors cannot take this person's
property, and so he or she does not need a bankruptcy.

This theory often holds true for people who are on Social Security or public
disability benefits, which are not reachable by most creditors anyway. If you
hope to improve your financial position in life, however, the theory is flawed.

If you are young and working and hope to improve your situation over time,
then a bankruptcy can help you. Without a bankruptcy, creditors continue to
lie in wait, and can always attach what you later acquire. In fact, their mere
existence can discourage you from actually acquiring anything of value. In
many cases, it may be better to get rid of the creditors once and for all. This of
course assumes that you know how to bankruptcy-proof yourself for the future.
That mostly involves saving for emergencies and operating with cash rather
than credit.

People Who Have Assets That Are Not Exempt But Do Not Have Much Income

As we just discussed, some assets are exempt or free from all unsecured creditor's
claims, even if you never file for bankruptcy. Someone in this position is referred
to as judgment-proof because they have no assets that can be reached by a person
with a judgment. If you have quite a few nonexempt assets, but not much income,
you will not be able to keep the property and also complete a successful consumer
bankruptcy case. You will lose the nonexempt property in a Chapter 7 case. In a
Chapter 13, you could keep the nonexempt property, but only if you can pay at
least its value to creditors under your plan. Without sufficient income, you will not
be able to do this. Thus, bankruptcy is not a good option.

People Who Have Incurred Large Debts through Fraud or Other Wrongdoing

If you have incurred large debts through fraud and other misdeeds, you should quickly flip to Chapter 11 of this book. That chapter discusses a series of debts that do not get discharged in bankruptcy. While some of these debts will be discharged in a completed Chapter 13 case filed before October 17, 2005, most people filing before that date will choose a Chapter 7.

You can discharge these types of debts, as long as you filed a Chapter 13 case before October 17, 2005. Chapter 7 does not discharge debts for fraud or intentional torts.

People Who Have Recently Tried to Hide Assets from Creditors By Transferring Them to Others

Sometimes people try to plan for their bankruptcies, by transferring assets to friends and family members, waiting a while, and then hoping that no one will find out about the transfers in their subsequent bankruptcy. This is a very dangerous strategy. You simply cannot file a bankruptcy unless you can fully disclose all the transfers you have made in the two years prior to your bankruptcy case (and longer in some cases). Full and complete disclosure of all your past financial dealings is absolutely necessary. In fact, it is a predicate to getting a bankruptcy discharge.

No one should file a bankruptcy case who is not willing to tell it all. Besides losing your discharge for nondisclosure, the bankruptcy will also undo some of these transfers (those over $600 to any one person), bringing these assets back into your bankruptcy estate for distribution to your creditors. If you have already done some of these transfers, you should look for options other than bankruptcy, even if you did not mean to do anything wrong. Speak to your lawyer for the specifics.

People Who Lost a Huge Sum of Money Recently

If you lost a huge sum lately, say $30,000 or more in the past year, you will not receive a discharge in bankruptcy. The law assumes the money is under your mattress and you will get no benefit out of a bankruptcy. One humorous reported case involved a man who lost (or could not explain the disappearance of) about $90,000. He tried, though. He told the judge he had spent it on "wine, women, and song." The judge did not believe him, again assuming it was hidden somewhere. If you have a legitimate explanation for a loss of funds, such as that one of your employees stole it, bankruptcy may still work for you. Don't make things up, though, or you could end up in jail.

People Who Have Already Received a Recent Bankruptcy Discharge

You cannot file for Chapter 7 bankruptcy if you obtained a bankruptcy discharge of your debts under Chapter 7 or Chapter 13 in a case begun within the past six years. However, if you obtained a Chapter 13 discharge in good faith after paying at least 70 percent of your unsecured debts, the six-year bar does not apply.

The six-year period runs from the date you filed for the earlier bankruptcy, not the date you received your discharge. *This period is being extended to eight years under the new law.*

Example

Mary Marks filed a Chapter 7 bankruptcy case on June 31, 2002. She received a discharge on September 25, 2002. Mary files another Chapter 7 bankruptcy on November 1, 2008. The second bankruptcy is allowed because six years have passed since the date the earlier bankruptcy was filed (even though fewer than six years have passed since Mary received a discharge in the earlier case).

This case would not be allowed to go forward and would instead be dismissed under bankruptcy reform.

People Who Had a Previous Bankruptcy Case Dismissed within the Previous 180 Days

You cannot file for Chapter 7 bankruptcy if your previous Chapter 7 or Chapter 13 case was dismissed within the past 180 days because:

- You violated a court order.
- You requested the dismissal after a creditor asked for relief from the automatic stay (11 U.S.C. § 109(g).).

Under the new law, bankruptcy will be far less advantageous for people who filed a case and then had it dismissed because they did not get all the paperwork right. Under the new law, your case can be automatically dismissed for a series of minor omissions, such as the failure to produce a tax return or other document required by the new law.

If you file a second case within one year of another case (one that presumably was dismissed because you failed or forgot to do something), the automatic stay goes into effect only for 30 days after the second filing, unless you can show that the second case was filed in good faith. It is your burden to meet this test.

If the second case is also dismissed, and a third case is filed within one year, the automatic stay does not go into effect at all in that third case, unless the court, upon a debtor's motion, finds that the debtor has proven that the new case was filed in good faith. The presumption is that the case was not filed in good faith.

People Who Had a Friend or Relative Cosign a Loan and Don't Want Them Subjected to Collection for the Loan

A friend, relative, or anyone else who cosigns a loan or otherwise takes on a joint obligation with you can be held wholly responsible for the debt if you don't pay it. If you receive a Chapter 7 bankruptcy discharge, you may no longer be liable for the debt, but your cosigners will be left on the hook. If you don't want this to happen, you'll need to use one of the alternatives to Chapter 7 bankruptcy that are outlined later. By arranging to pay the debt over time, you can keep creditors from going after your cosigners for payment.

People Who Can Afford to Pay a Chapter 13 Plan

If you qualify to file a Chapter 13 bankruptcy, the bankruptcy court may dismiss your Chapter 7 bankruptcy on the ground that granting a Chapter 7 discharge would be an abuse of the bankruptcy laws (11 U.S.C. § 707(b)). The Court can do this only if your debts are primarily consumer debts (not business debts).

Remember how you read earlier about the difference between a Chapter 7 case and a Chapter 13 case? Chapter 7 allows a person with few assets (or all exempt assets) to walk away from most unsecured debts without losing any property. Right now, under the old law, this is limited by a test that says that if you have money left over at the end of the month after paying your expenses, you can be forced to do a Chapter 13 payment plan instead, and thus pay off at least some of your otherwise dischargeable debts.

In the new law, this process of forcing a person to do a Chapter 13 if they can afford one is far more formalized. It is called the *means test*. Experts say that access to the walk-away Chapter 7 discharge will be far more limited. Thus, if you think that a Chapter 7 is best for you, you may want to at least consider filing before October 17.

You need not worry about the means test at all if your current income (measured by your actual income for the six months prior to your bankruptcy case) is below the median income for a family of your size in your state. Even if your income is above the median income, you cannot be forced into Chapter 13 unless you have at least $100 a month left over at the end of the month after deducting certain allowed expenses. This is covered in more detail in Chapter 13 of this book.

If you have $167 left over at the end of each month, you must do a five-year payment plan. However, if what is left over is between $100 a month and $166 a month, then you only have to do a Chapter 13 payment plan if doing so will result in payment of 25 percent of your unsecured creditors. Could this be any more complicated? I think not, which is probably part of the point here. We think Congress was attempting to discourage bankruptcy filing through this incomprehensible provision.

Of course, this is even trickier than we've made it sound, and for more information on this you need to read Chapter 13 of this book. The trickiest part is figuring out which expenses are allowed to come out of the income before you calculate what is left over at the end of the month. As it turns out, secured debts will lower what is left over. That means you can deduct your car payment and your house payment before figuring out what's left. The bigger these secured debts, the less likely that you'll be forced into a Chapter 13 plan against your will.

Renters, however, are far less likely to fare well under this test because they have no mortgage to deduct from their income. And overall, expenses can be severely limited. Moreover, under the new means test, all Chapter 13 cases for which the debtor falls within the means test range must be paid over five years, when in the past all debtors could choose a three-year Chapter 13 repayment plan.

People Who May Have Committed Tax Evasion

If you receive a lot of your income under the table, meaning you do not pay taxes on it, a bankruptcy could lead to huge problems on the tax evasion front. You cannot avoid telling your actual past income in your bankruptcy, so if you cannot disclose all your income without raising tax issues, do not file for bankruptcy. Being in debt is always better than being in prison, if you know what I mean.

People Who Have Made Recent Payments to Friends and Relatives and Do Not Want These Transfers Undone

If you recently paid back loans or made large gifts to your business colleagues or family members, which you don't want your creditors to be able to undo and recover from the people you paid back, then you should not file for bankruptcy. These types of transfers are called *preferential transfers* (or sometimes fraudulent transfers).

Preferential transfers are not a crime, are not evil, and are definitely nothing to be embarrassed about. It's just that the bankruptcy laws bring back all payments on loans made to these people for a whole year before the filing, so the money can be distributed equally to all of your creditors.

If you don't want them to ask Mom for that $2,500 you repaid her during the past year, do not file a bankruptcy.

People Whose Future Looks Even More Grim than Their Past

Bankruptcy is an opportunity that can be used only once in a while. You want to make sure you time your bankruptcy to get the most benefit out of it. It is generally not a good idea to file for bankruptcy while you are unemployed. You are likely to incur more debts while you are waiting to find a job, and the bankruptcy discharges only past debts, not future ones. Another bad time to file is while you are really sick. Ideally, you would file after you were well, so that you would not incur more medical costs after your bankruptcy. You clearly want to be looking at a brighter future when you discharge your old debts and reach for your new life and fresh start.

Having said that, there are times when you may just need immediate relief from your creditors even though the future is uncertain. Maybe you really need to stop a foreclosure or an eviction to keep from becoming homeless.* You need a future plan, and you are better off filing for bankruptcy after you have one.

This common strategy, that you need to time your bankruptcy perfectly so you can get the most benefit from it, is called into question by bankruptcy reform. Now it may be best to file before October 17, 2005, a topic we discuss in the next chapter.

---

*Keep in mind that the relief you get from these kinds of things is very temporary. See Chapter 9.

CHAPTER 7

The New Law versus the Old Law: If I Need to File, Should I File Now or Later?

If you are reading this book after October 17, 2005, you can skip this chapter. Obviously, there were certain advantages to getting a bankruptcy filed before the new law became effective. This does not mean you cannot benefit from a bankruptcy after October 17, 2005, as well. If it is after October 17, 2005, you should proceed now to Chapter 8.

As you now know, Congress just changed the bankruptcy laws to make it much harder for a debtor to get discharged from his or her debts. There has been a lot of press about the changes, all of which are aimed at curbing abuses of the bankruptcy system. Most people who are working in the system do not believe there was much abuse of the system, but nevertheless, Congress changed the old law.

The most famous part of the new law is the means test, which is supposed to force more debtors into Chapter 13 instead of allowing them to file a Chapter 7. The means test will probably force only a small number of debtors into Chapter 13. The complicated means test analysis, however, has to be completed by every individual debtor (meaning every debtor who is a living, breathing human being, as opposed to a corporation or a partnership).

There are actually many other important changes that will essentially affect all future bankruptcy debtors, at least those who file on or after October 17, 2005. These include tremendous new burdens on attorneys, which will likely discourage many from continuing to represent bankruptcy debtors.

There will be many more pieces of paper to file in every single case. Clients will need to have much more (and much more accurate) information to give to their attorneys.

Secured debts are also treated much more favorably under the new law, which will make it far harder for many debtors to do successful Chapter 13 cases.

How Can You Tell If You Need to File a Bankruptcy, or Whether You Can Instead Do Something Else?

For most people who need a bankruptcy, it will be better to file before October 17, 2005, if possible. However, we do worry that people who do not need a bankruptcy or who would not be good candidates for bankruptcy (see Chapter 6) will file one anyway while the rush is on. This could be a big mistake. There is nothing about the new law that makes bankruptcy more desirable for the people described in Chapter 6. If you have other options, such as borrowing from a relative, or cutting back on spending and paying off your bills, those options may be preferable to filing for bankruptcy either now or later. If you are still unsure whether you need a bankruptcy, reread Chapter 6. You should also go see a lawyer for a consultation.

If You Need to File and You Wait, It Could Be Much Harder to Find a Lawyer and Much More Expensive to File

Under the new law, there is much more paperwork for a bankruptcy debtor to file. Moreover, if you file your case and forget some of this paperwork, then your case will be dismissed. If you file a new case to fix the mistake, you also will be deprived of many of the benefits of bankruptcy in the new case, at least if the new case is filed within a year of the first one. This was changed so that people would be discouraged from filing multiple cases, but the new law also punishes people who make innocent mistakes.

This is such a precarious position for consumers because it makes it far more necessary than before to *use a lawyer*! We have never recommended filing a bankruptcy without a lawyer. There are legal aid offices that can file for people who truly have no money, and at least in the past, bankruptcy legal services have been quite affordable.

Now things are going to change for the worse. Because of the new obligations on attorneys, which include independently verifying the extensive financial data in each client's paperwork, it will be much more expensive for a person to file.

For example, in New Mexico, fees for a simple Chapter 7 are expected to double, going from about $1,000 to $2,000. The fees are much higher already in many parts of the country and will increase further after October 17, 2005.

Nevertheless, it would be completely crazy to file your own bankruptcy under the new law, and is not recommended even under the old law. You'll have a better chance of finding a good lawyer with affordable fees before October 17, 2005, due to the onerous requirements for attorneys under the new law.

For example, in a recent newspaper article about two Montana attorneys, both reported that they would stop handling personal bankruptcy once the new law went into effect. Why? First because the new law will require them to certify the accuracy of the information that they would normally get from their clients. As attorney Tom Trigg reportedly said:

> I make an awful pest of myself challenging the information they give me so I can put together as clean a package of paperwork as I can. But I count on my clients to be honest, and I can't go house to house throughout Western Montana estimating the values of sofas, rifles, and pick-up trucks.

As the news article reported, the law also requires lawyers to certify payment plans as successful. "How can I do that? I cannot predict which of my clients will be stricken by financial calamities," Trigg claimed. Lawyers also fear that as a result of these new requirements, malpractice insurance rates will be too high to make the practice profitable.

Obviously not all lawyers will leave the practice, but because the new law is so complicated, it is more important than ever that you find someone who is highly skilled in personal bankruptcy practice. Personal service is also a top concern.

When you're looking for a lawyer, we have two recommendations. First, and most important, call the attorney's office and see if he or she will answer your phone calls. If not, keep looking. Second, try to find a lawyer that has been certified as a bankruptcy specialist with the American Bankruptcy Certification Board. This means the person has taken a complex test on bankruptcy issues and is required to keep up with new developments in the law.

If You Need to File and You Wait, It Could be Harder to Pay Off Secured Debts

One really common reason people do a Chapter 13 payment plan is that they need to catch up on their house and car payments, which as you'll recall from Chapter 4, is secured debt. Chapter 7 liquidation cases do not help a person with secured debt, at least not very much (more on this in Chapter 13 of this book), but Chapter 13 has historically been really helpful.

A person has always been required to pay off their home mortgage in full, with make-up payments during the Chapter 13 plan. Cars, most unattached mobile homes, and household goods, have been treated very differently. These kinds of personal property (meaning not real estate) often depreciate very rapidly. This means you buy furniture for $1,000 but once you've used it for a while, it may be worth just $200. You may buy a new car for $20,000 but after you own it for just a few months, it is likely worth more like $15,000. Under the old law, for these items, a person could pay just the value of the item, not the full debt, in a Chapter13 plan.

You can imagine how helpful this can be. Sometimes car loans are twice as large as the value of the car. The bankruptcy laws (in the past) recognized that a person should not pay more than the value of the property they are keeping in their bankruptcy, because that's all a creditor would get if they sold it anyway. The rest of the creditor's debt (the part not supported by the value of the car) would be unsecured. It would be discharged in bankruptcy, and that is what happens to this debt after the debtor has paid a Chapter 13 plan. More on this in Chapter 15.

If you think about it, this makes sense, because the debt is secured only to the extent that there is value in the collateral. If the value is less than the loan, the loan is part secured and part unsecured. We call this *stripping down the lien* to the value of the collateral. Under the new law, consumers can no longer strip down the lien on cars or household goods and must instead pay the whole loan in full.*

If you have a car loan or a furniture loan, you should definitely go see a lawyer before the change in laws if you can. Many lawyers say that if a debtor's house is also behind, stripping down the other secured debts is often the only way to make it possible for the debtor to afford a Chapter 13 plan and keep both the house and the car.

Obviously, if you are reading this after October 17, 2005, you'll have to make do.

Means Testing: Fewer People Will Qualify for a Quick Discharge

Remember how you read earlier about the difference between a Chapter 7 case and a Chapter 13 case? Chapter 7 allows a person with few assets (or all exempt assets) to walk away from most unsecured debts without losing any property. Right now, under the old law, this test is rarely used, and most people are allowed to choose Chapter 7 if they like.

In the new law, this process of forcing a person to do a Chapter 13 if they can afford one is far more formalized, and experts say that access to the walk-away Chapter 7 discharge will be far more limited. Chapter 7 cases will be

---

*You can still strip down car loans that are more than two and a half years old (the loan, not the car), but a loan this old is unlikely to need to be stripped down because by then, the owner would probably have equity in the car rather than being "upside-down" (undersecured). Stripping down a lien helps only when the car (the collateral) is worth less than the debt on the car.

scrutinized to a far greater degree and will be far more expensive after October 17, 2005. There will be more paperwork and expense, and mistakes will really hurt if you have to refile a case after it is dismissed because of the mistake. *Thus, if you think that a Chapter 7 is best for you, you may want to at least consider filing before October 17.*

You need not worry about the means test at all if your current income (for the six months prior to your bankruptcy case) is below the median income for a family of your size in your state. Even if your income is above the median income, you cannot be forced into Chapter 13 unless you have at least $100 a month left over at the end of the month after deducting certain allowed expenses. This is covered in more detail in Chapter 14.

Under the new means test, if a debtor falls within certain means test guidelines, the debtor must pay his or her plan over five years. In the past, all debtors could choose a three-year Chapter 13 repayment plan. People who choose to do Chapter 13 payment plans but who fall below the median income for a family of their size in their state can still choose a three-year payment plan.

Note

At least in some cases, under this new means test there are fairly stringent limits on the expenses you'll be allowed to pay during your Chapter 13 case, which is another reason to file earlier than October 17 if you can. (Again, if it's already too late, you'll make do, through the guidelines set out in the rest of this book.)

Fraud Debts and Intentional Tort Debts

These debts are discharged under the old law but not the new one. If you have been in a fight or committed another intentional act against a person or his or her property; if you have obtained credit by giving out false financial information or through other fraudulent means; if you have charged a lot of luxuries right before your bankruptcy; or if you have committed fraud, in a fiduciary capacity or embezzlement, all of these debts (and more) are dischargeable in a current (pre-October 17, 2005) Chapter 13 repayment plan, though not in a Chapter 7. The plan can go on for just three years under current law, though you do need to pay down your debts to some extent during the case.

Under the new law, none of the types of debts mentioned in the preceding paragraph are dischargeable in any kind of personal bankruptcy case. Thus, if you have some of this debt, it makes sense to file before the new law becomes effective.

Making Mistakes Is More Costly Under the New Law

We talked previously about how a failure to file one document can cause a debtor to have his or her case dismissed. The old law requires far less paperwork and is also much more forgiving about mistakes. Normally, under the old or current law, a person has extra time to file what he or she may have forgotten or filed incorrectly before. Now, once any small mistake is made, the case is automatically dismissed, and there is a presumption that the next case filed is filed in bad faith.

If that is not bad enough, the automatic stay, which stops creditors from collecting from and harassing the debtor, will be terminated 30 days after a second case is filed, if it turns out that a prior case was pending within the year before the new case. This is true even if the first case was dismissed because of a mistake. If a third case is needed, the stay does not go into effect at all in the third case, unless the debtor can convince the court in a hearing to impose one.

In other words, mistakes are brutal and costly.

Credit Counseling

It is hard to imagine an industry that has suffered more scandal lately than the current consumer credit counseling industry. According to numerous news reports and IRS and other investigations, many of the ones in business as of the summer of 2005 are huge scam artists who rip people off and ruin their credit further.

Yet bankruptcy reform requires all bankruptcy filers to attend credit counseling before they file. There are limited exceptions, but even then, you must attend counseling after the filing. Additionally, all people who file are required to attend and pass an additional personal financial management course before they get a bankruptcy discharge.

Right now there are few reputable firms from which to get any of this counseling. (See http://money.com/2005/04/18/willis_tips.) All this counseling will also cost money for most people, something few bankruptcy debtors have in spades. Thus, you may want to avoid all this and file before October 17, 2005, if you plan to file at all.

CHAPTER 8

Preparing to File for Bankruptcy: Don't File without Reading This!

The Full Disclosure Requirements

In bankruptcy, you give up all of your financial privacy in exchange for some relief from your creditors. You must disclose all of your financial deals and all of your assets, even things you may not think of as assets. Maybe you think you could sue someone and get some money. That is an asset even if you never do sue.

Nothing at all can be hidden in your bankruptcy and all must be disclosed. If you are holding an asset for your grandmother, that must be disclosed. If your fiancé just gave you a diamond ring as a gift, that must be disclosed. This is serious business. It does not mean you will lose all these assets. To the contrary, you probably won't lose a thing, but everything must be disclosed.

If you won something of value in the mail or through the lottery, of course that must be disclosed, too. If you think you owe money to someone, you have to disclose that. If you have been involved in any financial transactions, made any payments to anyone, and so on, all must be disclosed.

I think you must be getting the picture here. If there are things in your financial life that you don't want anyone to find out about, please do not file a bankruptcy. If you fail to disclose something of significance, you can end up in jail. Sorry, but if you can't and won't tell all, you absolutely should not do this. For much more detail on what "everything" is in this context, please turn to Chapter 11 of this book.

Keep in mind that it is always better to provide more information rather than less information. This is true even if you have to repeat yourself in your bankruptcy paperwork over and over again in order to insure that the trustee does not believe that you are hiding anything. Believe us, there is no question that failing to mention something can have significant and very serious consequences. It can be a huge disaster and can even land you in jail, if the omission was intentional.

As a final point on this issue, here is one bankruptcy judge's explanation of the full disclosure rule:

I have noticed a disturbing trend among debtors and their counsel to treat the schedules and statement of affairs as "working papers" which can be freely amended as circumstances warrant and need not contain the exact, whole truth.

Notwithstanding execution under penalty of perjury, debtors and their counsel seem to think that they are free to argue facts and values not contained in the schedules or even directly contrary to the schedules. Some debtors have felt justified signing a statement that they have only a few, or even a single creditor, in order to file an emergency petition, knowing full well that the statement is false.

Whatever your attitude is toward the schedules, you should know that as far as I am concerned they are the sacred text of any bankruptcy filing. There is no excuse for them not being 100% accurate and complete. Disclosure must be made to a fault. The filing of false schedules is a federal felony, and I do not hesitate to recommend prosecution of anyone who knowingly files a false schedule.

I have no idea where anyone got the idea that amendments can cure false schedules. The debtor has an obligation to correct schedules he or she knows are false, but amendment in no way cures a false filing. Any court may properly disregard subsequent sworn statement at odds with previous sworn statements. I give no weight at all to amendments filed after an issue has been raised.

As a practical matter, where false statements or omissions have come to light due to investigation by a creditor or trustee, it is virtually impossible for the debtor to demonstrate good faith in a Chapter 13 case or entitlement to a discharge in a Chapter 7 case. I strongly recommend that any of you harboring a cavalier attitude toward the schedules replace it with a good healthy dose of paranoia.

Dated: September 10, 1997
Bankruptcy Judge Alan Jaroslovsky

The Filing Fees, Legal Fees, Deposits, and Other Money You Need to File

Bankruptcy can be expensive. Believe it or not, most people need to borrow money from a friend or family member or save up for their bankruptcy. The first thing you need is attorney's fees. These are about $800 for a simple Chapter 7 in Albuquerque, New Mexico, and much more in most other places. You also need about $200, give or take a little, for your court filing fee. This cannot be waived though it can sometimes be paid in installments.

You also may need to save up the equivalent of one to two months' worth of services for your phone and utility bills, to post as deposits. Ask your bankruptcy lawyer if you'll be needing this. In some places, if your bills are current, there is no need to pay a deposit.

Getting All Your Paperwork in Order

The bankruptcy disclosure paperwork requires that you disclose all of your assets (even things that may never be worth anything), all of your debts (even potential debts that you may never end up owing), all lawsuits to which you have been a party, certain payments to creditors (including family members), and more other stuff than you could ever imagine.

To get ready for your bankruptcy, you need to put all of your bills in one stack and then sort through them. Take the whole stack to your attorney.

If some accounts have been sent to collection agencies, save a copy of each different entity or agency that has contacted you, even if it is for the same debt.

Then, make as long a list as you can of all the other people who may claim that you owe them money, even if you don't think that you owe them anything. Bankruptcy works in a way that gives actual creditors as well as potential creditors notice that you will not pay their debts. If you forget to list someone in your paperwork, that person will not get the notice and their debt (or potential debt) will not be discharged.

You need the names and addresses of all the people to whom you could owe money, and this is not optional.

You also need a complete list of all of your assets, so you should start working on that as well. Household furniture can be lumped together, but think long and hard about other kinds of assets: anything that anyone owes *you*, any deposits you have given to anyone, tax refunds to which you are entitled, and so on. All of that will need to be listed and valued for your lawyer.

Also gather your tax returns for the past two years and your past few pay stubs. Your attorney can use these to put together your paperwork. If you have been a party to any lawsuits, you should bring in a copy of any paperwork you have from that as well. If you are a party to any contracts or leases for anything, you need a copy of those, as well as a copy of recent bank statements, statements for retirement and investment accounts, and any other paperwork showing what you own.

Admittedly, few people can get their hands on all of these pieces of paperwork, so just do your best. You can keep the cost of your bankruptcy down by gathering and organizing this paperwork.

Timing the Filing

The main thing to say here is that you probably want to file before October 17, 2005, for the reasons we set out in Chapter 7 of this book. For the rest of this chapter, we assume you are filing after that date. Both before and after, however, there are certain things you need to know to best time your case, assuming you have that luxury.

Transfers to (or Paying Back Loans from) Family Members

Have you borrowed money from anyone in your family or from a business associate during the past year and then paid some of it back? If so, assuming you paid back more than $600 to any one person, the money you repaid on these loans can be recovered by your bankruptcy trustee from the person you paid and then distributed to your creditors.

Charges for Luxury Goods and Cash Advances Taken Out Shortly before Your Bankruptcy Case Is Filed

Under the new law, charges incurred for luxury goods within 90 days of your bankruptcy are presumed to be fraudulent, meaning you did not intend to pay for the items when you charged them, as long as the individual creditor is owed at least $500 for these luxury goods. This means that unless you can prove that you did intend to pay for the items, you'll have to pay them despite your bankruptcy. Also, cash advances taken out within 70 days prior to the case, for which an individual creditor is owed $750 or more, are also presumed to be fraudulent.

Under the old law, the time limits were shorter and the amounts owed to creditors were higher, meaning that the presumption of fraud was far narrower. (See Chapter 11).

What is a luxury good? This is an amorphous and subjective concept if there ever was one. Some would say a fancy man's suit is a luxury good, while others would hotly disagree. The answer probably lies in what the suit was purchased for and its ultimate need. To avoid even having to deal with such issues, you should stop using your credit cards once you have decided to file for bankruptcy and, if possible, should also wait at least three months before filing after making a major purchase. The same rule applies to cash advances taken out on a credit card but for just 70 days. That means you need to wait 70 days after $750 or larger cash advance to file your case.

Timing the Filing with Your Paycheck

It is best to time the filing right after you have received your paycheck and used it to pay for the rent or mortgage, your lawyer, food, or whatever else you need. If you just have the right to be paid for prepetition services at the time you file, rather than the paycheck itself, then you will need to fit your paycheck within your exemptions. Your bankruptcy attorney can help you time the filing to avoid wasting your exemptions on your paycheck if you need all of your exemptions for other things.

Timing the Filing with Receipt of Your Tax Refund

Your tax refund is one of your assets, if you have not received it but are now entitled to it. You will need to disclose it in your bankruptcy paperwork and also fit it within your available exemptions. If you have quite a few nonexempt assets and not much room to fit in more, you may want to file your bankruptcy after you have received and spent your tax refund.

CHAPTER 9

Basics of Bankruptcy Law That Apply to All Bankruptcies

The rest of this book will get very technical because it is about bankruptcy law, a very technical area of the law. If it seems like more than you need to know at the moment, you can skip parts and come back to them when they are more relevant.

This area of the law is highly complex, especially for nonlawyers. When we introduce a new vocabulary word, we try to *italicize* it, and then define it right there. We hope this helps you understand the materials better. There is also a Glossary at the end of this book. If you run into a word you don't know, you can look it up there. Good luck!

The Automatic Stay

A bankruptcy filing dramatically changes things for both debtors and creditors. The change is drastic, too! The filing immediately stops all collection activity of creditors, including those embarrassing phone calls, and gives the debtor some relief. Without a bankruptcy, creditors can sue the debtor and then *execute* or try to seize the debtor's nonexempt assets. Under this process, the fastest creditor wins, which explains some of the earnestness with which they harass you.

By comparison, bankruptcy is a collective process. Its goals include equal distribution to creditors and providing the debtor a breathing spell from collection efforts.

The breathing spell is accomplished through the *automatic stay*, which is the equivalent of a temporary restraining order. This order requires that creditors leave the debtor alone. As soon as the debtor files his bankruptcy petition, all creditors must stop all collection efforts against the debtor or the debtor's property, regardless of where that property is located.

The automatic stay stops all kinds of creditor collection activities, including:

- *Any* attempt to collect on a debt including phone calls and letters.
- *Any* continuing lawsuit to collect a debt.
- *Any* repossession of a debtor's assets.
- *Any* attempt to exercise control over property of the debtor's estate (defined very broadly, as discussed in the next section).
- *Any* attempt to perfect a security interest.
- *Pretty* much anything else you can think of that would allow a creditor to improve their own position against the debtor compared to other creditors.

The automatic stay continues in place until the bankruptcy case is over, or until a creditor gets the stay lifted or removed, in order to pursue its own particular debt.

Getting the benefit of the automatic stay is the main reason people file for bankruptcy, at least the most immediate reason. It is a huge relief to have the phone stop ringing and to open your mailbox without being afraid of what you will find. Of course, getting most of your debts *discharged* and getting a clean slate is the more permanent reason, and we talk about that later in Chapter 12. Still, the importance of the automatic stay cannot be overemphasized. It is one good deal for the debtor, worthy of a long sigh of relief. Also, if a creditor continues to try to collect from you after you have filed for bankruptcy, they may have to pay you money damages.

Note

Bankruptcy reform, effective October 17, 2005, has made big changes to the automatic stay provisions!

Exceptions to the Automatic Stay

Under both versions of the stay, some things are not stayed at all, and others are stayed only temporarily. Criminal suits are not stayed. Lawsuits involving child support or marital support are not stayed.

Actions by governmental units to enforce police powers are also not stayed.

These are actions taken by federal, state, local, or tribal governments to protect the health and welfare of citizens. Examples include actions taken to stop a company from polluting or to stop ongoing dangerous activity. This exception is not as broad as you might think, though. Actions by governmental units merely to collect debts *are* stayed, and the line is hard to draw. Suffice it to say that virtually *all* collection suits must stop after a bankruptcy case is filed, even if the plaintiff is a governmental body, unless the suit is designed to stop a real danger to the public.

Changes in the Automatic Stay Resulting from Bankruptcy Reform

SERIAL FILING AND THE AUTOMATIC STAY   One big goal of bankruptcy reform is to discourage abusive filings. One category of abuse is what we call *serial filers*, or people who file one case after another, again and again, each time getting the benefit of the automatic stay, but frequently failing to do any of the things that are required in the bankruptcy cases. They would fail to do the paperwork, fail to appear at the creditors meetings, and so on. The case would be dismissed and they'd file another case, often frustrating a foreclosing creditor.

There is major disagreement about how often this type of thing happened, but it did happen some. The people who engaged in this type of behavior really ruined it for the rest of us. Congress overreacted to this serial filer and has severely limited a person's rights to refile their case, even if their first case was dismissed for very innocent reasons.

Here's how it works. Your case can be automatically dismissed for a series of minor omissions, such as the failure to produce a tax return or other document required by the new law. This is complex and everybody is bound to make mistakes. Heck, people still cannot even agree on what is required, so you know this is not easy!

If you file a second case within one year of the first case (one that presumably was dismissed because you failed or forgot to do something), the automatic stay only goes into effect for 30 days after the second filing, unless you can show that the second case was filed in good faith. It is your burden to meet this test, whatever it means. It is new so we don't know. No one else does, either.

If the second case is also dismissed, and a third case is filed within one year, the automatic stay does not go into effect at all in that third case, unless the court, upon a debtor's motion, finds that the debtor has proven that the new case was filed in good faith. The law presumes that the case was *not* filed in good faith.

STAY EXCEPTIONS FOR RESIDENTIAL REAL ESTATE LEASES   One activity that will no longer be stayed by the automatic stay imposed upon bankruptcy is an action to evict a tenant, in which the landlord has obtained a judgment for possession prior to the bankruptcy case.

This is a big departure from the prior law, where the stay would stop any eviction proceeding in its tracks, regardless of whether the landlord already had essentially *won* the case and obtained a judgment in eviction. That stay was only temporary, of course, because if the debtor could not pay the past due rent, he or she had to leave anyway. Still, the debtor had time to make other arrangements.

Practically speaking, on and after October 17, 2005, debtors just have to file their bankruptcy cases sooner. It takes a while for the landlord to get a judgment for possession, once an eviction action is started, so the debtor can at least wait to file for bankruptcy until he or she has been sued in eviction. It will be critical to get your bankruptcy filed before the landlord gets his or her judgment, though.

The second exception from the automatic stay for residential real estate leases is a quirky provision. It says that if an eviction is based upon endangerment of the rented property or an illegal use of controlled substances on the premises, the eviction case is not stayed as long as the eviction case was started before the bankruptcy, and as long as the endangerment or use of illegal substances on the premises occurred within 30 days of the bankruptcy filing.

Now we must admit, this seems awfully specific. We would be surprised if endangerment or use of illegal substances on the leased premises were all that common. In any event, as unlikely as it is that this last thing will apply to you, that is one of the new rules.

Most evictions, that is, those in which no judgment for possession has been issued yet, and where there is no endangerment or illegal substances in use, are still stayed.

STAY ISSUES REGARDING NOTICES SENT TO CREDITORS Prior to October 17, 2005, debtors are permitted to notify creditors of their bankruptcy cases at whatever address they have for the creditor.

Under the new law, however, debtors must notify creditors at the address used in at least two pieces of correspondence between the debtor and the creditor during the preceding 90 days, or at an address the creditor has filed with the court. Also, to be effective, the notice also must contain the account number of the debtor's account with the creditor.

Other notices sent to other addresses (or without account numbers) will not be considered effective notice of the case, and if the creditor violates the automatic stay after the debtor sent the notice to the wrong address, then the creditor will not have to pay any monetary damages for violating the stay.

In other words, the debtor and the debtor's attorney have to keep much better records, or a creditor will not get in trouble for violating the stay. The action taken in violation of the stay during the case can be reversed, but the creditor cannot be liable for money damages for violating the stay.

Relief from the Automatic Stay for Some Creditors

Even where the stay does go into effect, it can be removed by certain creditors, putting the debtor and the creditor back at square one, as if there had been no bankruptcy. In other words, sometimes creditors are able to have the automatic stay removed or lifted so that they can continue trying to collect the debt, just as if there was no bankruptcy. This right is granted only to *secured creditors* who can prove certain elements.

As mentioned earlier, a secured creditor is one who has collateral for his or her loan. Often, the creditor has loaned the debtor money to buy something specific and keeps that specific item as collateral on the debt. Being a secured creditor isn't enough to lift a stay, though. The creditor has to prove certain elements to get that special privilege. These elements essentially show that they are more entitled to the collateral than the debtor and the other creditors.

In a Chapter 7 bankruptcy, the most common situation in which the stay will be lifted is when a secured creditor is *undersecured* or *upside-down*.

Let's imagine a debtor gets a loan from a dealership to buy a car. As part of the standard contract, the dealership gets a security interest in the car in order to secure payment on the loan. Everything goes fine for a year and then hard times hit. The debtor can't make the payments and the dealership, as a secured creditor, is threatening to repossess the car. Hoping to get some relief, the debtor files a Chapter 7 bankruptcy.

If the secured creditor, in our example the car dealership, is owed $10,000 and the automobile, which is the collateral, is worth only $8,000, the bankruptcy court will usually lift the stay. In practical terms this means the dealership, which couldn't even call the debtor two paragraphs ago when he filed bankruptcy, can now repossess the car and sell it to satisfy at least part of its debt.

Why should this be allowed when the debtor went through the trouble to declare bankruptcy? The rationale is that realistically there is no value in the car for the estate, meaning the debtor's other creditors. In fact, the debtor has no equity in the car.

There is an important lesson here if you are thinking about filing a Chapter 7 bankruptcy. A Chapter 7 debtor who is behind on his obligations to secured creditors will find very little relief under a Chapter 7 case. If you file for a Chapter 7 case in a situation in which you are behind in your mortgage payments, the creditor will probably succeed in getting the stay lifted. If not, the case will be over in just three short months, after which time the automatic stay will disappear, leaving the creditor free to foreclose on your mortgage, anyway! That is why we said earlier that a Chapter 7 liquidation case does very little to help a debtor keep a house or a car on which the payments are not current.

If you want to save property that is subject to a security interest, and you are behind on those payments, you need a Chapter 13 payment plan. Think about whether the bulk of your financial problems relate to secured or unsecured debts when deciding what kind of bankruptcy to file. Chapter 7 is best for dealing with unsecured debts. If you are behind on your secured debts, you may need a Chapter 13 case.

In a Chapter 7 case, there is no time during which the debtor is allowed to make up for the past due payments on mortgages or car loans. Practically speaking, a debtor who is behind on the home mortgage will not be allowed to keep the home unless the bank payments are made up, or *cured*, within a very short period of time after the filing. Thus, most Chapter 7 debtors who are homeowners are current on their mortgage and should keep it that way.

Property of the Debtor's Estate

The Breadth of the Estate

When a bankruptcy case is filed, the *debtor's estate* is created. While it may seem ironic that yesterday the debtor couldn't pay any of his bills and today he has an *estate*, it is a fact of bankruptcy. The estate is *all* of the debtor's property as of the bankruptcy filing date, wherever located, and by whomever held. The estate is created for the benefit of creditors. Every possible interest of the debtor in any property, whether it is a contingent interest, a partial interest, a legal interest, or an equitable interest, goes into this estate. That means anything that you have any possible interest in at all, even if you have something that you own with someone else (including your spouse), must be listed on your bankruptcy paperwork, and valued for your bankruptcy trustee.

There are no exceptions here! All of the debtor's property goes into the estate. This isn't as scary as it sounds, though. As you will soon read when we talk about *exemptions*, just because something is in the estate does not mean the debtor will lose it.

It's important to note here that the concept of the estate applies to property owned or interest held *as of the filing date*. Most assets that you come into or begin to own after you file bankruptcy do not come into the estate, as explained later. The important thing to understand is that absolutely everything in which the debtor has any rights must be disclosed in the bankruptcy paperwork, and all of his assets come into the estate, at least initially.

Imagine a huge bag. Now try to visualize every possible kind of interest that the debtor has in anything at all, and put each item into the bag. Clothes, furniture, books, electronics, cars, homes, stocks, lamps, plants, upcoming plane tickets, Nintendo, art work, jewelry, savings accounts for the kids, and on and on. While later, many things will come back out of the bag, due to the debtor's exemptions, security interests of secured creditors, and other things, the estate initially contains every imaginable interest of the debtor in property as of the time the bankruptcy case is filed.

Legal and Equitable Interests in Property

Although everything the debtor owns any interest in must be disclosed, this does not mean that these assets will be taken by the *bankruptcy trustee*. The trustee is a person appointed by the court who acts as a sort of referee in bankruptcy. His or her job is to be impartial and fair and make sure every one of the creditors and the debtor follows the rules. It is up to the trustee to examine everything in the estate and decide what to do with each item.

Let's say that the debtor is holding a bank account in his name and his grandmother's. The bank account is for the sole benefit of his grandmother. It's all her money; none of it is his. Does it go into the estate? The answer is always *yes*!

This asset absolutely *must* be listed on the debtor's bankruptcy schedules. Now don't get upset. The trustee will not take Grandma's money, but this account must be disclosed. The trustee will not take this money to pay creditors because the debtor's interest in the bank account is solely a legal interest. The idea is that the trustee has a right to examine these items and make sure that the debtor is accurately determining whose money is in the account, and also is telling the truth about the facts.

Post-Petition Assets

In a Chapter 7 case, property that the debtor obtains *after* the case is filed does not become part of the debtor's estate. Rather than *estate property*, this is what we think of as *fresh start property*, or property that the debtor may keep as part of his or her fresh start.

Let's say you file for bankruptcy on May 1. On the evening of April 30, you owed $12,000 to various credit card companies and, after applying your state's exemptions that let you keep some cash, you had $900 in the bank from your last paycheck and $2,000 worth of electronics which were not exempt.

The bad news is your $900 and your electronics will be gone. The trustee will distribute the proceeds of those among your credit card creditors to pay off what they can of your debts.

But there is good news, too. That $12,000 in credit card debt is gone as well—discharged! May 5 rolls around and you get another paycheck. Guess what? It is all yours. You have a fresh start. No one—not the trustee or the judge or even the creditors—expect that money to go anywhere other than into your pocket. This is a very important rule. *All of the debtor's wages earned and property obtained after the bankruptcy is filed are his or hers to keep and do not become part of the debtor's estate in a Chapter 7.*

There are a couple of significant exceptions to this rule about property that the debtor obtains after the bankruptcy, or *post-petition*.

- If a debtor inherits money or property within six months after the bankruptcy filing, then this inheritance does become part of the estate.

- If a debtor receives marital property settlements that arise from a pre-bankruptcy divorce or separation, then that property does become part of the estate.
- Tax refunds that are for the prior year become part of the estate even if the debtor has not yet filed a return by the time of the bankruptcy.
- If a debtor receives proceeds and products of pre-petition property, those proceeds become part of the estate.

This *proceeds* concept can be a little tricky. Take the case of Deb Tore.

Deb Tore owned stock in General Electric (GE) when she filed her bankruptcy case on January 1. On February 14, that stock paid a nice big dividend. Imagine how sad Deb Tore was when she realized that, even though the dividend was money she would get post-bankruptcy, the dividend is estate property because it came directly out of an estate asset, that is, the GE stock that she owned prior to filing.

By coincidence, Deb Tore's mother gave her daughter stock in Home Depot on January 2, one day after her bankruptcy case. Since this was a gift Deb Tore received *after* she filed her case, it is a post-petition asset. On February 14, the Home Depot stock paid a dividend, and this time Deb Tore got to keep the whole amount for herself. Do you understand why? The Home Depot dividend is not estate property because the original asset (the Home Depot stock) was not an estate asset.

The moral of the story is that anything that became part of the estate upon the filing of a Chapter 7, which later produces some assets without the debtor having to add anything to it, is an estate asset as well.

Interestingly, in a Chapter 13 payment plan case, and even in an individual's Chapter 11 case under the new law, these post-petition (after the filing) assets *do* form part of the debtor's bankruptcy estate and thus must be used to pay creditors. This is even true of gifts the debtor receives after filing a Chapter 13 case.

Education Funds under the New Law

Under the new law, funds placed in an education retirement account or qualified state tuition program at least 365 days prior to your bankruptcy are not part of your estate. These funds must be for the benefit of a child or grandchild. There is a $5,000 limit on each such fund for each child.

Basic Bankruptcy Law, Courts, and Procedures

In this section, we tell you a little bit about the bankruptcy system and the federal bankruptcy law. It may be more than you feel you need to know at this point. If so, skip it until later.

Bankruptcy Law

Bankruptcy cases are governed by a federal statute called the Bankruptcy Code. We call this law either the *Bankruptcy Code* or just the *Code*. This is a long and complicated law enacted by Congress in 1978, tinkered with a bit here and there since then, and now changed very significantly for all bankruptcy cases filed on or after October 17, 2005.

Bankruptcy Courts

Bankruptcy cases are presided over by bankruptcy courts, which are federal courts. You may know that in every state in the United States there are courts that are part of a state court system, where state law issues such as family law and divorce, estate law, property law and other local laws are heard. Every state also has courts that are part of a federal system, which hear issues relating to federal law such as immigration law, tax law, bankruptcy law, patent law, and so on.

Bankruptcy courts are part of the federal system, and here in New Mexico, as an example, cases are heard by the Bankruptcy Court for the District of New Mexico, which usually sits in Albuquerque but also travels around the state to hear cases.

It is a little funny to say that bankruptcy courts *hear* bankruptcy cases because in the most common form of consumer bankruptcy cases, the Chapter 7 liquidation case, the debtor normally does not ever go before a court. The debtor goes only to his or her *creditors' meeting*, described later, which is not a court hearing.

In most Chapter 13 cases, the debtor will go to court once or twice in connection with approval of the payment plan.

The Bankruptcy Trustee

In both Chapter 7 and Chapter 13 cases, the case is run by a bankruptcy trustee. If you file a bankruptcy case, you will have a trustee as well.

What is the trustee's job? To look for assets to distribute to creditors, by carefully combing through your paperwork and asking questions about the values and other things. The trustee is a *fiduciary* for creditors, meaning that he or she is charged with trying to find assets to pay to creditors. If there are assets available that the trustee does not find, creditors can try to recover damages from the trustee. Moreover, the trustee gets a percentage of all the assets he or she distributes to creditors. You can see then why trustees are motivated to try to find assets to distribute to creditors.

In both Chapter 7 and Chapter 13 cases, the debtor's lawyer files all of the paperwork with the bankruptcy court, and the bankruptcy court sends notice of the case to all the debtor's creditors. About 30 days after the case is filed, the debtor is required to attend a meeting at the courthouse or another building, to which all the creditors are invited. It is named after the section of the bankruptcy law that requires the meeting, and is thus called a *Section 341 meeting* or simply a *341 meeting*, or even just a *creditors' meeting*.

Many of these meetings are scheduled at the same time and normally few creditors attend the meeting. The typical protocol is that the case trustee goes through all of the debtor's paperwork and makes sure it is all complete and accurate. In a Chapter 13 case, the trustee will also determine at this time whether the plan follows all the rules of Chapter 13.

BASIC CHAPTER 7 ADMINISTRATION   In a Chapter 7 case, the 341 meeting is run by the Chapter 7 trustee.* After the meeting, the trustee in a Chapter 7 case will set out to try to find assets to distribute to creditors, as he is a fiduciary for the creditors and is charged with finding whatever might be available for distribution to creditors. The trustee is aided in the search by the *schedules of assets and liabilities*, a long list of paperwork we discuss soon. If there is no property to distribute (what we call a *no asset* case), which is often the case, the case will be finished within three months of the filing, the debtor will be discharged from most debts, and the case will be closed.

If there are assets to distribute, the case can go on for several months or even years, though the debtor's discharge should still take just three months, assuming no unusual problems. (See Chapter 12.)

BASIC CHAPTER 13 ADMINISTRATION   In a Chapter 13, the 341 meeting is run by the Chapter 13 trustee's office. The Chapter 13 trustee is often a standing trustee, meaning that the same person is the trustee for every Chapter 13 case within the district. Most of the questions in a Chapter 13 Section 341 meeting center around income and expenses, the assets, and whether the repayment plan is feasible. The 341 meeting takes much longer in a Chapter 13 and is more detailed.

After the 341 meeting, the trustee will set out to determine if the proposed Chapter 13 plan meets the requirements of the Code. If it does, the trustee will allow the plan to go forward and be approved or *confirmed*. If there are problems, the trustee might object to confirmation of the plan. If the plan is not ultimately approved, the case will be dismissed. This means the bankruptcy has been denied. *A dismissed bankruptcy case is a failed bankruptcy case.*

---

*Technically, the first trustee appointed in the case is called the *interim trustee* and is just the temporary trustee. Creditors have the right to have someone other than the interim trustee appointed as the permanent trustee in the case. In practice, it is very rare for the interim trustee *not* to be appointed as the permanent trustee.

Exemptions

Remember earlier when discussing the breadth of the estate, we pictured a huge bag into which goes everything the debtor owns? You end up with a giant filled-up bag and a poor naked guy standing next to it. Of course, we can't leave poor Mr. Debtor like that, so some things get taken out of the bag and given back to Mr. D. The items that Mr. Debtor gets back out of the bag are called *exempt property*. There are two kinds of exemptions: federal exemptions and state exemptions.

In practical terms, every bankruptcy debtor gets to keep some of his or her property, even though he or she has failed to pay creditors. You might ask yourself why we have developed a system that allows bankruptcy debtors to keep a significant amount of their property, despite a stack of unpaid bills?

The federal and state exemption schemes allow people to keep enough assets to survive, and some provide much more than that. The theme of exemption law is that people with lots of debts can still live inside, drive a car, and wear their clothes, without fear that a creditor will try to take these necessities. If we allowed creditors to take all of a debtor's possessions, it would be difficult, if not impossible, to achieve any kind of realistic fresh start. *The exemptions were developed to establish a basic level of possessions that would allow a debtor to start fresh.*

State Law Exemptions

The exemptions spell out what a person in a particular state gets to keep, free from creditor claims, either inside or outside a bankruptcy case. Remember that in a bankruptcy, an automatic stay kicks in, which stops creditors from taking the debtor's property after the bankruptcy.

If there is no bankruptcy, creditors will be going to court and getting judgments against the debtor, and then executing on the judgments by getting the sheriff to take and sell assets that he or she can find. If the assets the sheriff finds are exempt, under the state law exemptions, then the sheriff is not allowed to take and sell them. For more on this go back and read Chapter 5.

Anyway, these state law exemptions vary quite a bit from state to state. A chart of the state exemptions, as of July 15, 2005, appears at the end of this book (Appendix B).

As we said back in Chapter 5, the primary role of the state law exemptions is to protect property from creditor executions in cases in which there is no bankruptcy case. These state law exemptions, however, can also be used in bankruptcy. Just so you know, the Bankruptcy Code has its own set of exemptions, which can be used *only* in a bankruptcy case. Those are discussed in the following section. In most states, these federal bankruptcy exemptions cannot be used at all, even in a bankruptcy, leaving the debtor with *only* the state exemptions. This is true because Congress allowed states to opt out of the exemptions provisions of the Bankruptcy Code.

Thus, the state law exemptions are always available to everyone, both inside and outside bankruptcy, and in some states, debtors can choose between the state and the federal exemptions in a bankruptcy case.

States that allow you to choose between state or federal exemptions are: Arkansas, Connecticut, the District of Columbia, Hawaii, Massachusetts, Michigan, Minnesota, New Jersey, New Mexico, Pennsylvania, Rhode Island, Texas, Vermont, Washington, and Wisconsin.

The Federal Exemption Scheme

Section 522(d) of the Bankruptcy Code contains the federal or Bankruptcy Code exemptions, which are available to debtors who live in the states listed in the preceding paragraph. People who live in these states can essentially choose the state or the federal scheme, based upon what assets the person has. One scheme may be great for one person, but horrible for another.

The amounts of the federal exemptions track the cost of living and periodically increase in a similar fashion. Like most state exemption schemes, the federal exemptions provide a specific item-by-item list of exactly what a debtor can and cannot keep once he or she is in bankruptcy, free from creditor claims. Because the exemptions are in specific items of property, not in just whatever items the debtor has, the debtor sometimes must choose among various items, much like ordering from a Chinese menu, one from category A and one from category B, and so on.

Compared to the state exemptions, the federal exemptions are probably average in generosity. As you can see in Table 9.1, the main benefit that the federal set of exemptions provides is a *wild card* category, which allows a debtor to protect absolutely anything including cash, investment accounts, gun collections, or fancy motorcycles. This is very rare among state exemption schemes and thus, the federal system is often better for debtors with cash or other moneylike, liquid assets. Married couples may double these exemptions to get a mathematically doubled exemption limit. Although there are more, the most commonly used federal exemptions are listed in Table 9.1. These numbers are effective through March 2006.

As set out in the table, most states do not allow bankruptcy debtors to use the federal exemptions. Each state may emphasize more protection for some things than others. These state exemptions can have massive benefits, or they can provide almost no relief at all.

The variances between jurisdictions can be so extreme that some debtors in the past have deliberately moved to a jurisdiction to get that state's exemptions. For example, Texas and Florida have no limit on the homestead exemption (the exemption for the home). This means that if you lived in Texas or

TABLE 9.1 Commonly Used Federal Bankruptcy Exemptions

Description of the Asset	Amount of Asset Protection	Bankruptcy Code Section
Homestead: Real property that the debtor uses as a residence, including a mobile home	Up to $18.450	11 U.S.C. § 522 (d) (1)
Motor Vehicle: Debtor's interest in one motor vehicle	Up to $2,950	11 U.S.C. § 522 (d) (2)
Personal Property: Debtor's interest in household furnishings, goods, clothing, musical instruments, and so on	Up to $475 per item $9,850 in total	11 U.S.C. § 522 (d) (3)
Jewelry: Held by the debtor or the dependant of the debtor	Up to $1,225	11 U.S.C,. § 522 (d) (4)
Wild Card: A debtor may use this for anything; additional exemption if the homestead is not completely used	Up to $975 for any item Up to $9,250 for any unused portion of the homestead	11 U.S.C. § 522 (d) (5)

Florida and had a $10 million home paid off, you could keep the home and file for bankruptcy.

Creditors would not get any of the value of the home. On the other hand, debtors in Florida cannot use the federal exemptions. Other than the house, a person can keep only $1,000 in other property.

Clearly, debtors who live in states in which they can choose their exemption scheme have more options and flexibility. As you'll read later, Congress has now limited the practice of moving from state to state to get better exemptions, by providing in the new law that a person can use only the exemption scheme of the state they moved from, until the debtor has lived in the new state for two years.

In those states where use of either state or federal exemptions are possible, the debtor has to choose one entire scheme and cannot pick and choose between the state and federal exemptions. The debtor's lawyer must carefully consider all the assets in choosing the best exemption scheme.

Under the pre-October 17, 2005, law you need only live in a state for six months in order to be eligible to use its exemptions.

Note

Under the new law, you have to reside in a state for two years to get the state's exemptions. That means residing in Texas or Florida for two years before being able to use their unlimited homestead exemptions.

If the debtor has moved around, then the court is to look to the period between two years and two and a half years prior to the filing to determine the relevant exemptions. At least in theory then, if the debtor lived in Texas or Florida during this random but legally relevant period (the six months falling between two and a half years and two years before the filing), it is possible that the debtor might be entitled to an unlimited homestead, even if the debtor now lives in New Mexico where the exemption is just $30,000 per person.

For homes purchased during the 1,218 days ($2\frac{1}{2}$ years) prior to the filing, there is an absolute cap of $125,000 on the homestead exemption offered by state law. That means that for homes purchased in the three years and four months prior to the bankruptcy, in states that otherwise allow a homestead exemption higher than $125,000 per person under state law, the homestead exemption is capped by federal law in bankruptcy cases at $125,000 per person. This new provision has no effect whatsoever on people who live in states where the state homestead exemption is less than $125,000.

If a person adds value to his or her existing homestead during the 1,215-day ($2\frac{1}{2}$-year) period preceding the bankruptcy, then regardless of intent, those amounts cannot be included in the homestead exemption unless they are transferred to this existing home from a prior home.

The homestead exemption is also capped at $125,000 if the debtor has been convicted of a felony, is guilty of state or federal securities fraud, has committed fiduciary fraud, racketeering crimes, or intentional torts or crimes that have caused serious bodily injury or death in the preceding five years. This absolute cap is inapplicable if the homestead property is reasonably necessary for the support of the debtor or the debtor's dependents. Again, this one strikes us as rather specific and quite odd.

The homestead exemption in all states and situations is reduced by any amounts that the debtor has added to the homestead's equity during the 10-year period preceding the filing, by selling nonexempt assets and converting them into home equity for the purpose of hindering, defrauding, or delaying creditors.

If any of these homestead exemption issues are raised in a debtor's bankruptcy case, this could delay the debtor's discharge.

We realize you probably need a translator to understand all of that but we do want you to know what has changed.

Valuation

Exemptions are based on a mathematical limit designating property that a debtor is allowed to keep. Since math is involved, you might wonder who determines the value of the debtor's property? Initially, the debtor is the one who determines what they believe their property is worth. The new bankruptcy reform requires attorneys to perform their own research and to oversee this valuation process, something that will drastically increase the cost of bankruptcy services and may even cause some attorneys to stop offering them. This is why they will be less expensive and easier to find before October 17, 2005.

The valuation numbers that the debtor chooses go directly into the petition, which becomes public record. Not only is this document open to the world, but it is specifically seen by the debtor's creditors and the trustee.

Value matters. Low values mean the debtor gets to keep more property.

A debtor can use many different methods for this exemption valuation. Each type of property requires a little different method of valuation. For the most part, homes require a recent appraisal, comparable prices in the area, or some other recent approximation of the home's value. As a general rule, debtors should not rely on property tax assessments to approximate the value of their homes. Property tax valuation is almost always low and, if disclosed as the source of the valuation, may draw an objection from the trustee or the debtor's creditors.

The valuation of a vehicle is much more straightforward because of the ease of book evaluations. These can be found in Kelly's Blue Book, www.nada.com, and other similar sources. It is very easy for a debtor to take the year, make, model, and options of their vehicle and determine the appropriate value to use.

There is, however, significant controversy over whether a debtor should use the wholesale or retail values for their valuation. Some courts have interpreted the value to be an average of the two. In a simple Chapter 7 bankruptcy, it is very unlikely a major valuation concern will arise over which value the debtor should have chosen unless the values are significantly different. Valuation conflicts like this occur much more frequently during the plan calculations in Chapter 13 bankruptcies because they have more of an impact on the outcome.

When it comes to the valuation of personal property, the debtor is given more slack. Because it would be totally inefficient to require a debtor to obtain an appraisal on all of their personal property (property that is not real estate), the court typically accepts the debtor's personal approximate of the value of his or her property. When calculating the value of a debtor's property, the debtor should use a value that would reflect the item's current market price for a used item.

It is a common mistake for debtors to approximate the value of their property at what they paid for it, or significantly close to it. For example if a debtor bought a $2,000 couch five years ago, it would be difficult to sell it today at $1,500. In fact, the debtor may not even be able to get $100 for it. The relevant question in a Chapter 7 case is what a trustee could raise for creditors by selling the item. He or she will not sell it, but this is how you arrive at an item's value.

It is very important to understand that personal property should be valued at used or garage sale prices when calculating the exemptions. This valuation process may have a direct effect on just how much property you can keep, and debtors notoriously overvalue their personal property. One judge told me he believes debtors regularly overvalue their personal property by 100 percent or more! On the other hand, if a valuation seems way out of whack (too low), the trustee will likely challenge it.

After the trustee receives all the valuation information, he or she will determine if the sale of any items over the exemptions would provide any significant amount of money to the creditors. When the trustee makes this decision, he or she will take into account the cost of sale to determine if selling the item will actually result in any payment to creditors. It is unlikely a trustee is going to take the time to sell an item just to receive a few dollars.

Naturally, your attorney will try his or her best to place as much of your property into these exemption categories. Imagine each exemption as being a very large plastic bin. Each plastic bin represents one category of an exemption. Your attorney will take things out of the big bag that constitutes your bankruptcy estate and try to fit all your assets into the bins. For example, there will be one very large bin for cars, another for the debtor's clothing, another for the debtor's cash, and so on. The debtor's attorney can be visualized trying to put as much property into each bin as possible.

Meanwhile, trustees and creditors' attorneys try their best to prevent as much of the debtor's property from getting into these exemption categories as possible. At the risk of mixing metaphors, you can imagine them as goalies protecting the bins. The more property they can keep out of the bins, the more that goes into their client's pockets. Picture a trustee following the debtor's attorney around to make sure everything in each bin belongs there and ensuring that the mathematical limit for each bin is not exceeded. The more property that finds its way into the bins, the less the debtor loses and the less there is to distribute to the creditors.

For the trustee, the way to gain more money for the creditors is to object to the debtor's valuation of an item as too low, in the hope it will be re-valuated high enough to justify its sale and distribution. In most consumer cases, however, there is no such objection.

Avoiding Liens That Interfere with Exemptions

An involuntary lien is a legal claim or charge against a debtor's property for satisfaction of a debt. This type of lien is created when a creditor executes on personal property or files a paper in the recorder of deeds office against a piece of real estate. The lien gives the creditor who obtained it the right to take the debtor's property or force a sale of the property until the debt is paid. These types of liens, as well as those in certain household goods, can sometimes be eliminated because they interfere with your exemptions. This topic is far too complicated to cover here, and we recommend you ask your attorney if these provisions of the law can be of any help to you.

Priorities

The Bankruptcy Code provides that if there are assets to distribute to creditors in a Chapter 7 case, some creditors should get their money before others. The priority scheme is found in Section 507 of the Bankruptcy Code and contains some of the law's most flagrant social engineering. The section proves that, as a society, we believe that some creditor claims are more important than others. We purposely give preference to those whom we feel need preference, as well as some who have simply asked for special treatment.

The claims that have priority under Section 507 are presumably those debts that society places the most value on and most wishes to be paid, even in bankruptcy. Some, however, are simply the result of effective lobbying. These claims include the trustee's fees and expenses in administering the bankruptcy estate, claims for alimony and child support, employee claims, deposit holders, claims for *some* taxes, and a few others. For individual debtors, the most common priority claims are support obligations and taxes.

The priority claims are not very important in Chapter 7 cases, but very important in Chapter 13 cases. This is because to be approved, a Chapter 13 payment plan must pay all priority claims in full. Sometimes the debtor does not have enough money or income to do this, so it really matters if a tax claim, for example, is really entitled to priority treatment or is instead just a regular unsecured claim, which need not be paid in full. This concept will be explored fully in Chapter 15 of this book.

The Avoiding Powers

Trustees and debtors-in-possession have almost magical powers to bring certain property that has been transferred away prior to a debtor's bankruptcy, back into the debtor's estate. These powers are called the *avoiding powers*.

Debtors most commonly avoid three types of transfers.

1. Preferential transfers.

2. Fraudulent transfers.

3. Transfers of security interest that are never *perfected*.

When a debtor makes one of these types of transfers, within the particular time set by the Code in each case, the trustee or the debtor-in-possession can avoid or undo the transfer, and thus bring the property, or its value, back into the debtor's estate for the benefit of all creditors.

The policy behind reversing these transfers of property is equality of treatment among creditors. Avoidance of such transfers softens the transition period between the pre-petition period, during which some creditors may have improved their position using the state court collection processes, and the post-bankruptcy period, which is marked by equality of treatment rather than a race to the courthouse.

In some cases, a creditor may have executed on property right before the bankruptcy. In other cases, the debtor may simply have transferred property or payments to another entity, either to keep them from taking action, or just because the debtor wanted to pay one creditor over another. Sometimes the debtor gives away property to avoid having to give it to creditors. At other times a debtor may simply sell something for less than its fair value. All of these transfers of property are subject to avoidance if certain elements are met. Remember that the debtor can transfer money or other tangible property outright or can transfer a security interest in something. All are subject to potential avoidance.

Note

Normally you will not care very much about any of this unless you have paid money or transferred property to a friend or a relative during the relevant time.

Preferential Transfers

Assume that the debtor pays their credit card bills for the past four months all at once, and a few weeks later files for bankruptcy. This is a transfer of money on account of a past due debt within 90 days of the bankruptcy petition. If the debtor was insolvent at the time of the transfer, then this transfer would be avoidable by the trustee or the debtor-in-possession under Section 547(b).

Section 547(b) contains the elements of an avoidable preferential transfer and requires exactly that, a transfer of property on account of a past due or antecedent debt made within 90 days before the filing (one year for transfers to insiders such as family members), while the debtor was insolvent. The transfer must allow the creditor to receive more than it would have received in a Chapter 7 case.*

Why is insolvency required in order for a transfer to be a preference? Perhaps because at the time of insolvency, even if insolvency precedes the bankruptcy filing, the policy of equality of treatment among creditors kicks in. More importantly, if the debtor is not insolvent at the time of a purportedly preferential transfer, there is no harm to other creditors because the remaining property should be sufficient to cover all creditors' claims.

The policy reasons behind preference avoidance should now be clear and they should help you remember the rule. Bring back the transferred property and allow it to be distributed among creditors equally, or at least according to the priority scheme.

In Chapters 7 and 13 cases, preferential transfers can be avoided, but this often makes less difference in the consumer case than it does in a business bankruptcy case. This is because payments made during the preference period tend to be smaller and thus have less of an impact on the case when they are recovered. This is not always the case, however. You might recall from our prior discussion that transfers to insiders can be avoided for a full year, rather than the usual 90 days for other transfers. The word "insider" is defined in Section 101(5) of the Code but in many consumer cases, the insider in question is a family member. Sometimes a parent has lent a child money and the child is paying it back over time.

These payments are avoidable by a trustee for a full year because, as the theory goes, an insider is more likely to be aware of the debtor's failing financial condition and thus was in a better position to avoid making the loan based upon this information. Such a creditor is also more likely to be preferred by the debtor. Moreover, we may even question the motivation of the so-called *loan*, assuming on some subconscious level that Mom really meant to make a gift here, right?

There are some exceptions to preference law: (1) for debts paid in the ordinary course of business (usually on-time monthly payments), (2) for new value given by a creditor after receiving a payment, and (3) for contemporaneous exchanges, which are not really payments on old debts.

Again you are most interested in this topic if you have paid back a loan to a relative or a business colleague during the year before your bankruptcy case.

Avoiding Fraudulent Transfers under the Bankruptcy Code

All states have laws allowing harmed creditors to avoid fraudulent transfers. Most of these laws allow the reversal of such transfers for a period of six years after the transfer is made.

---

*This last element means that if a bank lends money and takes back a security interest for the new debt, there is no preference through the grant of the security interest because in a Chapter 7, the bank would recover from the collateral and be no better or worse off as a result of the transfer.

Among the trustee's avoidance powers is the right to undo what we call *fraudulent transfers*. The Bankruptcy Code allows the trustee to set aside fraudulent transfers made by the debtor, while the debtor was insolvent, or that caused the debtor to become insolvent, that occurred within one year prior to the debtor's bankruptcy filing (two years under the new law). These transfers can be avoided where there is *actual fraud* (transfers made with actual intent to hinder, delay, or defraud creditors) and also where there is just *constructive fraud* (transfers for less than fair value).

The policy behind these laws is pretty clear. A person cannot give away property or sell it for less than it is worth, if doing so will harm her creditors by leaving them with less assets than are necessary to pay their claims. The law of fraudulent transfers is very detailed, however, and too complex to cover here. If this is an issue in your case, your attorney will explain it to you further.

Avoidance of Unperfected Security Interests under the Trustee's Strong-Arm Powers

If a secured creditor fails to do all of its paperwork correctly, it is possible to turn that creditor into an unsecured creditor. Essentially, *unperfected security interests* can be avoided in bankruptcy. We call this supernatural power to avoid certain liens the trustee's *strong-arm powers*, but that's not really important. What does matter is that these powers can turn a previously secured creditor into a general unsecured creditor. That makes the creditor much less powerful and you probably will not have to pay the creditor as much as you thought!

Let us elaborate on this just a bit. To be a voluntary secured creditor in a bankruptcy case, a creditor must have a contract signed by the debtor granting a security interest in certain property, to secure repayment of the loan. This process is similar to granting a bank a mortgage on your home to secure your repayment of the loan.

But just having a contract giving the debtor's approval is not enough. Usually, to be a secured creditor in a bankruptcy, the creditor also must do something to *perfect* this security interest. You need not be very concerned with exactly what this means. Generally, *perfecting* requires the creditor to give some sort of notice of the security interest to third parties, a task usually accomplished by filing a piece of paper with the Secretary of State's office. To make a long story short, you just need to know that an unperfected security interest is normally treated as an unsecured claim in a bankruptcy. Keep this in mind as you read the next chapter.

CHAPTER 10

The Treatment of Secured Creditors in Bankruptcy

A s you have read, the two main types of creditors are unsecured creditors and secured creditors. This section will take a closer look at how the secured creditor is treated in a bankruptcy.

Secured Credit in General

As we discussed in Chapter 5, secured creditors are those who have liens on certain property, real or personal, of the debtor. Liens arise under state law, not under the Bankruptcy Code, but the Bankruptcy Code recognizes them as property interests of the person holding the lien. The liens may arise in three different ways.

1. *Involuntary judicial liens.* These are created through the judicial process, in which a creditor gets a judgment, executes on the judgment, and has the sheriff levy on certain property of the debtor.

2. *Statutory liens.* These are created by statute (law made by a legislature). This type of lien arises because of the relationship of the parties, for example, the lien that a landlord has on the personal property of the tenant who is on the premises.

3. *Voluntary liens.* These arise from a voluntary act of the debtor, that is, the debtor grants to a creditor a security interest in some of his or her

property by creating a mortgage on real property or a security interest in some of his or her personal property.

As we just said in the previous chapter, to be a voluntary secured creditor in a bankruptcy case, a creditor must have a contract signed by the debtor granting a security interest in certain property to secure repayment of the loan. This process is similar to granting a bank a mortgage on your home to secure your repayment of the loan. In order to be enforceable in a bankruptcy, the lien also must be perfected. (We talked about this in the previous chapter.)

Secured Creditor Remedies Outside Bankruptcy

When a voluntary secured creditor's borrower is not in default and not in bankruptcy, the borrower pays the loan as promised, and eventually the creditor releases their security interest on the collateral and the debtor owns the property *free and clear*.

If the borrower does not pay the loan on time, and the loan instead goes into default, then the secured creditor has the right to repossess its collateral, sell the collateral to pay down the loan, and then pursue the debtor for a *deficiency judgment* (the part of the loan that was not paid off from the sale of the collateral). The creditor becomes an unsecured creditor for this deficiency judgment because the collateral is already gone.

There is no longer any collateral to cover the part of the loan that is still unpaid. If the creditor wants to get a judgment for this remaining debt, it will need to execute on other property of the debtor in order to be paid, just as any unsecured creditor would.

Secured Creditor Treatment in Bankruptcy

The state law theme of being paid upon default up to the value of the collateral continues into the bankruptcy process. In a Chapter 7 case, if the debtor is a business that has closed its doors, the secured party can get the automatic stay lifted in order to gain the right to repossess and sell its collateral, just as it would outside bankruptcy. If the debtor is an individual Chapter 7 debtor, then a number of things could happen. First, the debtor may just keep paying the loan and the creditor will not be affected by the bankruptcy. The debtor could also reaffirm the debt or redeem the collateral, something you'll read more about in Chapter 13 of this book.

Alternatively, if the debtor is in default (behind on the payments), the secured creditor may get the stay lifted and again gain the right to repossess and sell the collateral. If this happens, the creditor is limited in its recovery to the value of its collateral. Once the creditor has sold the collateral, the deficiency claim becomes an unsecured claim in the bankruptcy, and in most Chapter 7 cases, it is simply discharged. This assumes there are no assets to distribute to creditors, which is often, though not always, the case in Chapter 7 bankruptcies.

In a Chapter 13 case, the secured party gets paid over time under the debtor's plan. (Chapter 15 of this book goes into this treatment in greater detail.) As you will read, in a Chapter 13 case filed before October 17, 2005, the amount a secured creditor is paid is usually tied closely to the value of its collateral, not the amount it is owed.* After October 17, however, this will change drastically, and most debtors will need to pay the whole debt in a payment plan, not just the value of the collateral.

Note

It is definitely preferable to be a secured creditor rather than an unsecured creditor. Being a secured creditor in a bankruptcy—or outside a bankruptcy for that matter—can be a comfortable position. It certainly beats the alternative, which is to be a general or an unsecured creditor, with no collateral from which to be paid if there is a default.

From the debtor's perspective, however, it is far easier to deal with unsecured creditors. In a sense, the less secured debt you have, the more likely that your bankruptcy case will be successful for you.

Note: If you live in Alaska, Arizona, California, Idaho, Louisiana, Nevada, New Mexico, Puerto Rico, Texas, Washington, or Wisconsin, the way bankruptcy works (and the paperwork you need to fill out) will be a bit different from that in other parts of the country. Most of the differences relate to how your spouse's debts affect you and vice versa. In these states, known as *community property states*, your attorney will help you understand these unique community property concepts in bankruptcy.

---

*Pre-October 17, 2005, the debtor usually must *only* pay the lesser of the loan amount or the value of the collateral. This is a tremendous advantage.

CHAPTER 11

Basic Bankruptcy Procedures

This chapter contains a lot of detailed information (the nuts and bolts) of all types of consumer bankruptcy cases. As you prepare to do your bankruptcy, this information will come in handy.

The Paperwork

Now you are ready to begin the procedure of preparing for your bankruptcy. This starts by filling out a large amount of disclosure paperwork, which your attorney will then file with the court. To help you know what your attorney will need in terms of information, we have made a list of things you'll be disclosing.

The most complex paperwork consists of what we call *schedules of assets and liabilities* ("schedules"), *statement of affairs*, the bankruptcy *petition*, and, if you are doing a Chapter 13, a *Chapter 13 plan*.

The *schedules* are a snapshot, or "still life," if you will, of your financial condition at the time you file your bankruptcy. This paperwork asks for all your assets, all your debts or liabilities, all contracts to which you are a party, everyone who is also liable for your debts, your current income and expenses, and a list of the property you claim as exempt.

The statement of affairs, on the other hand, is not a still life or snapshot, but a look into the past. The statement of affairs tells a story about how you got into financial trouble. It starts by asking for a disclosure of your income from all sources (including public benefits and insurance) over the past few years, then asks about payments you've made to creditors, lawsuits to which you have been a party, things you have lost to fire, gambling, theft, things that have been repossessed, and so on. The idea is that the trustee and the creditors want to know what has gone on in your financial life during the past few years.

The bankruptcy petition itself is a fairly short document that contains your name, address, your approximate number of creditors, and how long you have lived in the district in which you are filing.

We discuss Chapter 13 plans later (in Chapter 15) of this book. A Chapter 13 requires significantly more paperwork and much more thought than a Chapter 7.

Disclosures for Schedules of Assets and Liabilities

The schedules of assets and liabilities are a series of charts. They are:

Schedule A   Real property that you have an interest in.

Schedule B   Personal property (all other things that you own or are owed).

Schedule C   Property you claim as exempt (property that you'd like to keep).

Schedule D   Creditors who are secured creditors (creditors who have collateral).

Schedule E   Creditors who have special priority (such as alimony, child support, certain taxes).

Schedule F   Creditors who do not have collateral or special priority (everyone else, credit cards, doctor's bills, most creditors).

Schedule G   Co-debtors (other people who are liable for your same debts, like husbands, wives, mothers, business associates, etc.).

Schedule H   List of contracts and leases to which you are a party.

Schedule I   Statement of current income (from any source).

Schedule J   Statement of current expenses.

Now let's go through each of these in some detail. If you don't need this information yet, just skip it.

ASSETS (SCHEDULES A–B)   You'll be disclosing all of your assets, and this is meant in the broadest way. But first we'll start with the obvious things.

Schedule A asks you to list all interests in real estate that you have, which will include your home, raw land, office spaces, a lease, and so on. You also must *value* the real estate on this schedule and disclose how you arrived at the value. In the past, a rough idea based upon what you have heard houses have sold for in your area has been enough. Under the new law, appraisals may be required.

Schedule B asks you to list all of your other assets, besides real estate. You can start with things like furniture and household goods, cars, motorcycles, guns, sporting goods, computers, appliances, and other things within your view when you walk through your home and garage.

Next, you need to think of less tangible assets, starting with all cash, all bank accounts, all retirement accounts, and all investments of any kind. For all of these things you need the approximate balance of the account and the account number.

Next, you really have to think broadly. Have you given a security deposit to anyone? Have you put down a deposit on something? Have you prepaid for any contracts for work around your house? Does anyone owe you money? Have you lent money to friends, business associates, family members? Do you have the right to sue anyone? Are you owed a tax refund? Is there any other thing or right of any value that you have that could be worth something? Think about this long and hard.

When Schedule B asks you to disclose all of your personal property, it really means all of your assets of any kind other than real estate. In a true test of your concentration, the forms ask you to disclose any interest in insurance policies, amenities, IRAs, ERISA, Keogh, or other pension or profit sharing plans, stocks and interests, incorporated and unincorporated businesses, interests in partnerships or joint ventures, government and corporate bonds and other negotiable and nonnegotiable instruments, accounts receivable, alimony, maintenance and support, property settlements, and believe it or not "other liquidated debts owing to debtor including tax refunds," "equitable or future interests, life estates, rights and powers exercisable for the benefit of the debtor other than those listed on the schedules of rule property," and finally, "contingent and non-contingent interests in an estate of a decedent, death benefit plan, life insurance policy, or trust."

Wow! They really do mean "everything"!

EXEMPT PROPERTY (SCHEDULE C)   Schedule C asks you to list all property that you claim as exempt. This means all property you are allowed to keep under either the state or the federal exemptions. Your lawyer will do the work for this one. His or her goal will be to try to get as many of the items listed on Schedules A and B to fit within your exemptions, and thus listed on Schedule C. Things that are listed on Schedules A and B, but not on Schedule C, are available for creditors to pay their claims. In other words, the debtor does not get to keep them. In the vast majority of bankruptcy cases, the debtor gets to keep all of his or her assets if the debtor wishes to do so. Otherwise, it may not make sense to file for bankruptcy.

DEBTS OR LIABILITIES (SCHEDULES D, E, F, G, AND H)   Schedules D through F ask you to list all of your debts. It is important to try to put everyone whom you could possibly owe money to on these lists. Otherwise, their claims may not be discharged and your bankruptcy will be less effective than it could be.

SCHEDULE D　　Schedule D asks for a list of all your secured creditors, along with their addresses, the approximate amounts of their claims, and their account numbers, if there are any.

If you have a mortgage or a home equity loan, those go here. So do car loans. You also may have furniture loans that are secured, if you borrowed from the store to pay for the items and gave the store back a security interest.

SCHEDULE E　　Schedule E asks for a list of priority claims. Most individuals have these types of claims only if they are behind on their taxes or their alimony or child support payments. Your lawyer will fill this out for you, so don't worry very much about it.

In a Chapter 7, what constitutes a priority claim does not make very much difference in most cases, but in a Chapter 13 payment plan, the plan has to pay all Schedule E claims in full. For this reason, your attorney may want to challenge the priority status of some of the taxes or other potential priority claims. Remember that not all taxes automatically have priority status.

In a Chapter 7, if there will be assets to distribute to creditors and if you do owe priority taxes, your lawyer may want to file a claim for the taxing authorities. That way, the taxes can be paid out of your bankruptcy rather than being still owed by you as a nondischargeable claim after your case is over. Not sure what we mean? Ask your lawyer.

SCHEDULE F　　This is where most of your debts or bills will be listed. To save time and money, and ensure that as many of your debts are discharged as possible, provide your attorney with copies of as many of your bills as you can. If some accounts have been sent to collection agencies, give those to your lawyer, too. In other words, bring in all the paperwork that you have.

If you have been sued, bring in copies of the complaint so your lawyer can list both the plaintiff in the suit and the plaintiff's lawyers.

Again, keep in mind that it is always better to provide more information rather than less information. This is true even if you have to repeat yourself in your bankruptcy paperwork, in order to insure that all creditors are notified and so that the trustee does not think you are hiding anything.

Believe us, there is no question that failing to mention something can have significant and very serious consequences. It can be a huge disaster if you fail to disclose an asset or to notify a creditor of your bankruptcy.

SCHEDULE G　　This is a list of the debts you have that other people are also liable for. An example would be a car that your mother co-signed for. You need the address of the creditor and the other person who is liable with you.

SCHEDULE H　　This is a list of all ongoing contracts and leases to which you are a party. You need the names and addresses of the other parties to the contracts and leases.

INCOME AND EXPENSES

SCHEDULE I Schedule I contains the current income of individual debtors. You will be required to disclose whether you are married or not as well as the first names and the ages of your children.

You will then be required to disclose your occupation, the name of your employer, how long you have been employed, and your employer's address. After that you will disclose all income from any source. This means any money that contributes to your monthly budget.

Please note that you will first state, if you are employed, your gross income, and then you will have to deduct all of your payroll deductions. The easiest way for you to provide the appropriate information to your lawyer is to provide a pay stub. *After bankruptcy reform on October 17, 2005, pay stubs are required of every debtor for the 60 days preceding the bankruptcy case.*

These figures taken off the pay stub or other proof of income will result in a net monthly take-home pay. You will then, if you run a business, have to disclose all of the expenses of your business on a separate sheet of paper.

If by chance your attorney does not request this information, be sure to provide it in any event. You will then be asked to disclose income from real property, interest and dividends, alimony and support payments, Social Security, and other government programs.

Finally, you absolutely should note any income that is not received on a monthly basis by somehow figuring that into Schedule I. For example, if you receive a bonus at your job, this amount should be noted somewhere on the form. Hopefully your attorney will know to do this.

SCHEDULE J The next schedule is Schedule J, the current expenditures of an individual debtor. This form is very critical to fill out and your attorney will help you.

It requires that you disclose your rent or home mortgage payment, all of your utilities, your expenses for food, clothing, laundry and dry cleaning, medical and dental expenses, transportation (not including car payments), recreation, charitable contributions, various forms of insurance, various taxes, various installment payments, such as your car or furniture, alimony, maintenance and support paid to others, payments made to support other dependents not living in your home, and all of your other monthly expenses.

Some people use Quicken or another financial program and can get their hands on this type of information easily, while others need to simply estimate these expenses.

Keep in mind that you would not include any payments on your credit cards or other installment debts that are not supported by collateral (meaning debts that are simply unsecured debts).

This Schedule J is critical on a number of levels:

1. It will determine (along with a whole bunch of other new paperwork under the new bankruptcy reform), whether or not you are eligible for a Chapter 7 case.

2. If you are attempting to pay off your home or your car over time in a Chapter 13 payment plan, this schedule will determine whether you have sufficient income to pay a Chapter 13 payment plan.

Schedule J is the last schedule in the schedule of assets and liabilities. Remember that this was part of the paperwork that contains a snapshot or still life of your current financial picture.

STATEMENT OF AFFAIRS We now move on to the statement of financial affairs, which is a lengthy disclosure explaining how you got into this situation.

1. In Statement of Affairs, question 1, you are required to disclose the amount of *income from employment or the operation of a business* that you and/or your spouse have received during the current calendar year, as well as the past two calendar years. The easiest way to get this information to your attorney is to provide your past tax returns and your most recent pay stubs.

   Under bankruptcy reform, a most recent tax return is required in all cases. This must be given to the trustee in your Chapter 7 case at least seven days before your Section 341 creditors' meeting.

2. Question 2 asks you to disclose income *other than from employment or the operation of the business*, which includes public benefits.

3. Question 3.a. asks you to disclose all payments on loans, installment purchases of goods and services, and other debts aggregating more than $600.00 to any creditor made within the 90 days immediately preceding the bankruptcy case. Obviously, if you've made payments to creditors in an amount less than $600.00 per payment, these do not need to be disclosed.

   Question 3.b. asks you to list all payments made within one year immediately preceding the case for the benefit of creditors who are *insiders*. *Insiders* are family members and business associates. Consequently, this is the part of the paperwork that the trustee will examine in order to determine whether there have been preferential transfers made by you to family members. (For more information on this, please read Chapter 9.)

4. Question 4 asks you to disclose all suits and administrative proceedings, executions, garnishments, and attachments to which the debtor has been a party. In a nutshell, this question asks your attorney to list all of the lawsuits to which you've been a party, and these may include

garnishments of your wages as well as attachments and executions on other pieces of property that you own.

5 Question 5 asks you to disclose all repossessions, foreclosures, and other transfers that you've made to creditors, either voluntarily or by force.

6. Question 6 asks you to disclose any assignments or receiverships, which essentially amount to state court bankruptcy proceedings. It is unlikely that you will have any of those to disclose.

7. Question 7 asks you to list all gifts or charitable contributions that you have made within a year prior to your case, except gifts made to family members in the ordinary course of business for less than $200.00 in value, and except charitable contributions aggregating less than $100.00 per recipient. These can be doubled if you are married. However, gifts to each other exceeding these amounts must also be disclosed.

8. Question 8 asks you to list all losses from fire, theft, other casualty or gambling within one year immediately preceding the commencement of the case.

9. Question 9 asks you to disclose all payments made to all attorneys or petition preparers who help you put your bankruptcy case together.

10. Question 10 asks you to list all property other than property transferred in the ordinary course of business that you have transferred away during the year preceding your bankruptcy.

11. Question 11 asks you to disclose the account numbers for all bank accounts you have closed during the past year.

12. Question 12 asks you to disclose all safe deposit boxes and their contents.

13. Question 13 asks you to disclose all setoffs that creditors have taken. Normally this means that you owed a bank money and the bank took what it was owed out of your checking account after you failed to pay in the normal way.

14. Question 14 asks you to disclose all property that you are holding for another person.

15. Question 15 asks you to disclose all your prior addresses for the prior two years. If you have moved around in the past two years, you will need to get this together before meeting with your attorney.

16. Question 16 asks you to disclose the names of any spouses or former spouses you've had during the past six years, but only if you live in Alaska, Arizona, California, Idaho, Louisiana, Nevada, New Mexico, Puerto Rico, Texas, Washington, or Wisconsin. These states are known as *community property* states and require additional disclosures.

The rest of the questions in the Statement of Affairs deal with businesses. If you are operating a business, your attorney will elaborate further on what you need to disclose in questions 17 thru 25.

You will notice that at the end of both the Statement of Financial Affairs and the Schedule of Assets and Liabilities, you will be asked to declare under penalty of perjury that you have read the answers contained in all of these pieces of paper, and that all of the information you have provided is true and complete.

I (Nathalie) once asked a perplexed client whether she knew what penalty of perjury *meant. She said she believed that it meant that you had to go to court, and that if you didn't show up you could end up in jail. This is* not *what it means to sign something under penalty of perjury. Penalty of perjury means that if you lie in any of these pieces of paper or if you intentionally fail to disclose something, then you may end up in jail.*

Special Chapter 7 Procedures

Statement of Intentions With Respect to Secured Debts

As we discuss in much greater detail in Chapter 13 of this book, when you file your bankruptcy paperwork, you will need to decide how you intend to pay your secured debts. If you file a Chapter 13, this decision is fairly simple, as you'll pay these debts over time in your Chapter 13 plan. However, if you intend to file a Chapter 7, you will essentially have two options after October 17, 2005.

First, you can redeem the property for its fair market value, a concept discussed further in Chapter 13 of this book. Second, you can reaffirm the debt, simply meaning you can agree to pay it as indicated.

Note about the new law: If you are filing for bankruptcy before October 17, 2005, you have a nice benefit that filers after that date will not have. In many places around the country (though not all), you can continue to pay your debt without signing on for the full obligation into the future, and then if you later decide you do not want to keep the secured property, you can simply return the secured property to the secured party. This is known as "ride-through" or "keep and pay."

This option is now available in a number of jurisdictions but it will not be available after bankruptcy reform, except for real estate mortgages. Again, for more information on this please turn to Chapter 13 of this book.

Needless to say, once you have prepared your bankruptcy paperwork, you should not do anything with any of your assets. You should simply file the paperwork, which reflects all of your assets and liabilities, and wait for the case to proceed.

The Rest of a Chapter 7 Case: The Section 341 Creditors' Meeting

So now you are starting to get the big picture of how a bankruptcy is accomplished, at least a Chapter 7. You will visit your attorney, will probably need to pay a retainer for his or her services, and then your attorney will prepare your paperwork. Next, the attorney will file the paperwork in the bankruptcy court in the district in which you have been living. Within 45 to 60 days of the filing of your case, you will need to attend a meeting of creditors.

All of your creditors, at least those who were listed on your bankruptcy paperwork, which should have been all of them, will also receive notice of your bankruptcy filing and notice of this meeting of creditors. You need not worry very much about having creditors go to your meeting, as normally no creditors attend the meeting.

Hopefully your attorney will get together with you before the meeting to go over the types of questions that the trustee will typically ask at the meeting. Most bankruptcy debtors are extremely nervous about attending their creditors' meeting. In a way, however, there is no need for that, as long as you have been honest on all of your bankruptcy paperwork.

The honesty that you used to fill out your paperwork should continue at the meeting, and, of course, it is absolutely critical that you answer every question that the trustee asks completely and honestly. If you do, your bankruptcy will be over before you know it.

What kind of questions will the Chapter 7 trustee ask? We'll go over that in a minute, but please understand that when you get to the room for your Section 341 creditors' meeting, you will see a lot of people. These are probably not your creditors, so don't worry. Normally, the trustee will schedule a number of Section 341 meetings at the same time, and therefore most of the people you see are actually other debtors and their attorneys. You will go into the room with the other debtors and their attorneys and sit and wait for your name to be called.

Hopefully your attorney has done a practice run of the creditors' meeting with you. If nothing else, you can ask your attorney to do this with you after having read about it in this book. *In any event, in a simple case, the whole creditors' meeting takes about five minutes, start to finish.*

As you sit at the actual meeting with your attorney, you will eventually hear your name called. They'll say "In re Patricia Smith," for example, and the next thing that happens is that you and your attorney will sit down at the table. The trustee will ask for a form of identification, as well as proof of your Social Security number. The easiest way to provide this proof is through your Social Security card. Be sure to bring this. I (Nathalie) am embarrassed to say that I have forgotten to tell clients to bring this card and the meeting has been postponed. Ouch!!

Once you have provided these two documents, the trustee will begin the meeting by saying something like this. "My name is Linda Bowman and I've been appointed by the Office of the United States Trustee, a part of the United States Department of Justice, to serve as interim trustee in this case. I will preside over this meeting and the others scheduled here today."

"The Bankruptcy Code requires that you be examined under oath with respect to the petition that you have filed, along with the other paperwork." He or she will probably go on to say. "All persons appearing must sign the appearance sheet, all persons questioning the debtor must state their name and who they represent for the record to state clearly. All examinations will be electronically recorded and testimony is made under penalty of perjury."

The trustee will then ask you to stand up and take an oath under penalty of perjury. You will stand up and put up your right hand and respond by saying yes to the following, "Do you solemnly swear or affirm to tell the truth, the whole truth, and nothing but the truth?"

After administering the oath, the trustee will ask you to verify that the signature that appears on the petition and the schedule is actually yours. The trustee will then note for the record that he or she has received proof of identification and proof of your Social Security number. He or she will say something like "I have viewed the original driver's license or passport and original Social Security card and they match the name and Social Security number on the petition."

Next, the trustee will began examining you, asking questions something like those that follow. Keep in mind, however, that every Section 341 meaning could be a little bit different:

1. Could you please state your full name and your address.
2. Do you own or rent your home?
3. If you own your home, where is it located?
4. How did you arrive at the value for your home?
5. What is your spouse's name?
6. What is your wife's maiden name?
7. Have you made any voluntary or involuntary transfers of real property or personal property within the past year?
8. Are there any debts from credit cards?
9. Have you returned or destroyed your credit cards?
10. I'm now showing you a copy of your schedule of assets and liabilities and statement of affairs.

    Is Schedule A a complete list of all your real estate?

    Is Schedule B a complete list of all your personal property?

Is Schedule C a complete list of all your exempt property?

Is Schedule D a complete list of all your secured creditors?

Is Schedule F a complete list of all your unsecured creditors?

Do you have a right to sue anyone?

Are you being sued by anyone?

Are you currently expecting a tax refund?

Have you paid back any loans to family members in the past year?

Did you receive a tax refund last year?

Are you current on your payments on your car?

Have you made any recent large payments to creditors or others?

Do you expect to receive any inheritance or any insurance proceeds?

Are you currently employed, and, if so, by whom?

Is all the information contained on Schedule I concerning your income correct?

Are all of your expenses as reflected on Schedule J correct?

Has your job or your income changed since you first filed your petition?

Did anyone help you prepare for your bankruptcy?

Is there anything else about your paperwork that you would like me to know?

How much did you pay for your bankruptcy services?

Sometimes a trustee may ask different questions of different people. If a debtor does not list a car, the trustee will often ask, "How did you get here?"

At the end of the meeting, or sometime during the meeting, the trustee may request that your attorney provide additional information with respect to some of the materials contained in the paperwork. This is not a cause for alarm, and you should not be worried. However, within a week or two you should call your attorney's office and ask whether or not this has been done. It is important to stay on top of these things, as some bankruptcy attorneys are very busy.

As we've discussed, one of the things the trustee is most likely to question is the values that you have placed on your assets. That is because certain property is exempt in bankruptcy, and if the trustee believes you have *undervalued* your assets, he may believe that there will be something for him to obtain for creditors by selling some of these pieces of property. For more information on this, see Chapter 9.

You need to understand that for the trustee, any asset that he or she can find to distribute to creditors will generate a fee for him. As a result, most trustees will look as hard as they can to find nonexempt assets for creditors.

If you don't have anything that's not exempt, however, there is nothing to worry about. If you do have some nonexempt assets, then it is very possible that you will eventually lose these items, but I presume that your lawyer will have explained this to you. Sometimes it is worth it to file even if you will lose some of your assets.

After the Creditors' Meeting, What Happens?

Now you are probably wondering what happens after you have attended your Section 341 creditors' meeting. In the vast majority of cases, you will now simply wait approximately 45 to 60 days, for a total of about 90 days from the time the case was filed, and you will then receive a piece of paper in the mail saying that you have received your bankruptcy discharge.

This is the piece of paper you have been waiting for, the event that says that you no longer owe any of the debts in your petition other than the ones that are not dischargeable (see Chapter 12) and those that are secured debts. If the case works out the way I have just described, this is a very, very happy time for you and you have accomplished exactly what you had hoped for.

In a small number of cases other things may happen, including that some creditors may object to the dischargeability of certain debts, for example those for fraud, intentional torts, embezzlement, and so on. Other creditors may, though this is very rare, object to your entire discharge. For more information on these you can look at Chapter 12. We doubt that this will be true in many cases, however, and thus Chapter 7 normally has a very happy ending.

Assuming that you are filing your case on or after October 17, 2005, there's a new barrier to your Chapter 7 discharge that was never there before. Specifically, your case can now be dismissed at the request of any creditor, the court, or a trustee if it is found to be an abuse of Chapter 7. This is a highly complex test that essentially makes it necessary for more people to file a Chapter 13 payment plan.

Chapter 13 Procedures

A Chapter 13 operates in much the same way initially that a Chapter 7 does. You will do the same paperwork that we talked about for the Chapter 7 case with your lawyer, as well as a Chapter 13 payment plan. The details of what needs to be included in a Chapter 13 payment plan are described in Chapter 15 of this book. You may want to look at that now to get some idea of what the plan looks like.

There is a Section 341 creditors' meeting in a Chapter 13 as well. The Chapter 13 trustee presides over this meeting who is often the same person for every Chapter 13 case in the district.

The Chapter 13 trustee will ask all of the same types of questions that the Chapter 7 trustee asks, as well as many, many questions about your income and your expenses. The Chapter 7 trustee will mention these items, but the Chapter 13 trustee's job is somewhat different. This person is charged with attempting to determine whether or not you have contributed enough of your money to your plan to pay creditors, and also whether or not you are able to pay your plan out of your current income.

The disposable income test requires the debtor to contribute all of his or her disposable income to the plan. The second part of the test is called the feasibility test. This requires that the debtor actually be able to make the plan. Pie-in-the-sky predictions are not acceptable to meet this test.

Once you have survived your Chapter 13 Section 341 meeting, you will usually need to go to court to get your plan approved. The court will hold a confirmation hearing where the court will approve your payment plan. If there are no issues in your Chapter 13 payment plan, then it is possible that the court will approve the Chapter 13 plan without an actual hearing.

More Information Required under New Law

At the Time of the Filing

On and after October 17, 2005, debtors in both Chapter 7 and Chapter 13 cases must provide additional information. The debtor and his or her attorney used to just worry about filing the *petition* for bankruptcy (a very short document), the *schedules of assets and liabilities*, and the *statement of affairs*, all discussed previously. Now the debtor also must file:

- A certification by the lawyer that the debtor was given an informational notice about bankruptcy options.

- Copies of all payment advices (basically pay stubs) or other evidence of income the debtor has received within the 60 days prior to the filing.

- A statement of the amount of the debtor's current monthly income, a quirky concept discussed later.

- A statement disclosing any reasonably anticipated increases in income or expenses over the 12-month period following the date of the petition.

- Practically speaking, this means that the filing package in every bankruptcy case will include the petition, the schedules of assets and liabilities, the statement of affairs, the informational notice from the attorney to the client, the pay stubs or other proof of income for the 60 days prior to the filing, the statement of current monthly income, and the statement of reasonably anticipated changes in income and expenses.

> ## Note
>
> This newly required document, the statement of current monthly income, sure sounds easy to produce. You just tell the court your monthly income, less taxes and other deductions, right? Wrong.
>
> The definition of *current monthly income* is not actually your real net income but an average of the income you have received over the past six months. Never mind that you might not be making this amount currently; this is what you are required to disclose. Even more startling, this is the number from which your expenses will be deducted to see if you are required to follow a repayment plan or can instead choose to discharge most of your debts.
>
> You'll learn more about this when we discuss the new *means test*.

Additional Paperwork Once Either a Chapter 13 or a Chapter 7 Case Is Filed

At least seven days prior to your section 341 meeting of creditors, you'll need to give your case trustee and any creditor who asks for it, a copy of your most recent tax return or a transcript in computer form for the tax return. Because the transcript does not contain all the private information that is found on a tax return, debtor's attorneys should become familiar with the transcript and the process of obtaining it.

If you do not produce the tax return or transcript, the court can dismiss your case automatically, unless the debtor can show that the failure to produce this information was beyond the debtor's control.

Also, any tax returns that come due and are filed with the IRS during your bankruptcy case, or those that were past due but are filed with the IRS during your bankruptcy case, have to be filed with the Bankruptcy Court. The transcript apparently will not do here, and this will leave the clerk's office of the Bankruptcy Court to figure out how to keep all this information private and confidential.

Audits in Consumer Cases

Starting in October 2006 (essentially a whole year later than the effective date of most of the rest of the new law), the U.S. Trustee's Office is required to perform random audits on bankruptcy paperwork in order to determine the accuracy, veracity, and completeness of the various bankruptcy documents. These will be something like an IRS audit, but the exact details of how this will work are unclear.

It's not clear what rules these auditors will use. The law requires that they use generally accepted auditing standards, but it's not clear what that means for individuals as opposed to business types of cases. Again, these audits will not start until October of 2006.

When they do go into effect, they will be serious matters. Bankruptcy debtors can be sent to jail for knowingly failing to disclose things and attorneys can be sanctioned for making mistakes.

Pre-Bankruptcy Debtor Counseling

Before a debtor can even file a bankruptcy case, he or she must receive, within 180 days of the bankruptcy filing, a briefing from a nonprofit budget and credit counseling agency approved by the U.S. Trustee's Office.

We told you in some detail in Chapter 6 to avoid nonprofit consumer credit counselors for the most part, because most are scams. Nevertheless, bankruptcy reform requires consumers to attend a briefing by such an agency before the person can file for bankruptcy.

The briefing must be done for free if the debtor cannot afford to pay for the services. The briefing must outline the opportunities for credit counseling and assist in performing a related budget analysis. The briefing can be done over the phone, on the Internet, and in a group as well as individually.

There is a narrow exception to the requirement that the debtor get the counseling *before* the bankruptcy. If a debtor has an emergency need for a bankruptcy, and has tried unsuccessfully to get the credit counseling within 5 days of the filing, the debtor can get the credit counseling within 30 days *after* the filing.

Note

In some parts of the country, credit counseling will not be required right away. Only agencies approved by the U.S. Trustee's Office in your particular court can provide this counseling, and in some places there may not be enough approved agencies by October 17, 2005. Ask your lawyer what the situation is in your courts.

This counseling will probably be most effective if there is competition and quite a few approved credit counselors. This credit counseling requirement seems to prevent individual debtors from being put into involuntary bankruptcy because this counseling is an eligibility requirement.

Post-Petition Financial Management Course

To get a discharge from the case in any chapter, an individual debtor must also complete a financial management course. This course would entail teaching people how to better manage their finances. It is something debtors will take *after* they file their bankruptcy case, but before the case is over.

Again, no one need complete this course unless and until the U.S. Trustee has found that there are enough of such courses available to satisfy this requirement. If there are not enough approved, then this requirement does not kick in until there are enough. Also, the program will be tested in just a few courts around the country. It is likely that the courses will not be required for a number of years. Having said that, most of what such a course would teach has already been provided to you in this book.

CHAPTER 12

The Chapter 7 Discharge and Its Limitations

This chapter discusses the bankruptcy discharge in a Chapter 7 case, along with the exceptions and objections that can be made to a debtor's Chapter 7 discharge.

The Chapter 7 Discharge: Some General Concepts

The *discharge* releases the debtor from most of his or her unsecured debts. The discharge works differently in the different kinds of bankruptcy, however.

In a Chapter 7, the discharge happens automatically at the end of the case as long as the debtor surrendered all of his or her nonexempt property to the trustee, and has been completely honest in the bankruptcy paperwork. The whole process takes only about 90 days from the date of the filing. So if the debtor has followed the rules, most of his or her unsecured debt will be forgiven at the end of three months. The discharged debts disappear forever.

In a Chapter 13, as well as a Chapter 12 (a case for a family farmer), the debtor does not receive a discharge until he or she has completed all of the plan payments and other obligations. This means that it takes three to five years to obtain a Chapter 13 discharge. If the plan is never finished, meaning that the debtor is unable to make the payments, the payments the debtor did make are essentially lost.* The debtor does not get any of his or her debts discharged.

---

*The payments are applied to the debt, but the rest of the debt is still owed.

In a typical Chapter 11 business case, most debts are discharged upon confirmation or approval of the plan, not upon completion of all plan payments.* Under the new law, if an individual files a Chapter 11 case, he or she does not get a discharge until the person has completed the plan payments, much as in a Chapter 13.

Only Pre-Petition Debts are Discharged

In a Chapter 7 case, only debts that arose prior to the bankruptcy are discharged, as the bankruptcy is designed only to clear up the debtor's pre-filing obligations. This makes sense. The debtor will list all of his or her pre-filing debts on the bankruptcy schedules of assets and liabilities and the statement of affairs. The creditors who are listed in the debtor's paperwork will receive notice of the bankruptcy case and thus receive due process in the case. Moreover, the debtor is expected to pay any debts that arise after the filing, just as a person who is not in bankruptcy would be.

Assume that a debtor files a Chapter 7 case in the morning and in the afternoon takes out a new car loan. Will the new car loan be discharged? Absolutely not. First, almost certainly, the auto will have a security interest on it that will allow the creditor to take the car back if the payments are not made. Second, the debtor will always owe the entire debt, not just the secured part, because the car was purchased after the filing. This will be a post-filing debt, for which the debtor will be liable. The filing will have no impact on this debt whatsoever.

These rules are modified slightly in Chapter 13 and Chapter 11 cases. As a result, some post-petition debts are sometimes included in the discharge in these other types of cases. In a Chapter 11, the confirmation order discharges all pre-confirmation debts, some of which will be incurred during the case. In a Chapter 13 case, all debts dealt with in the plan are discharged, and while most of those will be pre-bankruptcy claims, it is possible that some will be from the post-petition period as well.

Only Claims Are Discharged

A debt also must have risen to the legal level of a *claim*, as that word is described in the Bankruptcy Code in order to be discharged. The definition of a claim is very broad. There are things that you might think are not yet claims. They should not be listed on the bankruptcy paperwork that they probably are claims.

For example, if the debtor was in a car accident and it is not even clear whose fault it is, and no suit has been filed, the debtor should still list the

---

*In the case of an individual debtor, this rule may be an unintended glitch. Chapter 11 is usually sued by corporate or other legal entities as opposed to individuals, and in such a case, debts get discharged under Section 1141, but the debtor entity itself does not obtain a discharge. Part of the reason for this is that Congress does not want to create trafficking in corporate shells.

other party to the accident in his or her petition. If it turns out way after the bankruptcy case that the debtor is found liable for the accident in a negligence suit, the debt he owed to the other party in the car accident would be discharged in the bankruptcy!

Be overinclusive in your paperwork! It is better to be safe than sorry. When filing out your bankruptcy paperwork, it is important to take the time and consider every possible debt that you owe or might owe in the future based on the events leading up to the day you file for bankruptcy, because only the claims you list on the paperwork will be discharged.

Under the pre-October 17, 2005, law the bankruptcy discharge is far broader in a Chapter 13 than in the other chapters because Congress wanted to create incentives for people to try to pay back as much debt as they can through a Chapter 13. When deciding whether to file a Chapter 7 or a Chapter 13, this is one of the factors you would consider. On the one hand, a Chapter 13 would discharge more debts. On the other hand, a Chapter 7 would very quickly get rid of most of the debts, though not all, leaving the debtor with fewer debts to repay.

The new law essentially makes the discharges obtained in a Chapter 7 and a Chapter 13 almost identical, so the debtor can no longer discharge as many debts in a Chapter 13. (See Chapter 15 of this book.)

Exceptions to Discharge

As discussed previously, the primary and often the only reason that a debtor files a bankruptcy petition is because he wants to be discharged from debts. In most cases, the discharge is pretty much automatic. But, as you probably have guessed, it isn't that simple in some cases. Not all debts are discharged because there are exceptions to the dischargeability of debts.

Some of these debts are excepted from discharge because society has decided that these are the types of debts that people should be obligated to pay no matter what. *These include debts for alimony and child support, debts for recent taxes and some other taxes regardless of age, debts resulting from criminal restitution claims, debts arising from driving under the influence of alcohol, and student loans. These types of debts are not discharged in a case under Chapter 7, Chapter 13, Chapter 12, or Chapter 11.*

As this chapter shows, the Bankruptcy Code is a policy-driven law. As discussed earlier, the Code functions to give the debtor a fresh start through a broad discharge of various debts and obligations. However, the Code also has a counterbalancing policy designed to protect the interests of certain creditors.

While the bulk of the Code gives the debtor an opportunity to erase or discharge most debts, the Code limits the type of debts that can be discharged, and thus excludes certain debts from the discharge. While the Code lists 18 categories of debts that are nondischargeable, this book discusses only the most common exceptions to discharge.

Taxes

The Bankruptcy Code makes virtually all taxes that are *entitled to priority* nondischargeable. The key to determining whether taxes are entitled to priority, and thus are nondischargeable, is determining what type of taxes they are and when a return was due for them.

Since all priority taxes are nondischargeable in a Chapter 7, suffice it to say that a debtor with major tax problems will rarely gain relief in a Chapter 7. While the same taxes are also nondischargeable in a Chapter 13, Chapter 13 does provide some relief for taxes because they can be satisfied over the life of the plan. More importantly, once a Chapter 13 is filed, the taxes stop accruing interest, which can be a great help and thus a powerful incentive to file a Chapter 13.

In a Chapter 7, if the debtor's taxes are large and recent, filing a bankruptcy case will provide very little help. In some ways, this is similar to situations in which a debtor wants to file a Chapter 7 because he or she is behind on the mortgage. The case will ultimately accomplish nothing for the debtor. Thus, your tax liabilities may determine whether your case should be a Chapter 7 or a Chapter 13.

Marital Settlement Obligations

Debts for alimony, child support, or any type of support payment are not dischargeable in any bankruptcy. The thinking behind this policy is that a debtor may have obligations to former spouses or children that would, if discharged, have the effect of forcing these creditors to find public support.

DIFFERENCE BETWEEN SUPPORT OBLIGATIONS AND PROPERTY SETTLEMENT OBLIGATIONS Child support or alimony obligations flowing from a divorce are defined in the Bankruptcy Code as any debt "to a spouse, former spouse, child of the debtor, for alimony to, maintenance for, or support of such spouse or child, in connection with a separation agreement, divorce decree, or other order of a court of record." Debts that fall into this category *are not* dischargeable in a bankruptcy of any kind.

Property settlements on the other hand are treated differently, so the distinction is critical. Property settlement agreements sometimes are dischargeable and sometimes are not. The key is being able to tell the difference between support and a property settlement debt.

We know most people think of a property settlement as an agreement to split up property, but for many couples the property settlement part of the divorce also includes promises by one spouse to pay certain debts the couple incurred during the marriage. Generally speaking, promises to pay the mortgage, the car payment, the credit card bills, and other debts to third parties are part of a property settlement.

Because support payments are never dischargeable in any bankruptcy, every creditor receiving payments under a marital settlement agreement hopes that their debts will be characterized as support payments.

On the other hand, many bankruptcy debtors will try to argue the opposite, hoping to turn all obligations into potentially dischargeable property settlement debts. The Bankruptcy Court will look beyond the names given to obligations in the agreement itself to see what the payments are actually for. The names given to the obligations in the agreement are a starting point for analyzing the nature of the payments but will not determine, in and of themselves, if a debt is dischargeable in bankruptcy or not.

Treatment of Property Settlement Obligations in Bankruptcy

So far, we have been assuming that property settlement obligations can be discharged in bankruptcy, but this is only partially true. Actually, a debtor is *sometimes* required to pay these property settlement debts along with the support payments.

The pre-October 17, 2005, Bankruptcy Code provides a way out of paying these obligations that is not available for support payments. The Code provision dealing with this question is one of the most confusing provisions in the Code. The test seemed to boil down to deciding which of the two spouses is worse off financially. As one might expect, courts often find that the bankruptcy debtor is worse off than the spouse who is *not* in bankruptcy.*

In any case, this odd-ball provision is eliminated under the new law that becomes effective October 17, 2005. This means that after this date, property settlements are also nondischargeable in a Chapter 7 case, just like support obligations.

In a Chapter 13, the property settlement debts are discharged, however, making this distinction still important in some cases.

MARITAL OBLIGATIONS AND THE AUTOMATIC STAY The distinction between support and property settlements is also important in determining which state court actions are stayed by a bankruptcy filing. Actions to determine or collect alimony, maintenance, or support, are not stayed at all under the automatic stay. Actions to either establish or collect a property settlement *are* stayed. Practically speaking, once again, if you are not absolutely sure you are talking about support, it is safest for a creditor to request relief from the automatic stay before trying to collect any of this debt.

---

*I have no statistical support for this, and certainly the test is not supposed to favor the debtor spouse in every case, but it does seem that much of the time, the property settlement debt is deemed dischargeable.

Intentional Torts and Debts Stemming from Driving Under the Influence of Alcohol

For policy reasons, debts for intentional torts, such as battery, assault, and so on as well as debts for judgments resulting from driving while under the influence of alcohol are not dischargeable. Basically, at least in a Chapter 7, a debtor will not be excused from liability for behavior that society abhors.

Interestingly, as you will read in the discussions of the superdischarge in the Chapter 13 materials, intentional tort debts are dischargeable in a Chapter 13 under the old (pre-October 17, 2005) law. *After October 17, 2005, debts arising from intentional torts (like punching or stabbing someone) are not dischargeable under a Chapter 7 or a Chapter 13 case.*

DWI debts are never dischargeable, again reflecting the seriousness of such obligations.

Student Loans

If you are considering declaring bankruptcy because you owe thousands of dollars in student loans, forget it. The Code precludes the discharge of student loan obligations, except in *very* rare situations. Congress enacted this exception based partly on the fear that a student turned debtor would receive the benefit of an education, and then file for bankruptcy. This rule helps ensure that there will be more funds available to be used to educate future generations of students.

Congress also recognized, however, that in very rare situations, it might be necessary to allow student loans to be discharged. Under the technical language of the law, student loans may be discharged only if not discharging the loan "will pose an undue hardship on the debtor." The test looks to the debtor's likely future financial condition, not the debtor's unfortunate past. The test is extremely difficult to meet in most districts, which is what Congress intended.

Unlike the case with most other objections to the dischargeability of a debt, which are instituted by creditors, the debtor requests that the student loans be discharged, by filing a complaint. Thus, the debtor has the burden of proving that he or she meets the *undue hardship* standard.

Note

Under the new law, Congress has clarified that student loans, whether the lender is a nongovernmental, profit-making organization or the government, cannot be discharged outside the undue hardship test.

Fraud Debts, Including Credit Card Charges Close to Bankruptcy

In a Chapter 7 case, as well as a case filed by an individual under Chapters 11 or 12, there are many other debts that might not be discharged. These include:

1. Debts incurred by actual fraud.
2. Debts for luxury goods purchased within 60 (under the old law) or 90 (under the new law) days of the filing.
3. Debts incurred for cash advances within 60 (under the old law) or 70 (under the new law) days of the filing.
4. Debts for fraud in the fiduciary capacity.

The fraud exceptions to discharge embody one clear policy consideration, namely the notion that a debtor who obtains credit through fraudulent means should not be permitted to discharge the resulting debt. The goals of Congress in drafting the four fraud-based exceptions to discharge include protecting the defrauded creditor and not rewarding fraudulent behavior on the part of the debtor.

ACTUAL FRAUD   Debts obtained through fraud are not dischargeable. *Actual fraud* is proven by establishing the elements of common law fraud, and always requires the objecting creditor to prove actual intent to defraud. While the elements of fraud vary from state to state, one example of such a test for actual fraud would look like this.

1. The debtor made a representation.
2. The representation was false.
3. The debtor knew it was false at the time it was made.
4. The representation was made with the intention of deceiving the creditor.
5. The creditor actually and justifiably relied upon the representation.
6. The creditor sustained a loss or was damaged as a result of the false representation.

FRAUD THROUGH THE USE OF A FALSE FINANCIAL STATEMENT   There is another test for fraud that applies specifically to the fraudulent use of a false financial statement. In some ways, this test is less stringent. The creditor need not prove intent to defraud if a false financial statement is used, but can instead merely show that a written statement, for example a loan application, is incorrect and that the creditor relied on it in making the loan.

A real life example that meets all of the above criteria would be this. A debtor fills out a credit application and discloses her salary as $50,000 a year when actually her salary is just $32,000. This may seem like a harmless exaggeration, but the credit card company based the amount of credit it extended to the debtor based on income, which is enough to satisfy the last element required to prove actual fraud. In this example, any purchases made with the credit card obtained by the fraudulent application may be denied as dischargeable debts.

Note

Don't confuse the issue discussed here (nondischargeability, and the exceptions to discharge for particular debts) with *objections to discharge*, a phrase that refers to the process of objecting to a debtor's entire bankruptcy discharge, which is the subject of the next section.

A PRESUMPTION OF FRAUD FOR CHARGING LUXURY GOODS AND TAKING CASH ADVANCES   Under the pre-October 17, 2005, law debt incurred within 60 days of the bankruptcy filing, and used to buy luxury goods or services, is presumed to be nondischargeable on the basis of fraud. This is sometimes called *presumptive fraud*.

The theory behind this fraud-based objection to discharge is that a debtor who goes out and loads up on luxury goods right before filing for bankruptcy is aware, or should be aware, of the dire financial condition they are in, probably has no intention of paying the debt being incurred right before the bankruptcy, and thus should be required to pay the debt after the bankruptcy is completed.

Congress has now extended the presumption period from 60 days to 90 days for luxury goods charged prior to the bankruptcy. Also, a creditor must be owed just $500 under the new law for luxury goods ($1,225 under the old law).

The phrase "luxury goods or services" is not defined in the Bankruptcy Code, but essentially means goods not necessary to support the debtor or the debtor's dependants. As you can well imagine, interpreting this phrase involves a great deal of discretion on the part of the judge. Is a computer a luxury good? Does it depend on what you do for a living? How about food or a mastectomy? What about a new suit or new underwear?

The pre-October 17, 2005, Bankruptcy Code presumes that all cash advances totaling more than $1,225 from a single creditor within the 60 days prior to a bankruptcy filing are also nondischargeable on the basis of fraud, under the same logic just articulated.

The amount for cash advances has now been reduced to $750 and the period extended to 70 days, making more debts nondischargeable under this provision. The theory behind this presumption of fraud is that the debtor took the cash with full knowledge of his or her financial condition and with no intention of paying the debt back. Note that balance transfers (meaning transfers from one credit card to another), which credit card companies sometimes characterize as cash advances in their own bookkeeping, do not constitute cash advances for the purposes of this section.

Also remember that for this presumption of fraud to work for a creditor, the objecting creditor must be owed at least $500 for luxury goods or $750 for cash advances. (As we said previously, the numbers are even larger under prereform law).

Thus, if the debtor charges $300 worth of designer candles during the 60 days prior to her bankruptcy filing and then gets a cash advance from a different creditor of $600 to pay his or her mortgage, either creditor could rely on the *actual fraud* exception (the one we talked about earlier), but neither could use this *presumptive fraud* section. Not enough is owed to the creditor for luxury goods or services.

On the other hand, if the debtor charges $800 to his or her MasterCard for jewelry and then takes a cash advance for $1,000 from the same card, MasterCard could rely on the luxury goods exception. It is owed enough money for luxury goods or cash advances. This doesn't mean MasterCard will win. Remember that the debtor can rebut the presumption of fraud. Maybe the debtor had logical reasons that overcome the accusation of fraud. It is up to the judge to decide.

Tip

Keep in mind that the rule regarding nondischargebility of debts for luxury goods and cash advances merely creates a *presumption* that the luxury goods charged, or the cash advances taken, were done with no intent to pay back the debt—thus, through fraudulent means. This presumption can be rebutted by the debtor, essentially by proving that he or she had no intention of filing for bankruptcy at the time of the charge and had some reasonable belief that he or she could pay back the debt.

SUMMARY OF THE NEW LAW FOR CHARGES FOR LUXURY GOODS

- Now claims for fraud for things charged to a credit card within a short time before the filing are nondischargeable in both a Chapter 7 and a Chapter 13 case.

- The time periods have been increased and the maximum amounts decreased, to find a presumption of fraud for luxury goods charged and cash advances incurred near the time of the bankruptcy filing.

- The presumption covers luxury goods charged within 90 days (rather than the former 60 days), and amounts of just $500 (down from $1,225) owed to any one creditor.

- For cash advances the time period is now 70 days (up from 60), and the amount is $750 (down from $1,225).

Fraud in the Fiduciary Capacity, Embezzlement, or Larceny

The fraud referred to in this section is different from the fraud we have discussed previously. It deals not with the actual fraud or the debtor's purchases of luxury goods or services, but instead with fraud within a fiduciary relationship. It makes nondischargeable debts for fraud in the context of a unique position of trust and power.

For example, let's say you are treasurer for your local neighborhood association, and in your duties as treasurer you manage the group's funds through a checking account. In a moment of desperation, you use that checking account to pay your own bills. The group finds out and gets a judgment against you for $5,000. That debt, the judgment, is not discharged because it was created through fraud you committed in your duties to the association.

Debts for embezzlement and for larceny (basically theft) are also *not* discharged.

Forgetting or Simply Failing to List a Creditor in the Bankruptcy Paperwork

The importance of including every possible claim cannot be stressed enough. The reasons for it are tied directly to our Constitution. Specifically, the debtor's bankruptcy petition and accompanying documents, and the notices that are sent based upon the information contained in these documents, are designed to put all creditors on notice that a bankruptcy has been filed. This notice serves many practical purposes, including the due process required by the United States Constitution. Practically speaking, the notice tells creditors who receive it to stop all collection activity, informs them to file a proof of claim if there are assets in the case, and informs them of the deadline to object to the dischargeability of their debt or to the debtor's entire discharge. By providing these deadlines and this general notice of the case, the creditor has received the procedural due process required by the U.S. Constitution when a person's property (their right to recover their debt) is taken from him or her.

Win or lose, object or not, the creditor has received all the due process necessary by law if he or she has been listed on the petition and has received proper notice of the debtor's bankruptcy filing. On the other hand, debts that are not listed on the schedules of assets and liabilities are not dischargeable.

This includes debts that you forget to list that would have been discharged otherwise. The theory here is that by not listing the debt on the petition, the debtor has taken away the creditor's due process in the case by eliminating notice of the bankruptcy, the opportunity to object to the discharge of the debt, and the opportunity to file a claim. The practical result of such an omission is that the unlisted debt will not be discharged in the bankruptcy or otherwise affected by the bankruptcy.

Unlike the actual fraud exception, there is no mental intent requirement here. Whether the debtor furtively sought to leave a creditor off their schedules or whether the debtor just forgot, if the creditor and the debt are not on the schedule, that debt will not be discharged.

Objections to the Debtor's Global Discharge

Compared to the limited objections reviewed in the preceding section, which pertain to objections to the dischargeability of just one debt, this section discusses a far greater threat to the debtor's entire bankruptcy case, namely *objections to the debtor's general discharge.*

In some ways, this is like comparing a misdemeanor to a felony. To bring an objection to the debtor's general or global discharge, you have to really mean business.

The right to a discharge comes with obligations on the part of the debtor. These obligations include the responsibility to be honest in the case, to turn over nonexempt assets rather than trying to hide them, and to disclose absolutely everything that the bankruptcy paperwork requires. These obligations are not taken lightly. Failure to comply with any of these obligations will result in denial of the entire discharge.

Hiding assets and lying in the case are obvious reasons to deny a debtor a discharge, but a discharge can also be denied for less obvious behavior such as making a fraudulent transfer right before the case, not keeping records, or losing money without explanation. Also, giving all of your cash to a friend as a gift right before filing will most likely be seen as a fraudulent transfer.

The debtor must have done something that society really abhors to lose the right to a general discharge. The Code requires a very bad act, such as hiding assets, lying in your bankruptcy case, or destroying your business records.

A debtor's entire discharge can be denied only if the debtor essentially thumbs his or her nose at the whole system, or comes off as totally dishonest.

Because it is easy to confuse the two sections, we call objections to the discharge of a particular debt *objections to dischargeability* (referring to the debt), while calling objections to the general discharge *objections to discharge* (referring to the debtor himself or herself). If an objection to discharge is successful, none of the debtor's debts get discharged! From the debtor's standpoint, the entire case is a waste. Indeed, the debtor will be worse off because all of the debtor's nonexempt property will be gone and the debtor will still owe all of the debts that weren't paid by the trustee.

The justification for the objections to discharge, and the fairly severe punishment for noncompliance, is that in order to work, the bankruptcy system requires complete and total honesty and disclosure. Honesty and full disclosure are the two ethical and practical pillars of the system. These overlapping obligations are required of every debtor in exchange for the fresh start. The debtor who hides assets, or is dishonest about material obligations, is not entitled to a bankruptcy discharge. And, since getting a discharge is the raison d'etre of every debtor's entire case, denying a debtor a discharge is tantamount to taking away the entire benefit of the debtor's bankruptcy case. There are actually quite a few grounds for denying a debtor's entire discharge. This book covers the five most common grounds only.*

Knowing and Fraudulent False Oath in a Bankruptcy Case

A discharge can be denied if a debtor makes a "knowing and fraudulent false oath in or in connection with the case." The creditor objecting to discharge must prove that the false oath was made in the case, not prior to the case, or outside the case.

This objection goes to the very heart of the honesty and disclosure requirements. The false oath requirement refers to a statement made under oath, most commonly either in the written bankruptcy disclosure documents (the petition, the statement of affairs, or the schedules of assets and liabilities), or at the creditors' meeting or another bankruptcy court hearing. The debtor's statement must be false, of course, and the debtor must make it *knowing* that it is false. *Mistakes* are not knowing and fraudulent false oaths.

Inexplicable Loss of Money

A second ground for denial of a discharge is that the debtor has failed to explain satisfactorily, a "loss of assets or deficiency of assets to meet the debtor's liabilities." In essence, this means that the debtor has failed to explain what happened to income or property that he or she seemed to have before the financial trouble began. If you have $10,000 in the bank three months before you file for bankruptcy and $1,500 the day you file, you should be prepared to explain where the rest of the cash went or risk the loss of a general discharge.

Concealment, Loss, Destruction, Falsification, or Mutilation of Records, or a Failure to Keep Records

To destroy, mutilate, conceal, falsify, or even lose financial records create grounds for denial of a general discharge. It is easy to see why a bankruptcy debtor cannot receive a discharge if he or she destroys or hides records. It is a little harder to understand why people are punished for losing their records. The justification for this rule is that every bankruptcy trustee has a right to examine

---

*If the debtor is not an individual, then the debtor does not get a discharge. This means that corporations do not get a discharge, nor do they need one. They can just cease to exist. Other grounds to deny a discharge include that the debtor presented a false claim, withheld books and records from the trustee or the court, refused to obey an order of the court, invoked the Fifth Amendment against self-incrimination, and refused to testify about a material matter even after being granted immunity, or committed any of these acts in a prior bankruptcy case.

the financial records of his or her debtor, which can only be done if these records are kept and available. There is also a suspicion that if people do not safeguard these records, for whatever reason, they may be trying to hide something.

In one case, a debtor claimed that the garbage man must have taken all the debtor's business records, which he was storing in the garage near his trash can (*In re Harron,* 31 B.R. 466 [Bankr. D. Conn. 1983]). If you haven't already guessed, his debts were not discharged.

Furthermore, failure to keep records can be a ground for denying a discharge. It is likely that a court will deny a discharge based upon a failure to keep records when there is evidence that the failure was intentional and in contemplation of bankruptcy.

Courts have held that the recordkeeping requirement essentially applies only to businesspeople and not to the average consumer. The Code itself does not say this, but courts have interpreted the section in this way, perhaps in recognition that average people are not always organized.

Transfers Made with Intent to Hinder, Delay, or Defraud Creditors

As stated earlier, a person is not free to transfer or give away his assets to make himself insolvent or to avoid paying creditor claims. A fraudulent transfer can always be reversed if the debtor intended to hinder, delay, or defraud creditors, or even if there was no such intent if the debtor transferred an asset to another person for less than equivalent or fair value. Furthermore, outright gifts can be undone in this way, as can sales for less than the market value of the item sold.

The reason for the premises just stated is based on something informally known as *pre-bankruptcy planning.* Pre-bankruptcy planning is the process by which a person who is contemplating bankruptcy determines whether he or she is holding assets in a way that takes best advantage of the exemptions allowed under the Bankruptcy Code.

Susie lives in Florida, where residents are allowed to exempt all the equity or value in their homes no matter what the value! This means that Susie can have a home worth $200,000 with only a $50,000 mortgage on it. That means Susie has $150,000 in equity in her home. Additionally, no creditor can touch the $150,000 of equity Susie has in her home. No wonder they call it the Sunshine State!

On the down side, Florida does not allow a person to keep any cash from the reach of creditors. Too bad for Susie because she has a bank account with $20,000 in it. Susie decides to use the $20,000 in cash to pay down her home mortgage. Now the $20,000 has been converted to home equity, which is exempt under the Florida exemptions. One result of this transaction is that the debtor does not lose the $20,000. The other result is that creditors do not get the $20,000 in her bankruptcy. Isn't Susie smart?

The answer is a definite maybe. Some courts hold that pre-bankruptcy planning is acceptable if it is within reason, while others deny a discharge for relatively small transfers done in the spirit of pre-bankruptcy planning. The question is how lucky do you feel? Are you prepared to lose your entire bankruptcy discharge over it?

The fact is that these transfers can be undone, but that's not all! A person can also lose their entire bankruptcy discharge for doing something like this. Pre-bankruptcy planning is certainly not worth the risk!

Prior Bankruptcy Discharge Within the Past Six or Eight Years

You'll often hear people say that you can only file for bankruptcy once every six years.* Actually, you can file as often as you like, but if you received a discharge during the past six years, you cannot receive another one. Since the discharge is the purpose of the case, the common lore is more or less true.

A discharge is available only once every six years in a Chapter 7 or a Chapter 11 under pre-October 17, 2005, law. After October 17, 2005, one can get a Chapter 7 discharge only once every *eight* years.

Under the new law, one cannot receive a discharge in another Chapter 13 case filed within two years of receiving a prior Chapter 13 discharge or within four years of receiving a Chapter 7 discharge. Before the new law, you can file a Chapter 13 and get a Chapter 13 at any time, discharge regardless of any past filings.

The six-year or eight-year bar to a discharge in subsequent Chapter 7 cases is the only ground for denial of a discharge that does not involve a bad deed. No lies, no hidden assets, no evil intentions required.

For whatever reason, Congress merely decided that bankruptcy was something one could avail oneself of only once in a while. It is interesting that the biblical jubilee or sabbatical, which forgave debts every seven years, was more forgiving than Congress' new law!

Here is an irony! The six-year rule (and presumably the eight-year rule as well) has an interesting effect. Some lenders, especially used car dealers and small loan lenders, jump at the chance to lend to someone who has just filed for bankruptcy. This is because they know the debtor cannot get a discharge for six (or now eight) years.

Have you seen an advertisement that offers loans to debtors who have filed a bankruptcy petition? This is the reason! Discover credit cards even sends debtors a congratulatory greeting card, made especially for Discover by Hallmark, upon their discharge!

---

*Some people still say you can file only once every *seven* years, which was the rule under the old Bankruptcy Act.

CHAPTER 13

Keeping Secured Property in a Chapter 7 Case

This is going to get tricky. This section deals with treating secured debts in Chapter 7 cases. If you are having trouble remembering what secured debts are, these are debts secured by property or collateral, like a mortgage or a typical car loan. (Look back at Chapter 10 if you want more.)

As we have said before, a Chapter 7 rarely cures problems flowing from drastically past-due payments to secured creditors. Chapter 13 offers much better options for dealing with these past-due secured debts for property that the debtor would like to keep.

In a Chapter 7 case, however, the debtor does have at least two, and in some jurisdictions three, options for keeping property that is the subject of a security interest.

1. *Redemption*, which means essentially paying the value of the property in cash to the secured party and thus extinguishing the security interest.

2. *Reaffirmation*, which means essentially agreeing to honor the original loan agreement and paying the whole loan as promised, despite the bankruptcy.

3. *Ride-through*, which means that, at least prior to October 17, 2005, simply keeping the payments current without agreeing to all of the loan conditions.

The first two options are specifically allowed in the Code and the third, which is sometimes called "keep and pay" or the "fourth option,"* has been court-created. Some jurisdictions allow only the first two options.

Note

The Bankruptcy Reform Act specifically eliminates the ride-through or fourth option, at least for all property other than real estate. You can still use ride-through (in the places where it is permitted) with respect to real estate mortgages, even under the new law.

Redemption

The first option we discuss is redemption. This remedy has a religious connotation and sounds so cleansing, but actually all it means is that if the debtor has cash, the debtor can buy the secured property out from under the security interest for the lesser of the loan amount or the value of the property.

Note: This means that if a car is worth $5,000 but the debt on the car is for $10,000, then the debtor can redeem by paying the creditor the $5,000 in cash. The rest of the debt (the other $5,000) is discharged.

Needless to say, redemption is most helpful when the value of the property is far less than the amount of the loan because this allows the debtor to buy the property at a deep discount, compared to what he or she would have to pay under the regular loan terms. If the property has not depreciated, and the loan amount is lower than the value of the property, then there is little benefit to redeeming.

Reaffirmation: When Is It Necessary or Advisable?

Reaffirmation is another option for keeping collateral subject to a security interest. Just so you know, unsecured debts can be reaffirmed as well, although this is seldom a good idea.

General Principles of Reaffirmation

What is reaffirmation? Reaffirmation is a process by which the debtor agrees to pay a loan or debt, rather than having it discharged in his or her bankruptcy case. In essence, it is a voluntary waiver of the discharge of a particular debt.

At its most basic, a reaffirmation agreement is an agreement between the debtor and the creditor that a debt that otherwise would be discharged will be

---

*It actually called "the fourth," not the third, option, because another option for dealing with secured debt is to give back the collateral. Since that is the third option (one we would not highlight in a discussion of how to keep the collateral), keeping the payments current and *not* signing a reaffirmation agreement is called the *fourth option*.

repaid. The agreement can contain new terms of repayment, but most that we have seen simply restate the original loan terms and ask the debtor to agree to pay as originally agreed, with all interest, fees, due dates, and so on.

The Formal Requirements of Reaffirmation

There are pretty specific rules for reaffirmation:

- That reaffirmation occur prior to the discharge in the case.
- That a written reaffirmation agreement be filed with the court.
- That the debtor's attorney certify that the reaffirmation will not impose an undue hardship on the debtor.
- That the agreement state clearly that reaffirmation is not required and is voluntary on the part of the debtor.
- That the debtor be given 60 days to revoke the reaffirmation agreement.

If the debt is unsecured, the attorney also must certify that reaffirming is not an undue hardship for the debtor. These rules are stringent because in the past some creditors have abused the reaffirmation process, by trying to cajole the debtor into reaffirming, and by trying to achieve reaffirmation without the court's knowledge or blessing.

The requirement that the debtor's lawyer certify that the reaffirmation does not impose an undue hardship on the debtor is designed to make lawyers think before agreeing to let a client reaffirm a debt.

I mean, let's face it, reaffirmation is a bad idea. Why burden yourself with old debt? Let it go! Any reaffirmation will impair the fresh start, so it is a big deal. This is particularly true if the debt being reaffirmed is unsecured, in which case the attorney must find that the agreement is not an undue hardship on the debtor. Few self-respecting lawyers will sign off on that.

In cases in which the debtor is *not* represented by an attorney, the court itself sets a hearing to decide whether to approve the agreement. It will be approved only if the court finds it to not be an undue hardship on the debtor, and also finds it to be in the debtor's interest to sign the agreement.

Note

Reaffirmations are subject to onerous disclosures and requirements under the new law. Attorneys can also be held liable for debts that a debtor reaffirms and then does not pay.

Under the new law, the process of reaffirmation is subject to a complex mathematical analysis that requires the lawyer to determine if the debtor has the ability to pay the debt. The attorney must *certify* that the debtor can pay as well.

Reaffirmations have never been great for debtors and have now become highly risky for attorneys. We predict that reaffirmations will become far less common and that debtors will just give back the old cars and household goods and buy used items elsewhere. There may even become a huge glut of such items, which bankruptcy debtors can purchase at good prices.

A LITTLE HISTORY   In a famous case involving Sears, it was discovered that Sears was deliberately not filing reaffirmation agreements with the court because it feared that the agreements would not be approved by the court (*In re Latanowitch*, 207 B.R. 326 [Bankr. D. Mass. 1997]). In a two-year period, in the District of Massachusetts alone, Sears had knowingly failed to file reaffirmation agreements that it had solicited from unrepresented debtors in more than 2,700 cases. This ended up costing Sears more than $400 million in settlements, suggesting the importance of following the reaffirmation rules.

When Is Reaffirmation Necessary: The Keep and Pay Option

Many creditors send reaffirmation agreements to debtors, or if they are represented, to their counsel. In some jurisdictions, the debtor must sign the agreement in order to keep the secured party's collateral.

However, in some parts of the country, this is not required. The debtor can simply continue to make the payments without signing the agreement. This is a better option for the debtor where it is permitted, because if the debtor wishes to stop making the payments and return the goods to the creditor after the bankruptcy, he or she can do so at any time without being liable for the deficiency. *The deficiency (meaning the part of the debt that was undersecured and not covered by the proceeds of the sale of the collateral) will be deemed discharged by the prior bankruptcy.*

This is the "keep and pay" option briefly mentioned previously. In places that allow the debtor to keep paying the debt without reaffirming, judges think very poorly of attorneys who allow debtors to reaffirm debts. It is simply not necessary and is almost always against the debtor's best interest.

Note

The *fourth option*, or *ride-through*, has been eliminated for cases filed on or after October 17, 2005. *Ride-through has been eliminated for personal property, but not real property.* If the debtor fails to indicate if he or she intends to return personal property, reaffirm or redeem, then the stay is automatically lifted as to that property and the creditor is free to repossess it. In those jurisdictions where ride-though, or keep and pay, or the fourth option is permitted under pre-October 17 law, the option is still available for real property as the new law refers only to personal property.

CHAPTER 14

Dismissal of a Chapter 7 Case: The New Issue in Consumer Bankruptcy

While one alternative to getting a bankruptcy discharge is having a debtor's global discharge denied (or having an individual debt deemed nondischargeable), yet another alternative to discharge is having the case dismissed.

The debtor can almost always dismiss his or her own case. A debtor might choose to do so because he or she can now, unexpectedly, sell his or her assets for more than the existing debts.

Dismissal for Failure to Cooperate in the Case

More likely though, the trustee in a debtor's case will be the one to request dismissal because the debtor has failed to do what is required during the bankruptcy proceeding. The debtor is required to appear at the Section 341 creditors' meeting, and to accurately fill out the disclosure documents, among other things, in order to get a discharge. There are no exceptions, as this is the price the debtor pays for the discharge.

Most trustee-generated dismissal motions request dismissal because the debtor has failed to file the disclosure documents in the case, to appear at the Section 341 hearing, to produce requested information or documents to the trustee, or to comply with an order of the court in the case. If the case gets dismissed, the case disappears and the debtor gets no benefit from it.

Dismissal for Abuse of a Chapter 7: The Old Standard and the New

Means Test

After the 1978 Bankruptcy Code came into being, some creditors began complaining that the new bankruptcy scheme was too lenient on debtors. Specifically, consumer credit companies complained that many debtors who could afford to pay back some of their debts in a Chapter 13, were instead filing Chapter 7 cases and simply discharging their debts.

THE OLD TEST   The original Code had no requirement that a Chapter 7 debtor be *unable* to pay some debts under a Chapter 13 plan. In fact, the spirit of the Code was that the debtor could freely choose between a payment plan under Chapter 13 or a straight liquidation under Chapter 7.

Congress responded to the pressure from the consumer credit industry by adding Section 707(b) to the Code. The pre-October 17, 2005, version of the Bankruptcy Code ominously and somewhat vaguely states that the court may dismiss a case filed by an individual under Chapter 7 if the individual has primarily consumer debts and if the court finds that "the granting of relief would be a substantial abuse of the provisions of this Chapter."

Interesting, but what does it mean? After several years of interpreting this language, courts had developed two schools of thought to determine if a Chapter 7 case is a "substantial abuse" under the prior Section 707(b). Both recognize that, based on the Section's legislative history, the primary abuse Congress is talking about here is being able to afford to pay back some of one's debts.

The test is misnamed, which confuses people. The name implies that the debtor has done something evil in the heart, not simply chosen a liquidation case over a repayment plan. Yet even under the old law, *substantial abuse* simply meant the debtor had an ability to pay back some of one's debts.

Right now, pre-October 17, 2005, the test for dismissal of a Chapter 7 case is called the "substantial abuse" test. It is broad and vague and leaves a lot up to the court's discretion. A very large part of this test depends upon whether the debtor can afford to pay back some of his or her debts. Thus, an abusive case has always been understood to mean a case that was filed as a Chapter 7 (liquidation and easy discharge) case but really should be a Chapter 13 payment plan case.

THE NEW TEST FOR ABUSE UNDER SECTION 707(B): THE MEANS TEST   There is a new *abuse* test, effective on October 17, 2005. Congress decided that a big goal of bankruptcy reform would be to make people who can afford to do a repayment plan do one, rather than allowing debtors to do an easy Chapter 7 case.

The old test presumed that the debtor was the best person to decide what

DISMISSAL FOR ABUSE OF A CHAPTER 7

kind of bankruptcy case to file, and that debtors should not be forced to do repayment plans against their will. Part of the reason for this is that most Chapter 13 cases fail anyway because of the long time commitment needed to actually complete a payment plan and get a discharge.

The new law removes the presumption in favor of the debtor's choice of bankruptcy type and changes the standard from "substantial abuse" to just plain "abuse." It also sets forth one the most complex mathematical tests imaginable to determine whether there is "abuse."

Again, the idea is that a Chapter 7 case is an abuse, and should be dismissed or converted to a Chapter 13, if the debtor can afford to pay back some of his or her creditors. The new test is called the *means test*. This is probably the most famous part of the new bankruptcy reform bill.

Before we get into the ins and outs of the means test, you should know that a court or the U.S. trustee can always bring a motion for general abuse of Chapter 7 under a test called the *totality of the circumstances test* or the *general abuse test*. This is no different from prior law. This test is used when the debtor has done something to make the court, or the U.S. trustee, think that the case should not go forward. This original basis for objection to a Chapter 7 case is not available to other parties in the case, like creditors, and is not likely to be used much now that the means test has been passed.

Note

All abuse motions under Section 707(b) can be brought only against people whose debts are primarily consumer debts. Wealthier consumers with lots of business debts are not covered by the means test at all.

Under the new law, the main ground for dismissal for abuse under Section 707(b) is the means test. This test can be used by any creditor in the case or the case trustee, not just the court or the U.S. trustee.

To determine if a debtor can afford to pay some of his or her debts and has thus filed a Chapter 7 case that is an abuse of a Chapter 7, you need to:

1. Calculate the debtor's current monthly income.
2. Deduct some allowable expenses.
3. See what is left.
4. In some cases, compare what is left to how much the debtor owes creditors.

In sum then, think of it like this:

Currently monthly income – allowable expenses = money left for creditors

INCOME   We start by trying to calculate what the new law calls the debtor's current monthly income. If the debtor's income from all sources (including regular gifts from family members) is below the median income for a family of that size in the debtor's state, no one can assert the means test. Only judges and the U.S. Trustee's Office can assert the general abuse test we discussed briefly above.

What income?

The definition of current monthly income is not actually your real net income but an average of the income you have received over the past six months. Now never mind that you might not be making this amount now. This is the number from which your expenses will be deducted to see if you are required to pay a repayment plan or can instead choose to discharge most of your debts.

Calculating this income number can be quite complex. You include the debtor's income (and that of any nonseparated spouse in a joint case). You also include regular contributions that other family members make to the household. Social Security payments are not included, however, nor are victim's compensation payments. So older people on limited incomes primarily from Social Security fixed incomes are not affected by the means test at all. But they are, of course, affected by the other changes to the Code covered in this book, just like everyone else.

This current monthly income calculation is a very important number. Why? As just set out, if the debtor's household income is below that median income for a family of that size in the debtor's state, no one can assert the means test. *This is very, very critical!*

If the current monthly income is less than the median income for that state, the means test is over, and no one can claim presumptive abuse. Only the judge and the U.S. Trustee's Office can assert the general abuse part of the test, for reason's other than the debtor's general ability to pay creditors.

Median incomes for families of various sizes in all the different states. Since the Census does not compile income figures by household size and state every year, the current figures have to be extrapolated from the 2000 Census figures, which your lawyer will do by multiplying these Census 2000 figures by some amount for inflation. In other words, these amounts will increase annually for inflation from 2000 to January 1 of the current year.

ALLOWABLE EXPENSES   We'll assume for this next part that you do have an income that is higher than the median in that state as previously set out. Now we just have to figure out which expenses the debtor can deduct from his or her family income under the new means test. From the current monthly income figure, we now deduct some expenses.

Most of the allowable expenses are taken from the IRS collection standards. What are these? The IRS has developed living expense standards that are used by agents when working out payment plans with taxpayers for overdue taxes. To find these, go to http://www.irs.gov. Once you are there, click on information for Individuals. Then go to Collection Financial Standards.

These expenses are calculated in at least two different ways. In some cases, as with transportation and housing, the debtor puts his or her own expenses into the calculation, up to the amounts allowed by the IRS guidelines.

With food, clothing, personal care, and entertainment, the debtor can put into their budget the full amount allowed for these items by the IRS, even if he or she does not normally spend that much. The debtor can actually spend five percent more than these guidelines permit for food and clothing, if he or she demonstrates that these expenses are reasonably necessary.

Note

It appears (although there seems to be some disagreement) that secured debts are taken out of the income separately and as a result, a debtor with a large car payment or home mortgage need not fit those expenses anywhere within the IRS guidelines.

The means test also allows for *other necessary expenses*, which include other expenses one might incur. They include "actual care expenses for elderly or disabled members of the immediate family, private school of up to $1,500 per child per year, and additional home energy costs.

The new law also adds a number of extra deductions to this third category, including:

- Extra home energy cost not covered under the IRS guidelines.

- The actual expenses of caring for ill, elderly, or disabled members of the debtor's immediate family or household.

- Monthly private elementary or secondary school expenses (up to $1,500 per year per minor child).

- The actual monthly expenses of administering a Chapter 13 case (from tables to be published by the United States Trustee's Office).

There are other expenses that might fit into this third category of extra monthly deductions, but that covers most of it. If you are wondering if this could be more complicated, join the club.

Once all those things are deducted, $\frac{1}{60}$ of all of the payments on secured debts that come due within the next five years must be deducted as well, followed by $\frac{1}{60}$ of the total priority debts, that is, the taxes, child support, and other claims entitled to special treatment under the Bankruptcy Code, which we talked about in Chapter 9.

Finally, the debtor can deduct from the income continuing charitable contributions of up to 15 percent of the debtor's gross income. And that is a lot. It looks as though those need to be contributions that you made before your bankruptcy, too, not just a new way to avoid paying creditors.

Figuring Out What's Left

LESS THAN $100 LEFT, NO PAYMENT PLAN REQUIRED Whether a person has to pay a payment plan depends totally upon this last step, determining if any money is left at the end of the month, after taking the current monthly income and deducting all the expenses we just ran through.

If what is left is less than $100 per month, the debtor has passed the means test. There is no presumption of abuse.

As you can see, there is an enormous range of deductions for secured claims, priority taxes and support, charities, and so on, making it pretty easy on some level to get out of paying a Chapter 13 plan. Surely this cannot be what was intended.

BETWEEN $100 AND $166 LEFT PER MONTH, A FIVE-YEAR PAYMENT PLAN REQUIRED IF THE PLAN WOULD PAY AT LEAST A 25 PERCENT DISTRIBUTION ON UNSECURED CLAIMS If what is left is between $100 and $166, *and* if this amount times 60 is not enough to pay at least 25 percent of all of the debtor's general unsecured claims over five years, then the debtor has again passed the means test and there is no presumption of abuse.

Now obviously, for this part of the test, the more debt the better for the debtor. More debts mean less chance of having to pay a payment plan.

For example, if a person had $24,000 in debts, and $100 left per month, the person would have to do a payment plan. If the debtor's debts were just one dollar more, say $24,001, no payment plan would be needed. How random! This part of the test also seems to favor people who have larger debts, thus rewarding profligate spenders over frugal ones.

PAYMENT PLAN REQUIRED IF $167 OR MORE LEFT If the debtor makes $167 or more per month over all of the above deductions and expenses, then he or she always flunks the means test. This means there is a presumption of abuse and a presumption that the debtor must do a Chapter 13 plan. This will need to be a five-year plan. The debtor cannot choose a three-year plan.

How Can I Rebut the Presumption?

The only way to rebut the presumption of abuse created by the means test is for the debtor to swear to and document that there are "special circumstances" that would decrease the income or increase the expenses, so the debtor actually falls below the trigger points.

If the debtor lost his or her job so the income for the six months prior to the filing was higher than the current income, we would think that would do the trick and would allow the debtor to avoid a payment plan. Until the bill goes into effect and starts to be challenged, however, we won't really know how the presumption can be rebutted.

CHAPTER 15

Chapter 13 Payment Plan Cases

This chapter provides an overview of Chapter 13 bankruptcy cases. This is the type of bankruptcy that involves a three-year or a five-year payment plan. Some of this discussion is hard to understand, so bear with us. Don't get frustrated if you find it somewhat confusing and have a lot of questions after you have read it. This is just a very quick introduction to Chapter 13. Everything that is mentioned here will be discussed in detail later in this chapter.

An Overview of Complex Chapter 13

You definitely need a good lawyer to file a successful Chapter 13. No doubt about it, this is complex and even more so under the new law. As always, we never recommend filing for bankruptcy without an attorney. This is particularly true of a Chapter 13 case. Neither of us practices in this area for a profit, so we are not just trying to drum up clientele.

As discussed earlier, consumer bankruptcies (as well as business bankruptcies) can be either "sell out" or "pay out" cases. Chapter 7 cases are sell-out cases, even though most debtors never need to actually sell anything because their assets are all exempt. The Chapter 7 model is based on the debtor selling all nonexempt assets (if there are any) and walking away.

Chapter 13 cases, in contrast, are pay-out cases. Under the Chapter 13 model, the debtor typically does not sell his or her assets. Instead, the debtor can choose to file a Chapter 13 and use his or her future income to pay off some debts over time. The rest of the debts are typically discharged.

If Chapter 7 is like a form of heaven—forgiveness of debt and starting a new life—then Chapter 13 could be seen as a form of purgatory. The debtor agrees to pay back at least some of his or her debts over time. The idea is that the debtor will propose a plan of repayment called a "Chapter 13 plan," which will be approved by the court as long as it complies with a set of rules governed (not surprisingly) by Chapter 13 of the Bankruptcy Code.

Chapter 13 is for individuals only, not corporations or partnerships. However, many Chapter 13 debtors own small businesses, which are part of their bankruptcy estates.

Chapter 13 debtors must have regular income to qualify for Chapter 13, but this income can come from sources other than employment, including public benefits and even payments from other people. In other words, the income need not come from regular employment, even though Chapter 13 is sometimes called the "wage-earner" bankruptcy.

Under the pre-October 17, 2005, law the debtor was allowed in every case to choose between a three-year or a five-year Chapter 13 plan. Most chose a three-year plan because it was obviously less of a commitment than a five-year plan. In our experience, debtors complete three-year plans more often than five-year plans because the longer the commitment to pay past-due debts, the less likely it is that the debtor will be able to follow through.

One reason people sometimes choose a five-year plan voluntarily is because it will take them that long to pay off their secured debts over time, allowing them to keep their homes, cars, and so on. All of this is still true through October 17, 2005. *However, after October 17, 2005, debtors with family incomes over the median income for a family of their size in their state will be forced to pay a five-year Chapter 13 plan. These debtors will not get to choose between a three-year plan and a five-year plan.*

There are several good reasons for choosing a Chapter 13 over a Chapter 7, but the most common reason (pre-October 17, 2005) is that Chapter 13 allows the debtor to restructure secured debt that has become way past due, and thus keep the house, the car, or whatever the secured property may be. Remember that Chapter 7 accomplishes very little in such a situation. Chapter 13 may be the only way to save a house from foreclosure.

After October 17, 2005, some people will have no choice, and will be forced to do a Chapter 13 if they want to file for bankruptcy. (See Chapter 14.)

You'll recall that post-petition wages do not become part of the bankruptcy estate in a Chapter 7. The estate is comprised of the assets the debtor has an interest in at the time of the filing, and any income or proceeds flowing from those assets. In a Chapter 13, post-petition income as well as other assets become part of the estate. In fact, in order to qualify for a Chapter 13, the debtor *must* have future disposable income over and above his or her current living expenses. This leftover money will be used to fund the Chapter 13 plan. If there is no extra income over and above the everyday living expenses, the debtor cannot get a Chapter 13 plan approved. It's just not going to happen.

All *secured* debts must be paid in full under a Chapter 13 plan. However, because of the way a secured debt is defined, sometimes those debts need be paid only up to the value of the collateral. In those cases, the debtor can simply pay the value of the collateral, rather than the whole amount of the debt, with interest, over the life of the plan.* Additionally, Chapter 13 requires that all Section 507 priority debts be paid in full. If there is insufficient disposable income to cover these claims, there can be no Chapter 13 case. Also, the Chapter 13 trustee receives a percentage commission on every dollar that is paid through the case, so this must be budgeted for in the plan as well.

How much must unsecured creditors be paid in a Chapter 13 case? This depends on a few things. First, the debtor must contribute all of his or her disposable income to the plan. Under bankruptcy reform (after October 17, 2005), this disposable income will be determined under the new means test. If the debtor has enough disposable income (under the means test) to pay the secured and priority debts, as well as the Chapter 13 trustee's fees, and there is still money left over, this must be paid to the unsecured creditors under the plan.

Additionally, in a Chapter 13 case, the debtor is not required to give up his or her nonexempt assets. The model is one of pay-out, not sell-out.

The exemptions are still very important in a Chapter 13 because the debtor must pay the total value of all the nonexempt assets to creditors under the plan. In essence, the debtor is buying back the nonexempt assets by paying their value to the creditors who would realize that value upon sale if the case were a Chapter 7. This means that if the debtor owns $10,000 in unencumbered, nonexempt assets, he or she must pay at least $10,000 to unsecured creditors under the plan.

The plan also must be filed in good faith, a test with which you will become more familiar later. Finally, the Chapter 13 plan must be feasible in order to be approved.

The debtor's goal in a Chapter 13 is to get his or her plan approved, or as we say in the bankruptcy world, *confirmed*. A *confirmation hearing* is held by the court to decide whether to approve the plan. The Chapter 13 trustee, who will be the same person for many (if not all) Chapter 13 cases in the district,† will carefully review the plan, and perhaps suggest changes or question parts of it. The bankruptcy judge is unlikely to approve a plan if there is a serious objection by the Chapter 13 trustee. If the plan is confirmed, the debtor must then make every payment. At the end, if the debtor makes all the required pay-

---

*Home mortgages are treated differently, and they generally must be paid in full, regardless of the value of the collateral.

†In fact, in many bankruptcy districts, the Chapter 13 trustee is the same person in *every* case in the district. This person is then called the *standing Chapter 13 trustee*.

ments, the debtor is discharged from any unsecured debts that were not paid under the plan.*

Chapter 13 Eligibility

Chapter 13 is available to individuals with regular income who owe noncontingent, liquidated, unsecured debts of $307,675 or less, and secured debts of $922,975 or less.† Don't worry very much about what all these qualifying words mean. The gist is that the debtor cannot have debts higher than these, or he or she will be ineligible for a Chapter 13. The debts will be too high to qualify.

Stockbrokers and commodities brokers are ineligible for Chapter 13, but everyone else who meet these qualifications can file a Chapter 13 case. The regular income requirement is quite flexible. The money does not need to be earned monthly. It need not even be earned by the debtor. One recent case allowed the debtor's father to pay his plan. Public assistance benefits, as well as trust fund income, royalties, and similar earnings also qualify as regular income.

Secured Creditor Treatment Under Chapter 13

One of the most common reasons for a debtor to use a Chapter 13, as opposed to a Chapter 7, is to keep property subject to a security interest. You'll recall that in a Chapter 7, the only way to keep property subject to a security interest is to keep the payments to the secured creditor current, or to pay the value of the collateral in immediate cash to the secured party.‡

Both of these options are easier said than done. For many debtors, these options are not helpful. Few have the money to redeem the collateral by paying its cash value to the secured party. Moreover, many are already substantially behind on their payments, and cannot simply stay current.

Fortunately, Chapter 13 provides ready relief to those who are behind on their mortgage or car payments and would like to keep the property. Personal property such as cars and unattached mobile homes are treated somewhat differently from home mortgages, so they are discussed separately.

As always, whether the secured property is personal or real estate, a home or something else, secured creditors are always treated more favorably than unsecured creditors, in recognition that security interests are property interests. This is true in a Chapter 13 as well, which contains very explicit requirements for the treatment of secured debt.

Given these rules, and the fact that all secured debt must always be paid in

---

*Usually some debts do get discharged at this time, as it is unusual for a debtor to pay general unsecured creditors in full.

†This is as of April 1, 2005, and is revised annually by the Judicial Conference of the United States. See 69 Fed. Reg. 8482 (Feb. 24, 2004).

‡This is called redemption, as discussed more fully in Chapter 13 of this book.

full, with interest or something very much like interest, many Chapter 13 plans are structured around meeting these secured debt requirements.

Because it is possible to propose a plan that makes no distribution to unsecured creditors, and because many debtors have no priority debts, quite a few plans do nothing more than pay secured creditors.

Treatment of Personal Property Loans and Other Secured Loans That Are Not Home Mortgages

As you will very shortly read, up until October 17, 2005, a debtor can drastically reduce the amount that he or she pays on many personal property loans, such as car loans and mobile home loans, by paying the value of the secured property, along with interest, over the life of the plan. In many ways, this is like a Chapter 7 redemption that can be paid over time. Like a Chapter 7 redemption, the debtor can pay less than the full amount of the debt.

Chapter 13 has the added benefit of allowing that reduced amount to be paid in installments, rather than up front.

BIFURCATION AND STRIP-DOWN   Have you ever heard the saying that a new car is worth only half of what you paid for it the moment you drive it off the lot? While this is an exaggeration, there is some truth to it. Late model cars are almost always worth far less than the balance on the car loan. Like a new car, many personal property items depreciate very rapidly after they are purchased. Because of this depreciation, they are often worth far less than the amount still owed on them.

Here is what makes a Chapter 13 beneficial, particularly prior to October 17, 2005. The debtor can reduce the amount of money he has to pay on a piece of secured property down to the amount of the value of the collateral. The process of reducing the loan to the value of the collateral is called, in bankruptcy parlance, the *strip-down*. The word "strip-down" is a bankruptcy term of art with which every bankruptcy attorney is familiar. There is no more formal word for this concept. One of the biggest benefits of both Chapter 13 and Chapter 11 is the ability to strip down the secured debt to just the value of the collateral. There is no better way of describing this process.

Now back to our fictional new car for an example of strip-down. Assume you bought a car last month for $20,000 that is now worth $15,000. You have since fallen on tough times and need to file for a Chapter 13.

The secured party who gave you the car loan now has a claim that is *bifurcated* or split into two parts. One part of the claim, the $15,000, is a secured claim (only as large as the value of the collateral supporting the claim), and the other part, the $5,000, becomes an unsecured claim. The unsecured part will be treated just like any other unsecured claim in the case. It does not matter that the $5,000 was once part of a secured claim. This procedure has allowed you to strip down your secured claim to $15,000, or the current value of your property.

Chapter 13 now considers your secured debt on the car to be for $15,000, not $20,000. The secured claim has to be paid in full, but again it is defined by the value of the collateral, so it is just $15,000. That is the benefit of a Chapter 13. Only the stripped down amount has to be paid in full. Of course, the creditor has an additional claim for the other $5,000, but the debtor's plan does not have to provide that all of this unsecured claim will be paid.

In some cases the plan may provide that only a small portion of the unsecured debt or even none of it will be paid. So long as the plan provides for payment of the secured part (the $15,000), the debtor can keep the car. This $15,000 can be paid off over the life of a three to five year plan with a set amount deducted each week or month. As a result, the debtor may be able to keep the car, and indeed pay less for it than the original purchase price under a Chapter 13, while it is unlikely that the debtor could have come up with the $15,000 to redeem it under a Chapter 7.

The main thing to remember here is that paying the reduced or stripped down amount fulfills the Chapter 13's requirement that all secured claims be paid in full.

Note

Bummer! The strip-down thing was too good to last!

One of the huge benefits of Chapter 13 under the old law was the ability to strip down the debt, meaning to pay just the value of the underlying collateral, rather than the full debt.

Now assume a debtor's car is worth $5,000 and the debt on the car loan is for $10,000. Under the old Chapter 13 (pre-October 17, 2005), the debtor could pay $5,000 over the life of the plan.

Under the new law, in a drastic departure from the prior (pre-October 17, 2005) law, the debtor must pay the whole $10,000, unless the loan was taken out more than two and a half years before the filing.

All loans on other property, such as household goods, must be paid in full by the debtor, if incurred within one year of the filing, assuming the lien cannot be avoided under Section 522 because it impairs an exemption.

But strip-down is still permitted, of course, for loans on personal property other than cars that were taken out more than one year before the filing, and for car loans taken out more than two and a half years prior to the filing.

The new law adds another drastic change to secured creditor treatment under a Chapter 13. You may have to pay secured creditors some amount for your *use* of their stuff during the case, before you start your payment plan. These payments are known as *adequate protection payments*. The court can decide not to make you pay these adequate protection payments, but the general rule is that the creditor is entitled to these payments.

Valuation

Where a strip-down is still permitted, for example, for car loans that were taken out more than two and a half years ago, and on loans for other personal property taken out more than a year ago, the debtor must pay the creditor at the *replacement* (or *retail*) cost for used goods, without deducting the creditor's costs of sale.

Think back to the hypothetical about the $10,000 loan on the $5,000 car. We assumed quite a few facts in the hypothetical, including that $5,000 was a fair current value of the car you bought. In real life, valuation is probably the most common factual dispute decided by bankruptcy courts.

Imagine how much better the car lender's position would be if the value of the car had been $9,000 instead of $5,000. It would mean that the dealership would be getting an additional $4,000 in the payment plan.

On the flip side, imagine that you had evidence to prove the car was worth only $4,000. (You have to pretend there is no such thing as Kelly's Blue Book for this scenario to work.) Wouldn't it be worth arguing before the judge to get the value of the car set at that amount to lower the amount you had to pay back to the secured creditor? You bet. So how does the judge decide which number to go with?

Valuation is often accomplished through an appraisal of the property in question. Appraisals may vary greatly depending on the purpose of the valuation, as well as the assumptions made by the appraiser. Both you and the secured creditor will try to get the judge to use your own appraiser. Judges often pick the most credible appraiser. If both parties' appraisers are equally credible, then the court will often just split the values down the middle.

Normally only business assets and real estate are appraised. Smaller items of personal property are rarely appraised due to the cost of an appraisal. When it comes to vehicles and mobile homes, most parties use Kelly's Blue Book, National Automobile Dealers' Association (NADA), or a similar resource. When all sides have had their say, the court usually finds that the proper value of a debtor's used personal property, for strip down purposes, is the price at which the debtor could purchase a comparable used item. A good resource for this might be something as mundane as eBay.

Regardless of how it is determined, value is the single most important determination with respect to whether a debtor will be able to afford to pay the stripped down value of a big-ticket item under his or her plan. Of course, this is only relevant in situations where strip-down is still permitted.

THE PRESENT VALUE INTEREST RATE The other variable in determining the cost of paying off property that has been stripped down is the *present value* rate that the debtor will be required to pay. Actually, this present value rate is relevant for all secured claims, even those that cannot be stripped down.

The creditor is entitled to the value of that claim as if it were being paid all at once upon confirmation. Since the Code allows the payment over time, the debtor must compensate the creditor for the time value of money. A dollar paid a year from now is worth less than a dollar paid today. Thus, the debtor must pay the creditor for what the creditor loses in interest or other income by not receiving all of this money up front.

Practically speaking, the debtor must provide the secured party with the present value of its claim, and compensate the secured party by assigning an interest rate to the debt. We somewhat cavalierly refer to this as the *present value interest rate* or simply the *interest rate*, but it is not really interest. Rather, it is a payment to the secured party to provide it with the present value of its allowed secured claim.

Every court opinion on record discusses this concept in terms of *interest*, and many courts use prevailing interest rates as a guide to determine what rate will fairly compensate a secured party for the time value of its money. A recent Supreme Court case held that the correct rate is the prime rate plus a certain number of percentage points for the risk of the loan, often between 1 and 3 percent.

Treatment of the Home Mortgage in Chapter 13

The rules just described for stripping down secured loans do not apply to home mortgages. The home mortgage industry convinced Congress in 1984 that if people were allowed to strip down their home mortgages, the entire home lending market would collapse. The Bankruptcy Code specifically states that a person may not modify or otherwise effect a secured loan upon which the lender's only collateral is a home. This is called the *antimodification* clause.

As a result of this special rule, home mortgages are paid under a Chapter 13 in a totally different way. Moreover, as you'll soon see, a home mortgage payment that is in default will always require a larger payment in a Chapter 13 than the debtor was paying outside a Chapter 13. As a result, feasibility, or the debtor's ability to realistically keep up with the plan, is often in question. Many debtors cannot do what is required to cure the home mortgage, and thus cannot confirm or complete a plan.

Due to the antimodification section previously noted, the debtor must continue to make the regular monthly payment to the lender and also pay off all of the missed payments over the life of the plan.

Let's pretend your mortgage payment has always been $750 a month. Remember, there is no strip-down so that $750 is nonnegotiable—plan on paying it every month if you want to keep your house. However, in addition to the $750, you must also pay back all the money you owe for the payments you missed during your Chapter 13 plan. Say you are four payments behind when you file your Chapter 13 and owe $3,000 to the mortgage company. In addition to the $750 each month, you'll include an additional amount to make up the $3,000. If you have a three-year plan, that works out to $84.

But you're not done yet. Add some interest to the $84 to get it up to its present value. So for the life of your bankruptcy plan you are looking at an estimated $840 per month payment to your mortgage company: your original $750 payment, the $84 arrearage, plus some interest for the time value of money. You can see what we meant when we said a home loan in default will always require a larger payment in a Chapter 13. On the other hand, without the Chapter 13 option, you would most likely lose the home to foreclosure. If you are behind on your payments and want to keep your home, Chapter 13 is still a good solution.

Recognizing When Strip-Down Applies

I know your head probably hurts by now! You have now read several complex rules for treating secured claims in a Chapter 13 case, each in a vacuum depending upon the type of secured property that is at issue and the date the loan was taken out. You have read that all personal property loans can be stripped down prior to October 17, 2005, but real estate that is used as a principal residence cannot. You also have read that after October 17, 2005, some personal property loans also cannot be stripped down, depending upon when the loan was taken out.

It's an earful, we know, but your lawyer will get you through it. We just want you to be familiar with the basic law and the changes made as of October 17, 2005.

The Treatment of Priority Claims in a Chapter 13

Priority claims are treated almost as well as secured claims in a Chapter 13. Just like secured claims, priority claims have to be paid in full in order for the judge to confirm a Chapter 13 plan. There is one small difference. Unlike secured claims, the holders of these priority claims are not entitled to present value interest on their claims. Thus, to determine how much you must pay each month to satisfy the claim in full, your attorney needs only divide the amount of the priority claims by the number of months in the plan.

So what are the priority claims in a Chapter 13 likely to be? Some Chapter 13 debtors run businesses and thus owe priority employee claims and perhaps claims to suppliers and deposit holders. If you do not run a business, the most common priority claims will be:

- Taxes.
- Child support or alimony.
- Attorneys' fees for your Chapter 13.

A debtor that has large tax liabilities can save a great deal on interest by filing a Chapter 13 case. As soon as the case is filed, both the interest and any penalties that would normally accrue outside bankruptcy cease.

We said previously that one must divide the *allowed* priority claims by the number of months to calculate this part of the plan payment. But how does one determine how much of the claim is allowed?

Because many types of taxes get priority treatment only if they are recent, the issue of allowance comes up most often in that context. Not all taxes will need to be paid in full in every case. Some taxes lose their priority status because they are too old. Others fall into categories that simply get less priority than others. Thus, don't assume that all taxes are entitled to priority.

Another allowance issue comes up in the context of support payments under a marital settlement agreement. All past due support payments must, of course, be paid in full under a Chapter 13 plan, but what about past due property settlements? While property settlement agreements flowing from a marital settlement agreement sometimes are *not discharged* in a Chapter 7, they do not get any special *priority* in either chapter, so they do not have to be paid in full under a Chapter 13 plan.*

Note

The new law creates tremendous incentives for people to keep current on their marital and child support payments during their Chapter 13 cases. First, no one can get a discharge under Chapter 13 unless he or she is current on all marital support obligations. In fact, one cannot even get a Chapter 13 plan confirmed unless these payments are all current. Finally, the new law allows the nonfiling spouse to seek suspension of a debtor's driver's license as well as any professional license, if these payments are not kept current.

In sum, taxes, child support, alimony, and the fee your bankruptcy attorney charges you will all have to be paid in full in your Chapter 13 plan. Even though these are not claims secured by collateral, they are what the Bankruptcy Code has termed "priority" claims. In a Chapter 13 bankruptcy, the priority claim holder gets treated almost as well as secured creditors with the exception that they do not get interest on the debts.

---

*It is easy to confuse dischargeability with priority but the rules for each are different, as this example shows.

The Disposable Income Test in a Chapter 13

In order for a judge to approve your Chapter 13 bankruptcy, you must pass the *disposable income* test. This is also sometimes called the *best efforts* test. The disposable income test requires the debtor to contribute *all* of his or her projected disposable income to the plan. What is disposable income? The Bankruptcy Code (at least prior to October 17, 2005), defines it as income received by the debtor that is not reasonably necessary for the maintenance or support of the debtor and the debtor's dependents.

Note: There have been HUGE changes in this area after bankruptcy reform, so for the next few pages, we discuss just this test under the old law, that is, the law applicable to Chapter 13 cases filed before October 17, 2005.

The disposable income inquiry poses the most fundamental questions about the human condition, namely "what does a person really need?" American materialism and consumerism, as well as relative wealth compared to wealth in the rest of the world, make the question even more interesting. Can you imagine foreign societies in which private schools, music lessons, and summer camp are considered necessities?

This topic raises two dueling questions. First, what should a person who has not paid his or her debts be allowed to spend money on? At the same time, when a person is permitted to choose between walking away from his or her debts and paying some of them off over time, how attractive should we make a Chapter 13, in order to induce people to choose the repayment plan option? How stringent should we be, given that we would like to create an incentive to pay off at least some debts?*

Note: Under bankruptcy reform, we no longer have to make a Chapter 13 desirable because we will force people into a Chapter 13. Thus, under bankruptcy reform, some of these questions disappear.

At least under the pre-October 17, 2005 law, judges have a great deal of discretion in the area of approving what is and isn't disposable income. In the extremely fact-based area of disposable income, in which the debtors' expenses are scrutinized and judged, judicial discretion is at an all-time high. One judge might find a $50 hairdo outrageous, while another might find it a necessity. An animal lover might find pets to be a necessity while another judge might find their food and vet bills inappropriate for a bankruptcy debtor.

For items that are obviously a necessity, the issue becomes how much is reasonable to spend on food, medicine, car insurance, and so on. One Chapter 13 trustee told me that she considered $600 a month reasonable for food

---

*This policy is largely eliminated under the proposed bankruptcy reform because people can be forced into a Chapter 13. Incentives of this kind are no longer necessary.

for a family of four. However, a judge could question this, claiming that there is no way to say that $700 or even $800 might not be reasonable in some situations.

Does the household have teenagers in it? Does the debtor have enough cash flow to take advantage of buying in bulk? Do they live in a remote area where food is expensive? Does the category "Food" include toothpaste and toilet paper? Make-up for a teenage girl? What other expenses are reasonable? Is a $50 cable TV bill reasonable? As a nonsubscriber, I was surprised to learn that cable TV is a permissible expense for just about anyone.

Some things are specified in the Code as reasonable and not left to the judge's discretion. For example, the Code explicitly states that charitable contributions up to 15 percent of the gross income constitute reasonable and necessary expenses.

The Debtor's Budget and the Status Quo: Class Issues

As a debtor's economic class moves closer to or fully within the middle class, some judges will scrutinize his or her expenses more. On the other hand, many court opinions on the subject of the disposable income or best efforts test seem to allow the debtor to maintain the status quo. In other words, people who have always had high expenses will be allowed to continue to have high expenses, while really poor people will be allowed only the most basic expenses. For example, one court in Florida found private school tuition to be a reasonable and necessary expense as long as the cost was not excessive (whatever that means), and as long as the child had been attending the school for a considerable amount of time.

Another court in Texas flatly disagreed, finding private school to be a luxury and not a necessity. One court in Nebraska recently held that the debtor could not continue to pay high veterinary bills for his elderly horses and dogs. Ouch!

Braces, summer camp, and music and sports lessons for children have fueled similar debates. How much should children be required to pay for the sins (or credit indiscretions) of their parents? Can the children take piano lessons? Does it matter if they have always done so? If they are gifted? Can they go to summer camp? Have a nose job? There is no way to predict how the judge in your case will decide this issue. Keep this in mind when weighing whether or not to file a Chapter 13.

Payments to 401(k) Plans

Recently, courts have been faced with whether to allow a debtor in a Chapter 13 case to make contributions to a retirement plan. The cases seem to fall into two categories, those that say such contributions can wait until after the plan is finished, and those that allow some contributions, on a case-by-case basis, as long as they are reasonable. As far as these outright contributions are concerned, courts also are influenced by whether the employer will match a contribution, thus further improving the debtor's future, as well as by the tax implications of the contribution.

If there is no or little net benefit to creditors of discontinuing the contributions, then some courts will allow the debtor to continue making the contributions. Sometimes the debtor has borrowed money from his or her 401(k) plan and will suffer a large financial penalty if the money is not paid back. Some courts will allow those payments to continue and some will not, again based upon the incentives they hope to create in people and their financial behavior on the one hand, and the desire to pay creditors on the other.

The 401(k) cases pose questions about the future financial well-being of the debtors. Some would argue that encouraging people to save is important to their future rehabilitation and financial health. Others would naturally say that saving for the future is fabulous, once existing creditors are paid. And so the saga continues.

Note

The new law is much more generous in allowing consumers to protect their pension plans, which is good for people who have had the foresight to save. In fact, under the new rules for a Chapter 13, debtors can pay back loans they have taken from pension plans and 401(k)s while in bankruptcy and in some cases, can even continue to make contributions to their plans during bankruptcy. The new law also makes up to $1,000,000 per person in IRAs exempt.

Another issue courts have struggled with is whether the debtor should be allowed some extra money in the budget, in case of an emergency, as a contingency fund of sorts. Others have considered whether the debtor can save money for the sake of saving it during the plan. It seems that some plan for emergencies is wise and might even improve the chance of success under the plan. After all, unexpected expenses always come up. Courts are split on this issue, however, with some disallowing contingency funds or savings plans.

The Disposable Income Test Under the New Law

No area of bankruptcy law has been changed more radically by the reform than the disposable income test. As the previous discussion articulated, the disposable income test left judges with a huge amount of discretion to determine what expenses are reasonably necessary for a particular person or family.

In a sense, the old disposable income test is gone under bankruptcy reform, at least for debtors above the median income. The test is still named in the Code as a Chapter 13 requirement, but disposable income is now measured by the means test discussed in Chapter 14 of this book. That means if the debtor has no money left over after the IRS and other allowed expenses and after all secured and priority claims are accounted for, the disposable income test is met, even if the debtor has a $10,000 per month mortgage payment.

This is very different from the old law. There is little discretion left for the judge. The judge cannot question (at least under this test) the need for such a big house. Strange. We find it hard to believe that this was what Congress intended.

The Good Faith Test in Chapter 13

In addition to the disposable income test, there is another equally complicated Chapter 13 test. It is called the *good faith* test. This test requires simply that the plan be proposed "in good faith and not by any means forbidden by law." As simple as this sounds, the test is actually quite elusive.

The disposable income test was added to the Code in 1984. Prior to this time, the Code simply required that plans be filed in good faith. Many courts interpreted the good faith requirement to mean that the debtor had contributed all of the disposable income that he or she had. Once the disposable income test was added to the Code, this left the good faith test undefined. The good faith test means different things to different people. Some of those interpretations are discussed in the following subsections.

Overlap with the Disposable Income Test and Other Tests

When the debtor prepares his or her budget, some money falls to the bottom line as disposable income, or funds available to pay creditors. The debtor can then propose the plan. It is implicit in the Code's good faith requirement and disposable income test that the debtor will estimate all expenses in good faith and not inflate the expenses.

Under some interpretations of this test, at least under the pre-October 17, 2005 law, the debtor also should engage in some belt-tightening in the budget. If not, the plan may not meet the good faith test. Since the good faith test allows one to look at the debtor's overall behavior in a case, in terms of expenses, disclosures, and testimony, the test allows for an objection to the plan that is hard to define. In some ways it is like what Supreme Court Justice Potter Stewart has said about obscenity: "I can't define it but I know it when I see it."

Some of the following facts and factors may tip one off that good faith is at issue.

- The amount of the plan payments (i.e., small).
- The accuracy of the plan's statement of debts and expenses, and whether any inaccuracies are an attempt to mislead the court.

- The percentage repayment of unsecured debts.
- The extent of preferential treatment in the plan between classes of creditors.
- The extent to which secured creditor claims are modified, which is seen as a good thing.
- The type of debt sought to be discharged and whether any such debt is nondischargeable in a Chapter 7 (which is much less of an issue under the new law because the discharges in a Chapter 7 and a Chapter 13 are now identical).
- The existence of special circumstances, such as inordinate medical expenses.
- The frequency with which the debtor has filed for bankruptcy.
- The motivation and sincerity of the debtor in seeking Chapter 13 relief.
- The burden that the plan's administration would place on the Chapter 13 trustee.

We list these factors here just to give you a flavor for what a lack of good faith might mean. Again, judicial discretion is extensive.

Multiple Filings

The good faith test is often used as the basis for objection to a debtor's Chapter 13 plan when the debtor has filed more than one bankruptcy case. Here is an example of what a bad faith multiple filing would look like.

> Joe Shady, a home owner, finds out the bank is going to foreclose on his home because he has missed his last four mortgage payments. Joe decides to file a Chapter 13 in order to stop the home foreclosure, and the bank backs off. Joe doesn't really want to file for bankruptcy, but he wants to keep the bank at bay and knows that once he files, all creditors have to leave him alone under the automatic stay. Then, before filing a plan, Joe has the case dismissed. He just bought himself some relief for a month. As the bank gets close to foreclosing again, Joe files yet another case, and may or may not comply with Chapter 13 in the process. Do you see a pattern?

The case is filed for delay purposes only, and thus violates the good faith requirements of Chapter 13. This is quintessential lack of good faith. Although one or two previous filings could raise a flag and possibly an objection, it typically takes several to ensure success on a bad faith claim based solely on serial filing.

One controversial question is whether it is bad faith to file a Chapter 7 case followed by a Chapter 13. We sometimes call this a Chapter 20, meaning a 7 plus a 13. So why would anyone do something like this?

Filing a Chapter 7 would first allow a debtor to discharge all of the nonpriority unsecured debts, so that he or she could concentrate the Chapter 13 plan on just paying the priority and the secured debts. Can you see the advantage? Without any unsecured debt, the debtor gets to keep more of his disposable income.

In practical terms, by filing a Chapter 7 before a Chapter 13, you risk a judge rejecting your 13 on the basis of its failing the good faith test. Though the Code itself does not preclude one from filing a Chapter 7, followed by a Chapter 13, some courts still find doing so to be per se bad faith.

Multiple filings are very strongly curtailed under the new law. Thus, you can expect this multiple filing issue to become much less of a concern under the good faith test in the future.

Zero Percent Plans or Low Percent Plans

A zero percent plan is one that pays no distribution to unsecured creditors. Some courts permit this and some do not. But wait; if it is okay to have a Chapter 13 plan where unsecured creditors could receive no payments, also known as a zero percent plan, why should it be wrong to file a Chapter 7 first?

The answer is that courts disagree about whether it is acceptable to propose a plan that pays no distribution to unsecured creditors at all. Some say a zero percent plan is per se bad faith. Others say this is one factor to consider in analyzing whether a plan has been filed in good faith. Still other courts believe the zero percent plan does not raise good faith issues in and of itself, on the grounds that if the disposable income test is met, there is no issue of good faith. Some courts believe it is bad faith to file a plan with a small distribution as well.

Once again, the issue is left at the judge's discretion. If you are considering filing a Chapter 13, and you know you don't have enough disposable income to make some payments to your unsecured creditors, know that a judge may reject your plan.

Note: Experts predict that zero percent plans will become far more common under the new law, because debtors must pay more to secured debtors.

Debts That Would Be Discharged in a Chapter 13 but not a Chapter 7

When we discussed Chapter 7 bankruptcy, you might recall the very long list of debts that are nondischargeable in a Chapter 7 case. These debts include

- Taxes that are entitled to priority.
- Debts incurred through fraud or through recent credit card charges presumed to be incurred by fraud.
- Debts neither listed nor scheduled on the debtor's bankruptcy petition.
- Debts incurred through fraud or defalcation while acting in a fiduciary capacity.
- Debts for alimony and support.
- Debts for willful and malicious injury.

- Student loans.
- DWI-related debts.
- Debts for criminal restitution.
- Some marital property settlement debts.

Under the old law, one huge incentive for filing a Chapter 13 is that the discharge is far broader and more beneficial to the debtor. The Code creates great incentives for debtors to choose a Chapter 13, by making almost all debts dischargeable. All debts are discharged in a Chapter 13, except marital support obligations, certain taxes, and student loans.* This means that intentional tort debt and debts for fraud *are* dischargeable in a Chapter 13. Very interesting!

Under the new law, this incentive to file a Chapter 13 is completely eliminated. The debts that are not dischargeable in a Chapter 7 will not be discharged in a Chapter 13, either after October 17, 2005. Who needs incentives to do a Chapter 13 when people can be forced into a Chapter 13?

Under the old law, lots of fun questions arise. What if the Chapter 13 plan proposes to pay almost nothing on the claim that would not have been discharged in a Chapter 7? Isn't a Chapter 13 case like this tantamount to a Chapter 7 case where there is no distribution, and the creditor's nondischargeable claim gets discharged anyway? Some courts have found this very problematic, while others have been less concerned. In any event, the existence of debts that would otherwise be nondischargeable in a Chapter 7 is a factor in the good faith test. The test does not require any minimum to be paid on these claims, though cases have discussed this issue at length. In fact, these types of cases have become the most controversial good faith cases reported. *Again, after October 17, 2005, this will not be an issue.*

The Best Interest of Creditors Test

The disposable income test and the good faith test deal with how much the debtor must pay to unsecured creditors. We have focused on how much the debtor must give up in order to have the plan approved, or put another way, how much belt-tightening the debtor must engage in or how much the debtor must sacrifice.

The best interest test also goes to the same issue, namely how much must unsecured creditors get in a Chapter 13? How much do they get? This depends upon how much unsecured creditors would get if this person just filed a Chapter 7 instead.

Why do we care about this? Because if the creditors would get more in a Chapter 7, then the person should just file a Chapter 7. The money from a Chapter 7 liquidation would be a sure thing and the creditors are entitled to at

---

*Criminal restitution debts are also nondischargeable in a Chapter 13 but these are rare because they are debts flowing from the fruit of the crime.

least that much. We should not allow a debtor to file a Chapter 13 case if the creditors cannot get at least as much in the Chapter 13 plan as they would get from the sale and distribution of the debtor's nonexempt assets in a Chapter 7.

To put it another way, in a Chapter 13, the creditors must get at least what they would get in a liquidation. If not, the Chapter 13 case is improper. It does not present creditors with the best case bankruptcy scenario, and the Chapter 13 case would not be in their best interest. Rather, a Chapter 7 case would be in their best interest, thus the name *best interest of creditors* test.

The best interest test relates to one thing and one thing only! What would creditors have received in a Chapter 7? Disposable income, expenses, and so on, have *no* bearing on the best interest test. *None, Nada!*

The only thing the best interest test requires is that creditors get no less in a Chapter 13 than they would get in a Chapter 7. But how do we know what creditors would get in a Chapter 7? They would get to share the value of all the debtor's nonexempt assets. This is the minimum the debtor must pay in his or her Chapter 13 plan.

Remember that the debtor also must meet all the other tests we've talked about here, too, the feasibility test, the good faith test, the disposable income test, and so on.

Chapter 13 Plan Feasibility

The Bankruptcy Code requires the court to find that "the debtor will be able to make all payments under the plan and to comply with the plan." While it sounds quite daunting (that the debtor be able to make *all* payments), the test is quite lenient. This test, known as the *feasibility* requirement, simply requires that the plan proposed be realistic and that the debtor has a reasonable chance of completing it.

Do the Proposed Payments Meet the Plan Obligations?

One aspect of feasibility is quite stringent, namely that the payments proposed under the plan must actually add up to enough money to make the payments proposed in the plan. With the interest requirements and the trustee's fee, this can sometimes be tricky to calculate, but the Internet has sites that can help. Or you can just make the payment a little bit bigger and get some money back at the end. Your lawyer will know how best to do this calculation.

Can the Debtor Make the Payments?

The other aspect of feasibility relates to the debtor's likelihood of being able to make the payments required under the plan, based primarily on his or her income. This requirement relates to eligibility. You might recall that debtors need regular income to qualify for Chapter 13. The feasibility test is far easier to meet than one might imagine, because courts tend to give debtors a fair chance to rehabilitate their financial lives. However, if your monthly income is $2,000 and the plan payments are $1,800 a month, don't expect a judge to find your plan feasible. That is cutting it too close.

Modification of a Chapter 13 Plan or Dismissal of a Chapter 13 Case

Once the plan is proposed, is the debtor stuck with it? Not exactly. Prior to actual confirmation, the debtor can modify the plan freely. After confirmation, the court can order a modification at the request of the debtor, the trustee, or any other party-in-interest, to increase or decrease the payments or the payment period, or to increase or decrease the distributions to be paid under the plan. Obviously the modified plan must still comply with the Code.

What would justify such a modification? If the debtor is requesting it, perhaps there has been a drop in income or an increase in expense, either of which could justify modification. Perhaps the trustee or a creditor is requesting modification because the debtor is making more money now and is no longer in compliance with the disposable income test.*

If the debtor has missed a number of payments under the plan the trustee or a creditor may ask that the case simply be dismissed. The court may dismiss a Chapter 13 case or convert it to a Chapter 7 for cause, including a failure to make payments, unreasonable delay in proposing a plan or otherwise proceeding with the case, or for denial of confirmation, among other reasons.

As you might imagine, after the debtor has failed to pay the plan, the trustee or a creditor may move to convert or dismiss while the debtor might at the same time request modification. Believe it or not, if the debtor is really hit with hard times and has met the Code's most minimal requirements, such as paying off secured and priority claims, the debtor may be freed from all further payments due to unexpected hardship.

Still, it's best to assume you won't fall into the best case scenario when deciding whether or not to file a Chapter 13. Remember, the plans span from three-to five years. That is a long time to be tied to a plan, and if you fail to pay, even if you have been an angel the first two years of the plan, all that hard work can go down the tubes.

Overall, you should not agree to do a Chapter 13 plan unless you have a good chance of actually completing the plan. Having said that, we wish you luck in whatever you decide to do.

---

*The trustee requires that the debtor provide her with tax returns for each year of the plan, so any increased income will not go unnoticed.

Just a Bit More on the Chapter 13 Discharge Under the New Law

If you think about it, what Congress said in the new law is "we'll force people into Chapter 13 instead of allowing them to choose their chapter, and while we are at it, we will remove many of the old incentives provided by law to encourage people to go into Chapter 13."

The main incentive eliminated is the *super-discharge*, where the debtor could get fraud claims, embezzlement claims, claims for intentional torts, and for luxury goods charged or cash advances taken out, around the time of the bankruptcy, discharged by paying a Chapter 13 plan over as little as three years.

Now very few things are discharged in a Chapter 13 that are not also discharged in a Chapter 7. In effect, Chapter 13 no longer contains a super-discharge. Things that do get discharged in a Chapter 13 under the new law, but not in a Chapter 7, include willful injuries to property and debts for property settlements arising out of a divorce or other marital settlement agreement. These last debts for property settlements are not discharged in a Chapter 7, but are discharged in a Chapter 13.

CHAPTER 16

Business and Bankruptcy Law

As you certainly know by now, this book is primarily about consumer bankruptcy and primarily covers cases filed under Chapter 7 and Chapter 13. Chapter 13 claims to be for *individual* debtors only, meaning those who are real human beings with flesh and blood. While it is certainly true that a Chapter 13 cannot be used by corporations or partnerships, it can be used by individuals who own partnerships or even corporations. In essence, then, Chapter 13 can be used to address business problems.

In fact, a recent study shows that a Chapter 13 is very frequently used by struggling entrepreneurs, who are trying to deal with both business debt and personal debts. These personal debts are often personal guaranties that creditors have insisted the individual owners sign in order to fund the business.

Lately all of the press about bankruptcy has focused on individual debtors, who are supposedly guilty of irresponsible spending, and on big companies like Enron. There has been little if any press on the small businessperson trying to make a go of it. A recent study by professors from Harvard and the University of Nevada suggests that one in seven bankruptcy cases is filed by someone trying to cope with the collapse of a small business. This type of case is never featured in the press. It does not involve corporate scandals like Enron, nor does it involve thoughtless spending sprees. Rather, it is the case of an entrepreneur taking a chance. Sometimes you win, sometimes you lose.

Our entire economy was built through the entrepreneurial spirit, the things we do as a society to encourage people to take chances in business, and to add growth to the economy. One of the main reasons the United States has had such a forgiving bankruptcy system is that a forgiving system supports capitalism, risk taking, and entrepreneurialism.

In light of this, one must wonder why the new bankruptcy law is not more supportive of businesses, particularly small businesses. Part of the reason is that Congress did not know the extent to which individuals use the consumer bankruptcy system to address their business problems. The recent study makes that clear. Congress also may not think that promoting small business is a big priority in this country.

It should be, though, as far as we are concerned. Small businesses are a way out of poverty for many people. Small businesses also pay taxes and, surprisingly, employ (collectively) more people than any other size of business. More than Enron-sized companies. We need to be as supportive of small businesses in our society as we possibly can.

Many people have been concerned about the effects of bankruptcy reform on entrepreneurialism. Certainly, the new business bankruptcy provisions, which are beyond the scope of this book, require more paperwork of small businesses and also require them to restructure their debts more quickly than in the past. These are not particularly positive changes, if the goal is to fuel the entrepreneurial spirit.

On the other hand, if a person is using a Chapter 13 or a Chapter 7 to deal with business debt, the situation is not as grim as it may appear. First, the means test we talked about in Chapter 14 of this book does not apply to any person whose debts are primarily business debts. That means that if most of your debts arose out of your business, even if many appear to be individual credit card debts, you will never be forced into a Chapter 13 case under the means test. The test applies only to people whose debts are primarily consumer debts.

Second, without the means test, the main problems under bankruptcy reform will be finding and affording a good lawyer. We do not approve of the new law, but we do believe that competent and affordable attorneys will always be available regardless of how unfavorable the law becomes.

We have read quite a few blogs from people who say they will get out of business once bankruptcy reform passes because they can no longer take the risk of failure. We think this is an overreaction. We ask you to stay in business if you are already in it, and to remain optimistic about the future. After all, no law, regardless of how misguided, can kill a great business idea.

CHAPTER 17

Investing and Your Future

We've gotten you through some very tough materials in this book, and chances are you have been through or will soon go through some tough times financially. Otherwise, why buy this book, right?

However, we are optimistic that, armed with the new knowledge you now have, your future will be bright. One of the most exciting things that you can do now is read about and learn about investing, even if you have nothing to invest at this time. It is pure fun to watch your money grow and set yourself up for your future.

While investing can be somewhat scary, for the most part it feels really, really good. You could fit what we know about the subject into about two paragraphs, so we'll share our paltry thoughts and then leave you with a list of good sources for investment information.

We already told you that we got our start investing in no-load mutual funds, like those offered by the Vanguard Group. This has worked amazingly for us and is still our favorite place to stash cash. In fact, the past 10 years have been horrendous for investors. Pretty much everyone in the market lost money. The Vanguard STAR fund still paid 10 percent over that rough period. Might it come down in the future? Of course. You just have to find a place where you are comfortable with the level of risk and rewards.

We've made our share of mistakes, too. In 2001 or so, we took the profits from the sale of a home in Pennsylvania and invested them in individual stocks, like Nortel Networks, Intel, Cisco, McCloud, and other high-tech companies. I (Nathalie) had received advice from a relative who is an M.B.A., who said high-tech was *the* growth industry. Just our luck, the industry crashed and we lost 75 percent of our investment. We lost our money but gained a few lessons in the process. We learned that individual stocks are not for us.

We also learned that as individuals, we had very different investment ideas. I (Nathalie) wanted to get out right away when things started to turn. Stewart said once he makes a decision, he sticks with it.

Whoa! Invitation for disaster!! But it's okay. The marriage is fine and now we stick with mutual funds, unless someone else is managing the money. And some of the money *is* managed by others, but that is a subject for another day.

In closing we simply say, go out and save, and use some of the resources listed in the References section on page 219 to make your money grow! Good luck!

Chart of State Law Exemptions

Note: This chart summarizes complicated exemption schemes for every state in the nation. The law of any given state can be interpreted in more than one way and also can change at any moment. Thus, you should use this chart only as a guide and consult with an attorney about the exemptions available in your particular case. If a category is listed without a numeric amount, the exemption is unlimited for that category.

Alabama

Asset Type	Exemption
Homestead	$5000 in real property or mobile home, up to 160 acres; spouses may double
Personal Property	Books, clothing, family portraits, & pictures for debtor & family Burial plot & church pew for debtor and family
Tools of Trade	Uniforms, arms, & equipment for military personnel
Wild Card	$3000 of any personal property, except for wages; spouses may double
Wages	75% (or 30 times federal minimum hourly wage) of net earnings for consumer debt, 75% of unpaid, earned wages for other cases

Pensions	IRAs & other retirement accounts Judges (payments currently being received) Law enforcement officers State employees Teachers
Public Benefits	Aid to aged, blind, disabled, & other public assistance Crime victims' compensation Southeast Asian War POWs' benefits Unemployment compensation Worker's compensation
Insurance	$250 per month annuity avails or proceeds $250 per month average disability avails or proceeds Fraternal benefit society benefits Life insurance avails or proceeds Mutual aid association benefits
Miscellaneous	N/A
Federal Exemptions	Not allowed
Notes	Bankruptcy judge may authorize higher wage exemption for low-income debtors

Alaska

Asset Type	Exemption
Homestead	$64,800; joint owners may each claim a portion
Personal Property	$3600 in books, musical instruments, clothing, family portraits, household goods, & heirlooms Building materials Burial plot $1680 in cash/liquid assets, $2640 for sole wage earner household Deposit in apartment or condo owners' association Required health aids $1200 in jewelry $3600 in motor vehicle with total worth under $24,000 Personal injury & wrongful death recoveries, to extent wages exempt $1200 in pets Proceeds from lost, damaged, or stolen exempt property Tuition credits under an advance college tuition payment contract
Tools of Trade	$3360 in implements, books, & tools of trade
Wild Card	N/A
Wages	$420 in weekly net earnings, $660 for sole wage earner household; if not paid weekly or semimonthly, $1680 in cash or liquid assets paid monthly, $2640 for sole wage earner households

Pensions	Elected public officials, judicial employees, teachers (limited to benefits building up)
	Public employees (limited to benefits building up)
	ERISA benefits deposited over 120 days before filing
	Roth & traditional IRAs, medical savings accounts
	Other pensions being received to extent wages exempt
Public Benefits	Adult assistance to blind, disabled, & elderly
	Alaska longevity bonus
	Crime victims' compensation
	Federally exempt public benefits paid or due
	General relief assistance
	20% of permanent fund dividends
	Unemployment compensation
	Worker's compensation
Insurance	Disability benefits
	Fraternal benefit society benefits
	$12,000 aggregate cash surrender value in life insurance & annuity contracts
	Medical, surgical, or hospital benefits
Miscellaneous	Alimony, to extent wages exempt
	Child support payments made by collection agency
	Liquor license
	Property of business partnership
Federal Exemptions	Not allowed by statute, but allowed by case law
Notes	

Arizona

Asset Type	Exemption
Homestead	$100,000 in real property, apartment, or mobile home, proceeds exempt for 18 months
Personal Property	$4000 for 2 beds & bedding, 1 living room chair per person, dresser, lamp, table, dining room table & 4 chairs (plus 1 for every extra person), living room carpet or rug, couch, 3 lamps, 3 coffee or end tables, pictures, paintings, personal drawings, family portraits, refrigerator, stove, washer, dryer, vacuum, TV, radio, stereo, alarm clock
	$150 in bank deposit account
	$500 for Bible, bicycle, sewing machine, typewriter, burial plot, rifle, pistol, or shotgun
	$250 in books; $500 in clothing; $1000 in wedding & engagement rings; $100 for watch;
	$500 in pets, horses, dairy cows, & poultry; $250 in musical instruments
	6 month supply of food & fuel
	$5000 in funeral deposits
	Health aids

$5000 for motor vehicle, $10,000 if disabled
$1000 for rent or security deposit or 1½ times rent in lieu of
    homestead exemption
Proceeds from damaged or sold exempt property
Wrongful death awards

Tools of Trade	Arms, uniforms, & accoutrements of profession or office required by law $2500 in farm machinery, utensils, seed, instruments of husbandry, feed, grain, & animals Library & teaching aids of teacher $2500 in tools, equipment, instruments, & books
Wild Card	None
Wages	75% of earned but unpaid weekly net earnings or 30 times federal minimum hourly wage; 50% of wages for support orders
Pensions	Board of regents members, faculty, & administrative officers under board's jurisdiction District employees ERISA benefits deposited over 120 days before filing IRA Firefighters Police officers Rangers State employees retirement & disability
Public Benefits	Unemployment compensation Welfare benefits Worker's compensation
Insurance	Fraternal benefit society benefits Group life insurance policy or proceeds Health, accident, or disability benefits $25,000 in life insurance cash value or proceeds $20,000 in life insurance proceeds if beneficiary is spouse/child
Miscellaneous	Alimony & child support necessary for support Minor child's earnings, unless debt is for child
Federal Exemptions	Not allowed
Notes	Spouses may not double homestead exemption, may double personal property & tools of trade; IRA exemption allowed by case law Bankruptcy judge may authorize higher wage exemption for low-income debtors

Arkansas

Asset Type	Exemption
Homestead	(1) If married or head of household, unlimited exemption on real or personal property used as residence, up to ¼ acre in town, city, or village or 80 acres elsewhere; if

property is between ¼ to 1 acre in town, city, or village or 80 to 160 acres elsewhere, additional limit is $2500; homestead may not exceed these sizes

(2) $800 in real or personal property used as residence if unmarried, $1250 if married

Personal Property	Burial plot to 5 acres, if choosing homestead exemption option 2 Clothing $1200 in motor vehicle Prepaid funeral trusts Wedding rings
Tools of Trade	$750 in implements, books, & tools of trade
Wild Card	$500 in personal property if married or head of family, $200 if not married
Wages	Earned, but unpaid wages due for 60 days, not less than $25 per week
Pensions	Disabled firefighters Disabled police officers Firefighters & police officers $20,000 in IRA deposits if 1 year old at time of filing School employees State police officers
Public Benefits	Crime victims' compensation Unemployment compensation Worker's compensation
Insurance	Annuity contract Disability benefits Fraternal benefit society benefits Group life insurance $500 in life, health, accident, or disability cash value or proceeds paid or due Life insurance proceeds if beneficiary isn't the insured or if clause prohibits proceeds from use to pay beneficiaries' creditors $1000 in mutual assessment life or disability benefits Stipulated insurance premiums
Miscellaneous	None
Federal Exemptions	Allowed by statute, but not allowed by case law
Notes	Spouses may not double exemptions

California Option 1

Asset Type	Exemption
Homestead	Real or personal property occupied, including boat, community apartment, condo, mobile home, planned development or stock cooperative to: (sale proceeds exempt for 6 months)

$50,000 if single & not disabled
$75,000 for families who own no other homestead ($37,500 if
      only one spouse is filing & home is community property)
$150,000 if 65 or older or physically or mentally disabled
$150,000 if 55 or older, single, earn under $15,000 &
      creditors seek to force sale of home
May file homestead declaration

Personal Property	Appliances, furnishings, clothing, & food $2425 in bank deposits from Social Security, $3650 for spouses, unlimited if funds not commingled with other funds; $1225 in bank deposits for other public benefits, $1825 for spouses $2425 in building materials for home (may not be doubled) Burial plot Funds held in escrow Health aids Homeowners' association assessments $6075 in jewelry, heirlooms, & art (may not be doubled) $2300 in motor vehicle or auto insurance for loss or damage (may not be doubled) Personal injury & wrongful death causes of action Personal injury & wrongful death recoveries needed for support; 75% if receiving installments
Tools of Trade	$6075 in tools, implements, materials, instruments, uniforms, books, furnishings, & equipment, plus $4850 for commercial vehicle (vehicle code §260) Both may be doubled if both spouses use it in same occupation
Wild Card	None
Wages	Minimum of 75% of wages paid in 30 days prior to filing Public employees' vacation credits, minimum of 75% if receiving installments
Pensions	County employees County firefighters County peace officers Private retirement benefits, including IRAs & Keoghs Public employees Public retirement benefits
Public Benefits	Aid to aged, blind, disabled, & public assistance Relocation benefits Student financial aid Unemployment benefits Union benefits arising from labor dispute Worker's compensation
Insurance	Disability or health benefits Fidelity bonds Fraternal benefit society benefits Fraternal unemployment benefits Homeowners' insurance proceeds for 6 months after received, to homestead exemption amount Life insurance proceeds, if clause prohibits proceeds from use to pay beneficiaries' creditors

	Matured life insurance benefits needed for support $9700 in unmatured life insurance policy loan value (spouses may double)
Miscellaneous	Business or professional license $1225 for inmates' trust funds (spouses may not double) Property of business partnership
Federal Exemptions	Not allowed
Notes	For homestead exemption, see *In re McFall*, 112 B.R. 336 (9th Cir. B.A.P. 1990)

California Option 2

Asset Type	Exemption
Homestead	$18,675 in real or personal property used as residence, including co-op; unused portion may be applied to any property
Personal Property	$475 per item in animals, appliances, books, clothing, crops, furnishings, household goods, & musical instruments $18,675 for burial plot, in lieu of homestead Health aids $1225 in jewelry $2975 in motor vehicle $18,675 in personal injury recoveries, not including pecuniary loss & pain & suffering Wrongful death recoveries needed for support
Tools of Trade	$1875 in implements, books, & tools of trade
Wild Card	$1000 plus unused portion of homestead/burial exemption in any property
Wages	None, but federal nonbankruptcy wage exemption available
Pensions	ERISA benefits needed for support
Public Benefits	Crime victims' compensation Public assistance, Social Security, unemployment compensation Veterans' benefits
Insurance	Disability benefits Life insurance proceeds needed for support of family $9975 in accrued unmatured life insurance contract avails Life insurance policy other than credit
Miscellaneous	Alimony & child support needed for support
Federal Exemptions	Not allowed
Notes	Married couples may not double any exemption

Colorado

Asset Type	Exemption
Homestead	$45,000 for real property, mobile home, manufactured home, or house trailer occupied by debtor, sale proceeds exempt for 1 year Spouse or child of deceased owner may claim homestead exemption
Personal Property	One burial plot per family member $1500 in clothing $600 in food & fuel Health aids $3000 in household goods $1000 in jewelry & articles of adornment $3000 in motor vehicle or bicycle used for work; $6000 if used by debtor or dependent who is disabled or 65 or older Personal injury recoveries $1500 in family pictures & books Proceeds for damaged exempt property Security deposits
Tools of Trade	$25,000 in equipment, livestock or other animals, machinery, tools & seed, if debtor is engaged in agriculture $3000 for professional's library (if not included as tools of trade) $10,000 in books, electronics, equipment, fixtures, machines, stock in trade, supplies, tools & other business materials Military equipment owned by National Guard members
Wild Card	None
Wages	Minimum 75% of weekly net earnings or 30 times federal minimum hourly wage, whichever is greater, including pensions & insurance payments
Pensions	ERISA benefits, including IRAs & Roth IRAs Firefighters & police officers Public employees' pensions Public employees' deferred compensation Teachers Veterans' pensions for veteran, spouse, or dependents if veteran served in war or armed conflict
Public Benefits	Aid to aged, blind, disabled, & public assistance Crime victims' compensation Earned income tax credit Unemployment compensation Veterans' benefits for veteran, spouse, or child if veteran served in war or armed conflict Worker's compensation
Insurance	$200 per month in disability benefits, unlimited exemption if lump sum received Fraternal benefit society benefits

Group life insurance policy or proceeds
Homeowners' insurance proceeds for 1 year after received to
   homestead exemption amount
$50,000 cash surrender value of life insurance, except
   contributions to policy within past 48 months
Life insurance proceeds, if clause prohibits use to pay
   beneficiary's creditors

Miscellaneous	Child support Property of business partnership
Federal Exemptions	Not allowed
Notes	

Connecticut

Asset Type	Exemption
Homestead	$75,000 in real property, including mobile or manufactured home; spouses may double $125,000 for judgment arising out of services provided at a hospital after 1993
Personal Property	Appliances, bedding, clothing, food, & furniture Burial plot Health aids needed $1500 in motor vehicle Proceeds for damaged exempt property Residential security & utility deposits for one residence Spendthrift trust funds required for support of debtor & family Transfers to nonprofit debt adjusters Wedding & engagement rings
Tools of Trade	Arms, military equipment, musical instruments, & uniforms of military personnel Books, farm animals, instruments, & tools needed
Wild Card	$1000 of any property
Wages	Minimum of 75% of earned, unpaid weekly disposable earnings or 40 times the state or federal minimum hourly wage, whichever is greater
Pensions	ERISA benefits, including IRAs & Keoghs, to extent wages exempt Medical savings account Municipal employees Probate judges & employees State employees Teachers
Public Benefits	Crime victim's compensation Public assistance Social Security, veterans' benefits, & worker's compensation Unemployment compensation
Insurance	Disability benefits paid by association for its members Fraternal benefit society benefits

	Health or disability benefits
	Life insurance proceeds if clause prohibits use for beneficiary's creditors
	Life insurance proceeds or avails
	$4000 in loan value of unmatured life insurance policy
Miscellaneous	Alimony, to extent wages exempt
	Child support
	Farm partnership, animals, & feed reasonably required to run farm if 50% of partners are members of the same family
Federal Exemptions	Allowed
Notes	

Delaware

Asset Type	Exemption
Homestead	None
Personal Property	Bible, books, burial plot, clothing, including jewelry, church pew or seat in public place of worship & family pictures
	College investment plan account (higher of $5000 limit for year before filing or average of past two years' contributions)
	Income from spendthrift trust
	Pianos & leased organs
	Sewing machines
Tools of Trade	$75 in tools, implements, & fixtures in New Castle & Sussex Counties, $50 in Kent County
Wild Card	$500 in any personal property, except tools of trade, if head of family
Wages	85% of earned unpaid wages
Pensions	IRAs
	Kent County employees
	Police officers
	State employees
	Volunteer firefighters
Public Benefits	Aid to aged, disabled; general assistance
	Aid to blind
	Crime victim's compensation
	Unemployment compensation
	Worker's compensation
Insurance	$350 per month in annuity contract proceeds
	Fraternal benefit society benefits
	Group life insurance policy or proceeds
	Health or disability benefits
	Life insurance proceeds, if clause prohibits use for beneficiary's creditors
	Life insurance proceeds or avails

Miscellaneous	Child support
Federal Exemptions	Not allowed
Notes	A single person may exempt no more than $5000 total A married couple may exempt no more than $10,000 total Per *In re Hovatter*, 25 B.R. 123 (D. Del. 1982), property held as a tenancy in the entirety may be exempt against debts owed by only one spouse

District of Columbia

Asset Type	Exemption
Homestead	Any property used as a residence or co-op that debtor or debtor's dependent uses as a residence
Personal Property	$8625 or $425 per item in appliances, books, clothing, household furnishings, & goods, musical instruments & pets Cemetery & burial funds $50 in cooperative association holdings $400 in family pictures & library Food for 3 months Health aids Higher education tuition savings account $2575 in motor vehicle Payment for loss of person debtor or person depended on, including pain & suffering; wrongful death damages Residential condo deposit Uninsured motorist benefits
Tools of Trade	$300 in furniture, library, tools of professional, or artist $200 in mechanic's tools Seal & documents of notary public $1625 in tools of trade or business
Wild Card	$850 in any property plus $8075 of unused homestead exemption
Wages	Minimum 75% earned unpaid wages, pension payments $200 per month in nonwage earnings, including pension & retirement, for head of family; $60 per month for 2 months for others Payment for loss of future earnings
Pensions	ERISA benefits to maximum deductible contribution Any annuity, pension, profit sharing plan, or stock bonus Judges Public school teachers
Public Benefits	Aid to aged, blind, disabled; general assistance Crime victim's compensation Social Security & veterans' benefits Unemployment compensation Worker's compensation

Insurance	Disability benefits
	Fraternal benefit society benefits
	Group life insurance policy or proceeds
	Life insurance payments
	Life insurance proceeds, if clause prohibits use for
	    beneficiary's creditors
	Life insurance proceeds or avails
	$200 per month in other insurance proceeds for 2 months, for
	    head of family; $60 per month for 2 months for others
	Unmatured life insurance contract other than credit life
	    insurance

Miscellaneous	Alimony, child support
Federal Exemptions	Allowed

Notes	Property held as tenancy in the entirety may be exempt if
	    debts are owed by only one spouse per *Estate of Wall*,
	    440 F.2d 215 (D.C. Cir. 1971)
	Bankruptcy judge may authorize higher wage exemption for
	    low-income debtors

Florida

Asset Type	Exemption

Homestead	Unlimited value in real or personal property, including
	    mobile or modular home; can't exceed $1/2$ acre in
	    municipality, 160 acres elsewhere
	May file homestead declaration

Personal Property	Any personal property up to $1000 (spouses may double) Federal income tax refund or credit; health aids $1000 for motor vehicle Pre-need funeral contract deposits Prepaid college education trust deposits Prepaid medical savings account deposits
Tools of Trade	None
Wild Card	None

Wages	100% of wages, up to $500 per week, paid or unpaid, &
	    deposited into bank account for up to 6 months
	Federal government employees' pension payments needed
	    for support & received 3 months prior to filing

Pensions	County officers & employees ERISA benefits Firefighters Police officers State officers & employees Teachers
Public Benefits	Crime victim's compensation (unless attempting to discharge debt for treatment of injury incurred during crime) Public assistance & Social Security

	Unemployment compensation
	Veterans' benefits
	Worker's compensation
Insurance	Annuity contract proceeds; life insurance cash surrender value
	Death benefits payable to specific beneficiary, not the estate
	Disability or illness benefits
	Fraternal benefit society benefits
Miscellaneous	Alimony & child support needed for support
	Damages to employees for injuries in dangerous occupations
Federal Exemptions	Not allowed
Notes	Per *Havaco of America, Ltd. v. Hill*, 197 F.3d 1135 (11th Cir. Fla. 1999), property held as a tenancy in the entirety may be exempt from debts owed by one spouse

Georgia

Asset Type	Exemption
Homestead	$10,000 in real or personal property used as residence. Spouses may double
Personal Property	$5000 total, $300 per item for animals, appliances, books, crops, clothing, furnishings, household goods & musical instruments
	Burial plot, in lieu of homestead
	Health aids
	$500 in jewelry
	$7500 in lost future earnings needed for support
	$3500 in motor vehicle
	$10,000 in personal injury recoveries
	Wrongful death recoveries needed for support
Tools of Trade	$1500 in books, implements, & tools of trade
Wild Card	$600 plus $5000 of unused homestead exemption in any property
Wages	75% of earned unpaid weekly disposable earnings or 40 times the state or federal minimum hourly wage, whichever is greater, for private & federal workers
Pensions	Employees of nonprofit corporations
	ERISA benefits
	Public employees
	Payments from IRA needed for support
	Other pensions needed for support
Public Benefits	Aid to blind
	Aid to disabled
	Crime victim's compensation
	Local public assistance, Social Security & unemployment compensation

	Old age assistance Veterans' benefits Worker's compensation

Insurance	Annuity & endowment contract benefits
	$250 per month in disability or health benefits
	Fraternal benefit society benefits
	Group insurance
	Proceeds & avails of life insurance
	Life insurance proceeds, if policy owned by someone debtor
	    depends on or needs for support
	Unmatured life insurance contract
	$2000 in unmatured life insurance cash value, dividends,
	    interest, or loan value if debtor is beneficiary or
	    someone beneficiary depends on

Miscellaneous	Alimony & child support needed for support
Federal Exemptions	Not allowed
Notes	Bankruptcy judge may authorize higher wage exemption for low-income debtors

Hawaii

Asset Type	Exemption

Homestead	$30,000 for head of family or persons over 65; $20,000 for all
	    others; sale proceeds exempt for 6 months; spouses may
	    not double

Personal Property	Appliances, books, clothing, & furnishings Burial plot (250 sq. feet) plus tombstones, monuments & fencing $1000 in jewelry, watches, & articles of adornment $2575 in motor vehicle (wholesale value) Proceeds for sold or damaged exempt property (for 6 months)

Tools of Trade	Books, fishing boat, furnishings, implements, instruments,
	    motor vehicle, nets, uniforms, & other property needed
	    for livelihood

Wild Card	None
Wages	Unpaid earned wages from the past 31 days Prisoner's wages held by Dept. of Public Safety (except child support, restitution, & other claims)
Pensions	ERISA benefits deposited more than 3 years before filing Firefighters & police officers Public officers & employees

Public Benefits	Crime victim's compensation & special accounts created to
	    limit commercial exploitation of crimes
	Public assistance from Dept. of Health Services for work
	    done in home or workshop
	Temporary disability benefits

	Unemployment compensation $60 per month in unemployment work relief funds Worker's compensation

Insurance	Accident, health, or sickness benefits
	Annuity contract or endowment policy proceeds, if beneficiary
	    is insured's spouse, child, or parent
	Fraternal benefit society benefits
	Group life insurance policy or proceeds
	Life or health insurance policy for spouse or child
	Life insurance proceeds if clause prohibits use for
	    beneficiary's creditors

Miscellaneous	Property of business partnership
Federal Exemptions	Allowed

Notes	Per *Security Pacific Bank v. Chang*, 818 F. Supp. 1343 (D.
	    Haw. 1993), property held as tenancy in the entirety may
	    be exempt from debts owed by one spouse

Idaho

Asset Type	Exemption
Homestead	$50,000 for real property or mobile home; sale proceeds exempt for 6 months; may not be doubled

Personal Property	$5000 total, $500 per item in appliances, books, clothing,
	    family portraits, 1 firearm, furnishings, musical
	    instruments, pets, & sentimental heirlooms
	Building materials
	Burial plot
	College savings program account
	$1000 in crops on up to 50 acres; 160 inches in water rights
	Health aids
	$1000 in jewelry
	$3000 in motor vehicle
	Personal injury & wrongful death recoveries
	Proceeds for damaged exempt property for 3 months after
	    receipt

Tools of Trade	Arms, uniforms, & accoutrements that peace officer, National Guard, or military personnel are required to keep $1500 in books, implements, & tools of trade
Wild Card	$800 in any tangible personal property
Wages	75% of earned, unpaid weekly disposable wages, or 30 times the federal hourly minimum wage, whichever is greater
Pensions	ERISA benefits Firefighters Gov't & private pensions, retirement plans, IRAs, Keoghs, etc. Police officers Public employees

Public Benefits	Aid to aged, blind & disabled; general assistance Federal, state, & local public assistance Social Security & veterans' benefits Unemployment compensation Worker's compensation
Insurance	$1250 per month in annuity contract proceeds Death or disability benefits Fraternal benefit society benefits Group life insurance benefits Homeowners' insurance proceeds to amount of homestead exemption Life insurance proceeds, if clause prohibits use for beneficiary's creditors Life insurance proceeds or avails for beneficiary other than insured Medical, surgical, or hospital care benefits Unmatured life insurance contract, except credit life insurance $5000 in unmatured life insurance contract interest or dividends owned by debtor or person debtor depends on
Miscellaneous	Alimony; child support Liquor licenses
Federal Exemptions	Not allowed
Notes	Bankruptcy judge may authorize higher wage exemption for low-income debtors

Illinois

Asset Type	Exemption
Homestead	$7500 in real or personal property, including a farm, lot, & buildings, condo, co-op, or mobile home. Sale proceeds exempt for 1 year; spouses may double Spouse or child of deceased owner may claim homestead exemption
Personal Property	Bible, clothing, family pictures, & schoolbooks Health aids $1200 in motor vehicle $7500 in personal injury recoveries Pre-need cemetery sales funds, care funds, & trust funds Prepaid tuition trust fund Proceeds of sold exempt property Wrongful death recoveries
Tools of Trade	$750 in books, implements, & tools of trade
Wild Card	$2000 of any personal property, not including wages
Wages	85% of earned, unpaid weekly wages or 45 times the federal minimum hourly wage

Pensions	Civil service employees
	County employees
	Disabled firefighters; widows & children of firefighters
	ERISA benefits
	Firefighters
	General assembly members
	House of correction employees
	Judges
	Municipal employees
	Park employees
	Police officers
	Public employees
	Public library employees
	Sanitation district employees
	State employees
	State university employees
	Teachers
Public Benefits	Aid to aged, blind, & disabled; public assistance
	Crime victim's compensation
	Restitution payments for WWII relocation of Aleuts & Japanese Americans
	Social Security
	Unemployment compensation
	Veterans' benefits
	Worker's compensation
	Worker's occupational disease compensation
Insurance	Fraternal benefit society benefits
	Health or disability benefits
	$7500 in homeowners' proceeds in home destroyed
	Life insurance, annuity proceeds, or cash value, if beneficiary is insured's child, parent, spouse, or other dependent
	Life insurance proceeds to a spouse or dependent of debtor to extent needed for support
Miscellaneous	Alimony; child support
	Property of business partnership
Federal Exemptions	Not allowed
Notes	Bankruptcy judge may authorize higher wage exemption for low-income debtors

Indiana

Asset Type	Exemption
Homestead	$7500 in real or personal property used as residence; spouses may double; homestead plus personal property exemptions may not exceed $10,000, excluding home health aids
	Property held as tenancy in the entirety may be exempt from debts owed by one spouse

Personal Property	Health aids Money in medical care savings account Spendthrift trusts $100 of any intangible property, except money owed to debtor
Tools of Trade	Arms, equipment, & uniforms for National Guard
Wild Card	$4000 in real estate or tangible personal property; wild card plus homestead exemptions cannot exceed $10,000
Wages	75% of earned, unpaid weekly disposable earnings, or 30 times the federal hourly minimum wage
Pensions	Firefighters Police officers Public employees Public or private retirement benefits & contributions Sheriffs State teachers
Public Benefits	Crime victim's compensation, unless seeking to discharge the debts for which the victim was compensated Unemployment compensation Worker's compensation
Insurance	Employer's life insurance policy on employee Fraternal benefit society benefits Group life insurance policy Life insurance policy, proceeds, cash value, or avails, if beneficiary is insured's spouse or dependent Life insurance proceeds if clause prohibits use for beneficiary's creditors Mutual life or accident proceeds
Miscellaneous	Property of business partnership
Federal Exemptions	Not allowed
Notes	Bankruptcy judge may authorize higher wage exemption for low-income debtors

Iowa

Asset Type	Exemption
Homestead	Unlimited value in real property or apartment; cannot exceed $1/2$ acre in town or city, 40 acres elsewhere; spouses may not double May record homestead declaration
Personal Property	$5000 in accrued wages, motor vehicle, musical instruments, & tax refund; no more than $1000 from tax refund & wages $2000 in appliances, furnishings, & household goods $1000 in bibles, books, portraits, pictures, & paintings 1 acre burial plot $1000 in clothing & its containers

Health aids
$500 in residential security or utility deposit or advance rent
Rifle, musket, or shotgun
Wedding or engagement rings

Tools of Trade	$10,000 in farming equipment, including livestock & feed $10,000 in nonfarming equipment
Wild Card	$100 of any personal property, including cash

Wages	Expected Annual Earnings	Amount Not Exempt per Year
	$0 to $12,000	$ 250
	$12,000 to $16,000	$ 400
	$16,000 to $24,000	$ 800
	$24,000 to $35,000	$1000
	$35,000 to $50,000	$2000
	Over $50,000	10%

Wages not exempt from spousal or child support
Wages or salary of a prisoner

Pensions	Disabled firefighters & police officers (payments being received) Federal government pension Firefighters; police officers Peace officers Public employees Other pensions, annuities, & contracts fully exempt; contributions made within 1 year prior to filing not exempt to extent they exceed normal & customary amounts Retirement plans, Keoghs, IRAs, Roth IRAs, ERISA benefits
Public Benefits	Aid to dependent children Adopted child assistance Any public assistance benefit; Social Security; unemployment compensation Veterans' benefits Worker's compensation
Insurance	Accident, disability, health, illness or life proceeds or avails; life insurance proceeds paid to spouse, child, or other dependent (limited to $10,000 if acquired within 2 years of filing) Disability or illness benefit Employee group insurance policy or proceeds Fraternal benefit society benefits Upon death of insured, $15,000 total proceeds from all matured life, accident, health, or disability policies exempt from beneficiary's debts contracted before insured's death Life insurance proceeds, if clause prohibits use for beneficiary's creditors

Miscellaneous	Alimony & child support needed for support Liquor licenses

Federal Exemptions	Not allowed
Notes	

Kansas

Asset Type	Exemption
Homestead	Unlimited value in real property or mobile home debtor occupies or intends to occupy; cannot exceed 1 acre in a town or city, 160 acres on a farm
Personal Property	Burial plot or crypt Clothing, food, & fuel to last 1 year Funeral plan prepayments Furnishings & household equipment $1000 in jewelry & articles of adornment $20,000 in motor vehicle; unlimited if designed or equipped for disabled person
Tools of Trade	$7500 in books, documents, furniture, equipment, instruments, breeding stock, grain, seed, & stock National Guard arms, equipment, & uniforms
Wild Card	None
Wages	75% of disposable weekly wages or 30 times the federal minimum hourly wage per week, whichever is greater
Pensions	Appointed & elected officials in cities with populations between 120,000 & 200,000 ERISA benefits Federal government pension needed for support & paid within 3 months of filing (only payments being received) Firefighters Judges Police officers Public employees State highway patrol officers State school employees Payments under an annuity, pension, profit-sharing, stock bonus, or similar plan or contract on account of age, death, disability, illness or length of service, to extent reasonably necessary for support
Public Benefits	Crime victim's compensation General assistance Social Security & veterans' benefits Unemployment compensation Worker's compensation
Insurance	Disability & illness benefits Fraternal life insurance benefits

	Cash value of life insurance; not exempt if obtained within one year of filing with fraudulent intent
	Life insurance proceeds
Miscellaneous	Alimony, maintenance, & support
	Liquor licenses
Federal Exemptions	Not allowed
Notes	Bankruptcy judge may authorize higher wage exemption for low-income debtors

Kentucky

Asset Type	Exemption
Homestead	$5000 in real or personal property used as residence; sale proceeds exempt
Personal Property	$5000 in burial plot, in lieu of homestead
	$3000 in clothing, jewelry, articles or adornment, & furniture
	Health aids
	Lost earnings payments needed for support
	Medical expenses paid & reparation benefits received under motor vehicle reparation law
	$2500 in motor vehicle
	$7500 in personal injury recoveries (excluding pain & suffering & pecuniary loss)
	Prepaid tuition payment fund account
	Wrongful death recoveries for person debtor depended on, needed for support
Tools of Trade	$1000 in furnishings, instruments, & office equipment of attorney, chiropractor, dentist, minister, physician, surgeon, or veterinarian
	$2500 in motor vehicle of attorney, auto mechanic, chiropractor, dentist, mechanical or electrical equipment servicer, minister, physician, surgeon, or veterinarian
	$3000 in equipment, livestock, poultry, & tools of farmer
	$300 in tools of nonfarmer
Wild Card	$1000 in any property
Wages	75% of disposable weekly earnings or 30 times the federal minimum hourly wage per week, whichever is greater
Pensions	ERISA benefits, including IRAs, SEPs, & Keoghs deposited more than 120 days before filing
	Firefighters
	Police officers
	State employees
	Teachers
	Urban county government employees
Public Benefits	Aid to aged, blind, disabled; public assistance
	Crime victims' compensation

Unemployment compensation
Worker's compensation

Insurance	$350 per month in annuity contract proceeds Cooperative life of casualty insurance benefits Fraternal benefit society benefits Group life insurance proceeds Health or disability benefits Life insurance policy, if beneficiary is married woman Life insurance proceeds, if clause prohibits use for beneficiary's creditors Life insurance proceeds or cash value, if beneficiary is someone other than insured
Miscellaneous	Alimony & child support needed for support Property of business partnership
Federal Exemptions	Not allowed
Notes	Bankruptcy judge may authorize higher wage exemption for low-income debtors

Louisiana

Asset Type	Exemption
Homestead	$25,000 for property debtor occupies; if debt is result of catastrophic or terminal illness or injury, limit is full value of property as of 1 year prior to filing; cannot exceed 5 acres in city or town, 200 acres elsewhere; may not be doubled Spouse or child of deceased owner may claim exemption; spouse given home in divorce gets homestead
Personal Property	Arms, bedding, clothing, dishes, family portraits, glassware, military accoutrements, musical instruments, silverware (nonsterling), utensils; bedroom, living room, & dining room furniture; poultry, 1 cow, household pets; heating & cooling equipment, freezer, iron, refrigerator, sewing machine, stove, washer, & dryer Cemetery plot monuments $5000 in engagement & wedding rings Spendthrift trusts
Tools of Trade	Books, instruments, & tools; $7500 in motor vehicle; $500 in one firearm; needed for work
Wild Card	None
Wages	75% of disposable weekly earnings or 30 times the minimum hourly wage per week, whichever is greater
Pensions	Assessors Court clerks District attorneys ERISA benefits, including IRAs & Keoghs, if contributions made over 1 year prior to filing Firefighters

	Gift or bonus payments from employer to employee or heirs
	Judges
	Louisiana University employees
	Municipal employees
	Parochial employees
	Police officers
	School employees
	Sheriffs
	State employees
	Teachers
	Voting registrars
Public Benefits	Aid to aged, blind, disabled; public assistance
	Crime victim's compensation
	Unemployment compensation
	Worker's compensation
Insurance	Annuity contract proceeds & avails
	Fraternal benefit society benefits
	Group insurance policies or proceeds
	Health, accident, or disability proceeds or avails
	Life insurance policy proceeds or avails; if policy issued within 9 months of filing, exempt to $35,000
Miscellaneous	Property of minor child
Federal Exemptions	Not allowed
Notes	Bankruptcy judge may authorize higher wage exemption for low-income debtors

Maine

Asset Type	Exemption
Homestead	$35,000 in real or personal property used as residence; $70,000 if debtor has minor dependents in residence; $70,000 if debtor is over 60 or mentally or physically disabled; proceeds of sale exempt for 6 months; joint debtors may double
Personal Property	$200 per item for animals, appliances, books, clothing, crops, furnishings, household goods, & musical instruments
	Balance due on repossessed items; must be under $2000 financed
	Burial plot in lieu of homestead exemption
	Cooking stove; furnaces & stoves for heat
	Food to last 6 months
	Fuel: up to 10 cords of wood, 5 tons of coal, or 1000 gallons of heating oil
	Health aids
	$750 in jewelry; no limit on one wedding ring & one engagement ring
	Lost earnings payments needed for support
	Military arms, clothes, & equipment
	$5000 in motor vehicle

$12,500 in personal injury recovery

Seed, fertilizers, & feed to raise & harvest food for one
   season

Tools & equipment to raise & harvest food

Wrongful death recoveries needed for support

Tools of Trade	Commercial fishing boat, 5 ton limit $5000 in books, materials, & stock One of each farm implement & its maintenance equipment needed to harvest & raise crops
Wild Card	$400 plus $6000 in unused portion of homestead exemption; or unused exemption in animals, appliances, books, clothing, crops, furnishings, household goods, musical instruments, personal injury recoveries, & tools of the trade in any property
Wages	None; use federal bankruptcy wage exemption
Pensions	ERISA benefits Judges Legislators State employees
Public Benefits	Crime victim's compensation Maintenance under the Rehabilitation Act Public assistance Social Security Unemployment compensation Veterans' benefits Worker's compensation
Insurance	$450 per month in annuity proceeds Death benefit for police, fire, or emergency medical personnel who die in the line of duty Disability or health proceeds or avails Fraternal benefit society benefits Group health or life policy or proceeds Life, endowment, annuity or accident policy, proceeds or avails $4000 in life insurance policy, accrued dividends, interest or loan value for policy from person you depended on Unmatured life insurance policy, except credit insurance policy
Miscellaneous	Alimony & child support needed for support Property of business partnership
Federal Exemptions	Not allowed
Notes	

Maryland

Asset Type	Exemption
Homestead	None
Personal Property	$500 total in appliances, books, clothing, furnishings, household goods, & pets

Burial plot
Health aids
Perpetual care trust funds
Prepaid college trust funds
Lost future earnings recoveries

Asset Type	Exemption
Tools of Trade	$2500 in appliances, books, clothing, instruments, & tools
Wild Card	$5500 in any property ($3000 may be cash); must claim exemption within 30 days of levy or attachment
Wages	75% or $145 per week, whichever is greater in earned, but unpaid wages; in Kent, Caroline, & Queen Anne's or Worcester counties, the greater of 75% or 30 times the federal minimum hourly wage
Pensions	ERISA benefits, except IRAs State employees
Public Benefits	Baltimore police death benefits Crime victim's compensation General assistance Unemployment compensation Worker's compensation
Insurance	Disability or health benefits, including arbitrations, court awards, & settlements Fraternal benefit society benefits Life insurance or annuity proceeds or avails, if beneficiary is insured's dependent, child, or spouse $145 per week or 75% of disposable wages in medical insurance benefits deducted from wages, plus medical insurance payments
Miscellaneous	None
Federal Exemptions	Not allowed
Notes	Per *In re Birney*, 200 F. 3d 225 (4th Cir. 1999), property held as tenancy in the entirety is exempt against debts owed by one spouse

Massachusetts

Asset Type	Exemption
Homestead	$300,000 in property debtor occupies or intends to occupy, including mobile home; $300,000 if over 65 or disabled Must record homestead declaration before filing, if statement of homestead is not in title Spouse or children of deceased owner may claim exemption Property held as tenancy in the entirety may be exempt from debt for nonnecessity owed by one spouse
Personal Property	$125 in bank deposits; $200 total in bibles & books; $200 in sewing machine; $75 per month in cash for fuel, heat, water or light; $200 per month for rent, in lieu of homestead; $100 for cooperative association shares; $300 in food or cash for food; $3000 in furniture; $700 in

	motor vehicle; beds & bedding, burial plots, tombs & church pew, clothing, heating unit, 2 cows, 12 sheep, 2 swine, & 4 tons of hay Moving expenses for eminent domain $500 in trust company, bank, or credit union deposits
Tools of Trade	Required arms, accoutrements, & uniforms $500 in fishing boats, tackle, & nets $500 in materials debtor designed & procured $500 in fixtures, implements, & tools
Wild Card	None
Wages	$125 in earned, but unpaid wages
Pensions	Credit union employees ERISA benefits, including IRAs Private retirement benefits Public employees Savings bank employees
Public Benefits	Public assistance Aid to families with dependent children Unemployment compensation Veterans' benefits Worker's compensation
Insurance	$400 per week in disability benefits Fraternal benefit society benefits Group annuity policy or proceeds Group life insurance policy Life or endowment policy, proceeds, or cash value Life insurance police if beneficiary is married woman Life insurance or annuity contract proceeds, if clause prohibits use for beneficiary's creditors Medical malpractice self-insurance
Miscellaneous	Property of business partnership
Federal Exemptions	Allowed
Notes	

Michigan

Asset Type	Exemption
Homestead	$3500 in real property, including condo; property cannot exceed 1 lot in town, village, or city or 40 acres elsewhere; spouse or children of deceased owner may claim homestead exemption
Personal Property	$1000 in appliances, books, furniture, household goods, utensils $1000 par value in building & loan association shares, in lieu of homestead

Burial plots, cemeteries, church pew, slip, seat for entire
family
Clothing, family pictures, food & fuel to last family for 6 months
2 cows, 100 hens, 5 roosters, 10 sheep, 5 swine, & feed to
last 6 months

Tools of Trade	Required arms & accoutrements $1000 in apparatus, horse & harness, implements, materials, motor vehicle, stock, team, & tools
Wild Card	None
Wages	60% of earned, unpaid wages for head of household (minimum $15 per week), plus $2 per week per nonspouse dependent; others may keep 40% (minimum $10 per week)
Pensions	Firefighters, police officers ERISA benefits, except contributions within last 120 days IRAs, except contributions within last 120 days Judges, probate judges Legislators Public school employees State employees
Public Benefits	Crime victims' compensation Social welfare benefits Unemployment compensation Veterans' benefits for Korean War veterans Veterans' benefits for Vietnam veterans Veterans' benefits for World War II veterans Worker's compensation
Insurance	Disability, mutual life, or health benefits Employer-sponsored life insurance policy or trust fund Fraternal benefit society benefits Life insurance Life, endowment, or annuity proceeds, if clause prohibits use for beneficiary's creditors
Miscellaneous	Property of business partnership
Federal Exemptions	Allowed
Notes	Per *In re Smith*, 246 B.R. 540 (E.D. Mich., 2000), property held as tenancy in the entirety may be exempt against debts owed by only one spouse

Minnesota

Asset Type	Exemption
Homestead	$200,000 in home & land on which it is situated; $500,000 if homestead is used for agricultural purposes; cannot exceed $1/2$ acre in city, 160 acres elsewhere; may not be doubled Unlimited for manufactured home

Personal Property	$8100 in appliances, furniture, jewelry, phonograph, radio, & TV Bible & books Burial plot; church pew or seat Clothing, 1 watch, food & utensils for family $3600 in motor vehicle; $36,000 if vehicle has been modified for disability Personal injury & wrongful death recoveries Proceeds from damaged exempt property
Tools of Trade	Farm machines, crops, implements, livestock, & produce $9000 in furniture, instruments, library, machines, stock in trade, & tools Total for 1st two categories cannot exceed $13,000 total Teaching materials of college, public school, public institution, or university teacher
Wild Card	None
Wages	75% of weekly disposable earnings or 40 times the federal minimum hourly wage, whichever is greater Wages paid within 6 months of returning to work, after receiving welfare, or after incarceration; includes earnings deposited in a financial institution in the past 90 days Wages deposited into bank accounts for 20 days after depositing
Pensions	$54,000 in present value in ERISA benefits or IRAs needed for support Public employees State employees State troopers
Public Benefits	Crime victim's compensation Public benefits Unemployment compensation Veterans' benefits Worker's compensation
Insurance	Accident or disability proceeds Fraternal benefit society benefits $36,000 in life insurance proceeds plus $9000 per dependent, if beneficiary is spouse or child of insured Police, fire, or beneficiary association benefits $7200 in unmatured life insurance contract dividends, interest or loan value, if insured is debtor or person debtor depends on
Miscellaneous	Earnings of minor child
Federal Exemptions	Allowed
Notes	Unlimited exemptions may be unconstitutional in Minnesota & limited to a "reasonable amount" of property. Current exemption amounts available at www.comm.media.state.mn.us/bookstore/stateregister.asp (changed every 2 yrs)

Mississippi

Asset Type	Exemption
Homestead	$75,000 in property owned & occupied by debtor; debtors over 60 and married or widowed may claim a former residence; property cannot exceed 160 acres; sale proceeds exempt May file homestead declaration
Personal Property	$10,000 in tangible personal property: any item worth under $200; appliances, books, clothing, crops, dishes, domestic animals, furniture, kitchenware, health aids, household goods, motor vehicles, 1 radio & 1 TV, 1 firearm, 1 lawnmower, tools of the trade, wedding rings; excludes antiques, art, electronic entertainment equipment, or jewelry $20,000 in mobile home $10,000 in personal injury judgments Sale or insurance proceeds from exempt property
Tools of Trade	See personal property
Wild Card	None
Wages	All earned, unpaid wages for 30 days; after 30 days, 75% of earned, unpaid weekly disposable earnings or 30 times the federal hourly minimum wage, whichever is greater
Pensions	ERISA benefits, IRAs, Keoghs deposited 1 year before filing Firefighters & police officers Highway patrol officers Law enforcement officers' & volunteer firefighters' death benefits Private retirement, to extent they are tax-deferred Public employees' retirement & disability benefits State employees Teachers
Public Benefits	Assistance to aged Assistance to blind Assistance to disabled Crime victim's compensation Social Security Unemployment compensation Worker's compensation
Insurance	Disability benefits Fraternal benefit society benefits $75,000 in homeowners' insurance proceeds Life insurance proceeds if clause prohibits use for beneficiary's creditors
Miscellaneous	Property of business partnership
Federal Exemptions	Not allowed

Notes	Per *In re Cobbins*, 234 B.R. 882 (S.D. Miss. 1999), mobile home does not qualify as homestead, unless debtor owns land it is located on
	Bankruptcy judge may authorize higher wage exemption for low-income debtors

Missouri

Asset Type	Exemption
Homestead	$15,000 in real property or $1000 in mobile home; may not be doubled
Personal Property	$1000 in animals, appliances, books, clothes, crops, furnishings, household goods & musical instruments $100 or 1 acre in burial grounds Health aids $500 in jewelry $1000 in motor vehicle Personal injury causes of action Wrongful death recoveries for person debtor depended on
Tools of Trade	$2000 in books, implements, & tools of trade
Wild Card	$1250 in any personal property if head of household, others $400; head of family may claim additional $250 per child
Wages	75% of weekly earnings, 90% for head of household, or 30 times the federal hourly minimum wage, whichever is more
Pensions	Employee benefit spendthrift trust Employees of cities with over 100,000 people ERISA benefits needed for support, payments being received Firefighters Highway & transportation employees Police department employees Police officers & employees State employees Teachers
Public Benefits	Crime victim's compensation Public assistance & Social Security Unemployment compensation Veterans' benefits Worker's compensation
Insurance	Assessment plan or life insurance proceeds Disability or illness benefits $5000 in fraternal benefit society benefits or life insurance dividends, interest or loan value, if bought over 6 months before filing Life insurance proceeds if policy owned by a woman & insures her husband Life insurance proceeds if policy owned by a woman & insures her father or brother Stipulated insurance premiums Unmatured life insurance policy

Miscellaneous	$500 per month in alimony & child support Property of business partnership
Federal Exemptions	Not allowed
Notes	Bankruptcy judge may authorize higher wage exemption for low-income debtors Per *In re Eads*, 271 B.R. 371 (Bkrtcy. W.D. Mo. 2002), property held as tenancy in the entirety may be exempt against debts owed by only one spouse

Montana

Asset Type	Exemption
Homestead	$100,000 in real property or mobile home debtor occupies; sale, condemnation, or insurance proceeds exempt for 18 months Must record homestead declaration before filing
Personal Property	$4500 total, $600 per item in animals with feed, appliances, books, clothing, crops, household furnishings & goods, firearms, jewelry, musical instruments, & sporting goods Burial plot $500 in cooperative association shares Health aids $2500 in motor vehicle Proceeds from sale or for damage or loss of exempt property for 6 months after receipt
Tools of Trade	$3000 in books, implements, & tools of trade Arms, accoutrements, & uniforms needed to carry out government functions
Wild Card	None
Wages	75% of earned unpaid weekly disposable earnings or 30 times the federal hourly minimum wage, whichever is greater
Pensions	ERISA benefits deposited over 1 year before filing or up to 15% of debtor's gross annual income Firefighters IRA contributions & earnings made before judgment filed Police officers Public employees Teachers University system employees
Public Benefits	Aid to aged, disabled needy persons Crime victim's compensation Local public assistance & Social Security Silicosis benefits Subsidized adoption payments to needy persons Unemployment compensation Veterans' benefits Vocational rehabilitation to blind needy persons Worker's compensation

Insurance	$350 per month in annuity contract proceeds
	Disability or illness proceeds, avails or benefits
	Fraternal benefit society benefits
	Group life insurance policy or proceeds
	Hail insurance benefits
	Life insurance proceeds, if clause prohibits use for beneficiary's creditors
	Medical, surgical, or hospital care benefits
	$4000 in unmatured life insurance contracts
Miscellaneous	Alimony & child support
Federal Exemptions	Not allowed
Notes	Bankruptcy judge may authorize higher wage exemption for low-income debtors

Nebraska

Asset Type	Exemption
Homestead	$1200 for married debtor or head of household; may not be doubled; cannot exceed 2 lots in city or village or 160 acres elsewhere; sale proceeds exempt 6 months after sale
Personal Property	$1500 in appliances, books, furniture, household electronics, household goods, musical instruments, & personal computers
	Burial plot
	Clothing
	Crypts, lots, niches, tombs, & vaults
	Health aids
	Perpetual care funds
	Personal injury recoveries
	Personal possessions
Tools of Trade	$2400 in equipment or tools, including a vehicle used for commuting to principal place of business; spouses may double
Wild Card	$2500 in any personal property except wages, in lieu of homestead
Wages	85% of earned, unpaid weekly disposable earnings or pension payments for head of household; for others, 75% of earned, unpaid weekly disposable earnings or 30 times the federal minimum hourly wage, whichever is greater
Pensions	County employees
	Deferred compensation to public employees
	ERISA benefits needed for support
	Military disability benefits
	State employees
Public Benefits	Aid to aged, blind, disabled; public assistance
	General assistance to poor persons

	Unemployment compensation
	Worker's compensation
Insurance	$10,000 loan value in fraternal benefit society benefits, unless beneficiary convicted of crime related to benefits
	$10,000 loan value in life insurance or annuity contract proceeds
Miscellaneous	None
Federal Exemptions	Not allowed
Notes	Bankruptcy judge may authorize higher wage exemption for low-income debtors

Nevada

Asset Type	Exemption
Homestead	$200,000 in real property or mobile home; may not be doubled
	Must record homestead declaration before filing
Personal Property	$10,000 in appliances, furniture, home & yard equipment, & household goods
	$1500 in books; keepsakes & pictures
	Burial plot purchase money & funeral service contract money held in trust
	One gun
	Health aids
	Metal-bearing ores, geological specimens, art curiosities & paleontological remains; must be arranged, classified, catalogued, & numbered in reference books
	Mortgage impound accounts
	$15,000 in motor vehicle; no limit on vehicle equipped for disabled person
	$16,500 in personal injury compensation
	Restitution received for criminal act
	Wrongful death awards to survivors
Tools of Trade	Arms, uniforms, & accoutrements debtor is required to have
	Cabin or dwelling of miner or prospector; $4500 in mining claim, cars, appliances, & implements (for working claim only)
	$4500 in equipment, library, materials, supplies, & tools
	$4500 in farm equipment, seed, stock, tools, & trucks
Wild Card	None
Wages	75% of disposable weekly earnings or 30 times the federal minimum hourly wage per week, whichever is more
Pensions	$500,000 in ERISA benefits, deferred compensation, SEP IRA, or IRAs
	Public employees
Public Benefits	Aid to aged, blind, disabled; public assistance
	Crime victim's compensation
	Industrial insurance (worker's compensation)

Public assistance for children
Unemployment compensation
Vocational rehabilitation benefits

Insurance	$350 per month in annuity contract proceeds Fraternal benefit society benefits Group life or health policy or proceeds Health proceeds or avails Life insurance policy or proceeds, if annual premiums under $1000; spouses may double Life insurance proceeds if the debtor is not the insured
Miscellaneous	Alimony & child support Property of business partnership
Federal Exemptions	Not allowed
Notes	Bankruptcy judge may authorize higher wage exemption for low-income debtors

New Hampshire

Asset Type	Exemption
Homestead	$100,000 in real property or manufactured housing (& land it's on, if owned by debtor)
Personal Property	Beds, bedding, & cooking utensils $800 in bibles & books Burial plot, lot Church pew Clothing Cooking & heating stoves; refrigerator 1 cow, 6 sheep & their fleece, 4 tons of hay $300 in domestic fowl $400 in food & fuel $3500 in furniture 1 hog or pig or, if slaughtered, its meat $500 in jewelry $4000 in motor vehicle Proceeds of lost or destroyed exempt property Sewing machine
Tools of Trade	Arms, equipment, & uniforms of military member $5000 in tools of debtor's occupation Yoke of oxen or horse needed for farming or teaming
Wild Card	$1000 of any property, plus $7000 in unused portions of exemptions for bibles & books, food & fuel, furniture, jewelry, motor vehicle, & tools of trade
Wages	Earned, unpaid wages of spouse 50 times the federal minimum hourly wage per week
Pensions	Federally created pensions (limited to benefits building up) Firefighters Police officers Public employees

Public Benefits	Aid to aged, blind, disabled; public assistance Unemployment compensation Worker's compensation
Insurance	Firefighters' aid insurance Fraternal benefit society benefits $5000 in homeowners' insurance proceeds
Miscellaneous	Jury, witness fees Property of business partnership Wages of minor child
Federal Exemptions	Allowed
Notes	

New Jersey

Asset Type	Exemption
Homestead	None
Personal Property	$1000 in any kind of personal property & possessions, stock, or interest in corporations Burial plot Clothing $1000 in furniture & household goods
Tools of Trade	None
Wild Card	None
Wages	If annual income is under $7500, 90% of earned unpaid wages; if annual income is over $7500, judge decides exemption amount Wages or allowances received by military personnel
Pensions	Alcohol beverage control officers City boards of health employees County employees ERISA benefits for city employees Firefighters, police officers, traffic officers IRAs Judges Municipal employees Prison employees Public employees School district employees State police Street & water employees Teachers Trust containing personal property created pursuant to federal tax law, including 401(k) plans and higher education savings plans
Public Benefits	Old age, permanent disability assistance Unemployment compensation Workers' compensation

Insurance	$500 per month in annuity contract proceeds
	Death or disability benefits for a military member
	Death, disability, hospital, or medical benefits for civil
	    defense workers
	Disability benefits
	Group life or health policy or proceeds
	Health or disability benefits
	Life insurance proceeds, if clause prohibits use for
	    beneficiary's creditors
	Life insurance proceeds or avails, if debtor is not the insured

Miscellaneous	None
Federal Exemptions	Allowed

Notes	Per *Freda v. Commercial Trust Co. of New Jersey*, 570 A.2d
	    409 (N.J. 1990), survivorship interest of a spouse in
	    property held as tenancy in the entirety is exempt from
	    creditors of a single spouse
	In re Yuhas, 104 F.3d 612 (3rd Cir. 1997) allows an
	    exemption for IRAs

New Mexico

Asset Type	Exemption
Homestead	$30,000; spouses may double

Personal Property	Books, clothing, furniture, & health aids
	Building materials
	Cooperative association shares, minimum amount to be
	    member
	$2500 in jewelry
	Machinery, materials, & tools to complete, dig, drill,
	    operate, or repair gas well, oil line, or pipeline
	$4000 in motor vehicle

Tools of Trade	$1500 in tools of trade
Wild Card	$500 in any personal property $2000 of any real or personal property, in lieu of homestead
Wages	75% of disposable earnings or 40 times the federal minimum hourly wage, whichever is more
Pensions	Pension or retirement benefits Public school employees
Public Benefits	Crime victim's compensation (through 2006, unless renewed) General assistance Occupational disease disablement benefits Unemployment compensation Worker's compensation
Insurance	$5000 in benevolent association benefits Fraternal benefit society benefits Life, accident, annuity or health benefits, withdrawal or cash value, if beneficiary is a New Mexico resident Life insurance proceeds

Miscellaneous	Ownership interest in unincorporated association
	Property of business partnership
Federal Exemptions	Allowed
Notes	Bankruptcy judge may authorize higher wage exemption for low-income debtors

New York

Asset Type	Exemption
Homestead	$10,000 in real property, including co-op, condo, or mobile home; spouses may double
Personal Property	$5000 in exemptions, including personal property, limited annuity, & tools of trade; $50 in bible, schoolbooks, & other books; church pew or seat; clothing, cooking utensils, & tableware, dishes, furniture, pictures, radio, refrigerator, sewing machine, TV, wedding ring; 60 day food supply; stoves with 60 day fuel supply; $450 in domestic animal with 60 day food supply; $35 watch
	Burial plot without structure to $1/4$ acre
	$2500 in cash, including savings bonds, bank & credit union deposits, & tax refunds; or up to $5000 after personal property exemptions taken, whichever is less in lieu of homestead
	College savings program trust fund
	Health aids, including service animals with food
	Lost future earnings recoveries needed for support
	$2400 in motor vehicle; spouses may double
	Personal injury recoveries for 1 year after receipt
	Recovery for injury to exempt property for 1 year after receipt
	$600 in savings & loan savings
	Security deposits to landlord, utility companies
	Spendthrift trust fund principal, plus 90% of income, if not created by debtor
	Wrongful death recoveries for person debtor depended on
Tools of Trade	Farm machinery, food & team for 60 days; $600 in books, instruments, & professional furniture
	Arms, emblem, equipment, horse, medals, sword, & uniforms of member of military
Wild Card	None
Wages	90% of earned unpaid wages received within 60 days before filing or anytime after
	90% of dairy farmer's sales to milk dealers
	100% of pay of noncommissioned officer, private, or musician in U.S. or N.Y. state armed forces
Pensions	ERISA benefits, IRAs, Keoghs, & income needed for support
	Public retirement benefits
	State employees
	Teachers
	Village police officers

	Volunteer ambulance workers' benefits Volunteer firefighters' benefits
Public Benefits	Aid to aged, blind, disabled Crime victim's compensation Home relief, local public assistance; Social Security; unemployment compensation Public assistance Veterans' benefits Worker's compensation

Insurance	Annuity contract benefits due the debtor, if debtor paid for the
	    contract; $5000 limit if purchased within 6 months of
	    filing & not tax-deferred
	$400 per month in disability or illness benefits
	Life insurance proceeds left at death with the insurance
	    company, if clause prohibits use for beneficiary's creditors
	Life insurance proceeds & avails if the beneficiary is not the
	    debtor or debtor's spouse has taken out policy

Miscellaneous	Alimony & child support Property of business partnership
Federal Exemptions	Not allowed
Notes	

North Carolina

Asset Type	Exemption
Homestead	$10,000 in real or personal property, including co-op, used as residence

Personal Property	$3500 in animals, appliances, books, clothing, crops,
	    furnishings, household goods, & musical instruments;
	    may add $750 per dependent, for up to 4 dependents;
	    must have been purchased over 90 days before filing
	$10,000 in burial plot, in lieu of homestead
	Health aids
	$1500 in motor vehicle
	Personal injury & wrongful death recoveries for person
	    debtor depended on

Tools of Trade	$750 in books, implements, & tools of trade
Wild Card	$3500 in unused portion of homestead/burial plot exemption in any property $500 in any personal property
Wages	Earned, unpaid wages received 60 days before filing, if needed for support
Pensions	Firefighters & rescue squad workers IRAs Law enforcement officers Legislators Municipal, city, & county employees Teachers & state employees

Public Benefits	Aid to blind Crime victim's compensation Public adult assistance under Work First Program Unemployment compensation Worker's compensation
Insurance	Employee group life policy or proceeds Fraternal benefit society benefits Life insurance on spouse or children
Miscellaneous	Property of business partnership $10,000 in support received by a surviving spouse for 1 year
Federal Exemptions	Not allowed
Notes	Per *In re Chandler*, 148 B.R. 13 (E.D.N.C., 1992), property held as tenancy in the entirety may be exempt against debts owed by only one spouse

North Dakota

Asset Type	Exemption
Homestead	$80,000 in real property, house trailer, or mobile home; spouses may not double
Personal Property	All debtors may exempt: $100 in bible, schoolbooks, or other books Burial plots & church pew Clothing & family pictures Crops/grain raised by debtor on 160 acres where debtor resides Food & fuel to last 1 year Insurance proceeds from exempt property $1200 in motor vehicle; $32,000 for vehicle modified to accommodate owner's disability $7500 in personal injury recoveries $7500 in wrongful death recoveries Head of household may exempt: (if not claiming crops/grain) $5000 of any personal property, or: $1000 in beds & bedding, household, & kitchen furniture $1500 in books & musical instruments $4500 in farm implements & livestock $1000 in library & tools of professional, tools of mechanic, & stock in trade Nonhead of household may exempt: $2500 of any personal property, unless claiming crops/grain
Tools of Trade	See personal property
Wild Card	$7500 in any property, in lieu of homestead
Wages	75% of disposable weekly earnings or 40 times the federal minimum hourly wage, whichever is greater
Pensions	Disabled veterans' benefits, except military retirement pay $100,000 per plan in ERISA benefits, IRAs, Keoghs; no limit if more needed for support; total exemption, including life insurance surrender value, cannot exceed $200,000

	Public employees' deferred compensation Public employees' pensions
Public Benefits	Crime victim's compensation Old age & survivor insurance program benefits Public assistance Social Security Unemployment compensation Worker's compensation
Insurance	Fraternal benefit society benefits Life insurance proceeds payable to deceased's estate, rather than a specific beneficiary $100,000 per policy in life insurance surrender value, if beneficiary is insured's dependent & policy was owned for 1 year prior to filing; limit can be exceeded if needed for support
Miscellaneous	Child support payments
Federal Exemptions	Not allowed
Notes	Bankruptcy judge may authorize higher wage exemption for low-income debtors

Ohio

Asset Type	Exemption
Homestead	$5000 in real or personal property used as residence
Personal Property	$1500 total ($2000 if no homestead exemption); $200 per item in animals, appliances, books, crops, firearms, furnishings, household goods, hunting & fishing equipment, & musical instruments; $400 for 1 piece of jewelry, $200 each for others; spouses may double $200 per item in beds, bedding, clothing Burial plot $400 in cash, money due within 90 days, tax refund, bank, security & utility deposits; spouses may double $300 each for cooking unit & refrigerator Health aids Lost future earnings needed for support received during year prior to filing $1000 in motor vehicle $5000 in personal injury recoveries received during year prior to filing Tuition credit or payment Wrongful death recoveries for person debtor depended on or needed for support, received during year prior to filing
Tools of Trade	$750 in books, implements, & tools of trade
Wild Card	$400 of any property
Wages	75% of disposable weekly earnings or 40 times the federal hourly minimum wage, whichever is greater

Pensions	ERISA benefits needed for support Firefighters, police officers IRAs & Keoghs needed for support Public employees Public safety officers' death benefit Public school employees State highway patrol employees Volunteer firefighters' dependents
Public Benefits	Crime victim's compensation received in 12 months before filing Disability assistance payments Public assistance Unemployment compensation Vocational rehabilitation benefits Worker's compensation
Insurance	$5000 in benevolent society benefits $600 per month in disability benefits Fraternal benefit society benefits Group life insurance policy or proceeds Life, endowment, or annuity contract avails for debtor's spouse, child, or dependent Life insurance proceeds for a spouse Life insurance proceeds, if clause prohibits use for beneficiary's creditors
Miscellaneous	Alimony & child support needed for support Property of business partnership
Federal Exemptions	Not allowed
Notes	Bankruptcy judge may authorize higher wage exemption for low-income debtors Per *In re Pernus*, 143 B.R. 856 (N.D. Ohio, 1992), property held as tenancy in the entirety may be exempt against debts owed by only one spouse

Oklahoma

Asset Type	Exemption
Homestead	Unlimited value in real property or mobile home, cannot exceed 1 acre in city, town, or village or 160 acres elsewhere; $5000 limit if more than 25% of total square foot area used for business purposes; ok to rent out homestead, as long as no other residence is acquired
Personal Property	Books, portraits, & pictures Burial plots $4000 in clothing College savings plan interest Deposits in IDA (Individual Development Account) Federal earned income tax credit 1 year supply of food & seed for growing 1 gun

Health aids

Household & kitchen furniture

Livestock for personal or family use: 5 dairy cows & calves under 6 months, 100 chickens, 10 hogs, 20 sheep, 2 horses, bridles & saddles; feed & forage to last 1 year

$3000 in motor vehicle

$50,000 in personal injury & wrongful death recoveries

Prepaid funeral benefits

War bond payroll savings account

Tools of Trade	$5000 in implements needed to farm homestead, apparatus, books, & tools
Wild Card	None
Wages	75% of wages earned in 90 days before filing; bankruptcy judge may allow more with showing of hardship
Pensions	County employees Disabled veterans ERISA benefits, IRAs, Roth IRAs, Education IRAs, & Keoghs Firefighters Judges Law enforcement employees Police officers Public employees Tax exempt benefits Teachers
Public Benefits	Crime victim's compensation Public assistance; Social Security Unemployment compensation Worker's compensation
Insurance	Annuity benefits & cash value Assessment or mutual benefits Fraternal benefit society benefits Funeral benefits, if prepaid & placed in trust Group life policy or proceeds Life, health, accident, & mutual benefit proceeds & cash value, if clause prohibits use for beneficiary's creditors Limited stock insurance benefits
Miscellaneous	Alimony, child support Beneficiary's interest in statutory support trust Liquor license Property of business partnership
Federal Exemptions	Not allowed
Notes	

Oregon

Asset Type	Exemption
Homestead	$25,000 ($33,000 for joint owners) in real property debtor occupies or intends to occupy; $23,000 ($30,000 for joint

owners) for houseboat or mobile home on debtor's property; $20,000 ($27,000 for joint owners) for mobile home not on debtor's property; property cannot exceed 1 block in city or town or 160 acres elsewhere; sale proceeds exempt for 1 year, if debtor intends to purchase another home

Real property of a soldier or sailor during time of war

Personal Property	$7500 in bank deposits; cash for sold exempt property $600 in books, musical instruments, & pictures; spouses may double Building materials for construction or improvements Burial plot $1800 in clothing, jewelry, & other personal items; spouses may double $1000 in domestic animals, pets, & poultry plus 60 days of feed Federal earned income tax credit Food & fuel supply for 60 days, if debtor is householder $3000 in furniture, household items, radios, TVs, & utensils Health aids $7500 in higher education savings account Compensation for lost earnings for debtor or someone debtor depended on, to extent needed; spouses may double $1700 in motor vehicle; spouses may double $10,000 in personal injury recoveries; spouses may double $1000 in pistol, rifle, or shotgun owned by person over 16
Tools of Trade	$3000 in library, tools, & team with 60 day food supply; spouses may double
Wild Card	$400 in any personal property not already covered by existing exemption; spouses may double
Wages	75% of disposable wages or $170 per week, whichever is greater Wages withheld in state employees' bond savings accounts
Pensions	ERISA benefits, including IRAs & SEPs Public officers & employees
Public Benefits	Aid to blind Aid to disabled Civil defense & disaster relief Crime victim's compensation; each spouse may claim General assistance Injured inmates' benefits Medical assistance Old age assistance Unemployment compensation Veterans' benefits Vocational rehabilitation Worker's compensation
Insurance	$500 per month in annuity contract benefits Fraternal benefit society benefits Group life policy or proceeds, if not payable to insured Health or disability proceeds or avails Life insurance proceeds per cash value if debtor is not the insured

Miscellaneous	Alimony & child support needed for support Liquor licenses
Federal Exemptions	Not allowed
Notes	Per *In re Pletz*, 225 B.R. 206 (D. Or., 1997), tenancy in the entirety is not exempt, but is subject to rights of nondebtor spouse Bankruptcy judge may authorize higher wage exemption for low-income debtors

Pennsylvania

Asset Type	Exemption
Homestead	None
Personal Property	Bibles & schoolbooks Clothing Military uniforms & accoutrements Sewing machines
Tools of Trade	Seamstress' sewing machine
Wild Card	$300 of any property, including cash, proceeds from sale of exempt property, real property & securities
Wages	Earned, unpaid wages Prison inmates' wages Wages of victims of abuse
Pensions	City employees County employees Municipal employees Police officers Private retirement benefits, to extent tax deferred, if clause prohibits proceeds from use to pay beneficiary's creditors, limited to deposits of $15,000 per year made at least 1 year prior to filing; deposit limit does not apply to rollovers from other exempt funds or accounts Public school employees State employees
Public Benefits	Crime victim's compensation Korean conflict veterans' benefits Unemployment compensation Veterans' benefits Worker's compensation
Insurance	Accident or disability benefits Fraternal benefit society benefits Group life policy or proceeds $100 per month in insurance policy or annuity contract payments, cash value, or proceeds, if insured is the beneficiary Life insurance annuity policy cash value or proceeds, if beneficiary is insured's dependent, child, or spouse

	Life insurance & annuity proceeds, if clause prohibits use for beneficiary's creditors No-fault automobile insurance proceeds
Miscellaneous	Property of business partnership
Federal Exemptions	Allowed
Notes	Per *In re Martin*, 259 B.R. 119 (M.D. Pa. 2001) property held as tenancy in the entirety may be exempt against debts owed by only one spouse

Rhode Island

Asset Type	Exemption
Homestead	$150,000 in land & buildings debtor occupies or intends to occupy as principal residence; spouses may not double
Personal Property	$8600 in beds, bedding, furniture, household goods, & supplies; spouses may not double $300 in bibles & books Burial plot Clothing $50 in consumer cooperative association holdings Debt secured by promissory note or bill of exchange $1000 in jewelry $10,000 in motor vehicle Prepaid tuition program or tuition savings account
Tools of Trade	Library of practicing professional; $1200 in working tools
Wild Card	None
Wages	$50 in earned, unpaid wages Earned, unpaid wages due military member on active duty Earned, unpaid wages due seaman Wages of any person who had been receiving public assistance exempt for 1 year after going off assistance Wages of spouse & minor children Wages paid by charitable organization or fund providing relief to poor
Pensions	ERISA benefits Firefighters; police officers IRAs Private employees Public employees
Public Benefits	Aid to aged, blind, disabled; general assistance Crime victim's compensation Family assistance benefits State disability benefits Unemployment compensation Veterans' disability or survivors' death benefits Worker's compensation

Insurance	Accident or sickness proceeds, benefits, or avails Fraternal benefit society benefits Life insurance proceeds, if clause prohibits use for beneficiary's creditors Temporary disability insurance
Miscellaneous	Earnings of a minor child Property of a business partnership
Federal Exemptions	Allowed
Notes	

South Carolina

Asset Type	Exemption
Homestead	$5000 in real property, including co-op; joint owners may double
Personal Property	$2500 in animals, appliances, books, clothing, crops, furnishings, household goods, & musical instruments $5000 in burial plot, in lieu of homestead $1000 in cash & other liquid assets, in lieu of burial or homestead exemption College investment program trust fund Health aids $500 in jewelry $1200 in motor vehicle Personal injury & wrongful death recoveries for person debtor depended on for support
Tools of Trade	$750 in books, implements, & tools of trade
Wild Card	None
Wages	None; use federal nonbankruptcy wage exemption
Pensions	ERISA benefits; debtor's share of pension fund plan Firefighters General assembly members IRAs Judges, solicitors Police officers Public employees
Public Benefits	Aid to aged, blind, disabled; general relief Crime victim's compensation Local public assistance; Social Security; unemployment compensation Veterans' benefits Worker's compensation
Insurance	Accident & disability benefits Benefits accruing under life insurance policy after death of insured, if proceeds left with insurance company pursuant to agreement; benefits not exempt from action to recover necessaries if parties agree

Disability or illness benefits
Fraternal benefit society benefits
Group life insurance proceeds; $50,000 cash value
$4000 in life insurance avails from policy for person debtor
    depended on
Life insurance proceeds from policy for person debtor
    depended on or needed for support
Proceeds & cash surrender value of life insurance, payable to
    beneficiary other than insured's estate & for the express
    benefit of insured's spouse, children, or dependents, if
    purchased 2 years prior to filing
Proceeds of life insurance or annuity contract
Unmatured life insurance contract, except credit life policy

Miscellaneous	Alimony & child support Property of business partnership
Federal Exemptions	Not allowed
Notes	

South Dakota

Asset Type	Exemption
Homestead	Unlimited value in real property or mobile home, if mobile home registered at least 6 months prior to filing and larger than 240 square feet at its base; property cannot exceed 1 acre in town or 160 acres elsewhere; $30,000 in sale proceeds exempt for 1 year, unlimited for debtors over 70 or widow/widower who has not remarried; spouses may not double Gold or silver mine, mill, or smelter not exempt Spouse or child of deceased owner may claim exemption Debtor may file homestead declaration
Personal Property	$200 in bibles, schoolbooks, & other books Burial plots, church pew Cemetery association property Clothing Family pictures 1 year food & fuel supply
Tools of Trade	None
Wild Card	$6000 in any property for head of household; $4000 for others
Wages	Earned unpaid wages from 60 days prior to filing, if needed for family support Wages of prisoners in work programs
Pensions	City employees $250,000 in income & distribution from ERISA benefits Public employees
Public Benefits	Crime victim's compensation Public assistance

	Unemployment compensation
	Worker's compensation
Insurance	$250 per month in annuity contract proceeds
	$2000 in endowment, life insurance, or policy proceeds; $20,000 cash value if policy issued by mutual aid or benevolent society
	Fraternal benefit society benefits
	$20,000 in health benefits
	Life insurance proceeds, if clause prohibits use for beneficiary's creditors
	$10,000 in life insurance proceeds, if beneficiary is surviving spouse or child
Miscellaneous	None
Federal Exemptions	Not allowed
Notes	

Tennessee

Asset Type	Exemption
Homestead	$5000; $7000 for joint owners; spouse or child of deceased owner may claim homestead exemption
	2–15 year lease
	Life estate
Personal Property	Bible, clothing, & storage containers, family pictures, portraits, & schoolbooks
	Burial plot to 1 acre
	Health aids
	Lost future earnings payments for debtor or person debtor depended on
	$7500 in personal injury recoveries; $10,000 in wrongful death recoveries; $15,000 total for crime victim's compensation, personal injury & wrongful death recoveries
	Wages of debtor deserting family, if in hands of family
Tools of Trade	$1900 in books, implements, & tools of trade
Wild Card	$4000 in any personal property, including deposits on account with any bank or financial institution
Wages	75% of disposable weekly earnings or 30 times the federal minimum hourly wage, whichever is greater, plus $2.50 per week per child
Pensions	ERISA benefits, IRAs, & Roth IRAs
	Public employees
	State & local government employees
	Teachers
Public Benefits	Aid to blind
	Aid to disabled

$5000 in crime victim's compensation; $15,000 total for crime victim's compensation, personal injury, & wrongful death recoveries

Local public assistance; Social Security; unemployment compensation

Old age assistance

Relocation assistance payments

Veterans' benefits

Worker's compensation

Insurance	Accident, disability, or health benefits for resident & citizen of Tennessee Disability or illness benefits Fraternal benefit society benefits Life insurance or annuity
Miscellaneous	Alimony & child support owed for 30 days prior to filing Educational trust funds & prepayment plans
Federal Exemptions	Not allowed
Notes	Per *In re Arango*, 992 F.2d 611 (6th Cir. 1993), property held as tenancy in the entirety may be exempt against debts owed by only one spouse Bankruptcy judge may authorize higher wage exemption for low-income debtors

Texas

Asset Type	Exemption
Homestead	Unlimited; property cannot exceed 10 acres in city, town, or village or 100 acres elsewhere (200 for families); sale proceeds exempt for 6 months after sale; renting is allowed if another home is not acquired If no homestead declaration filed, court will file & charge debtor
Personal Property	$60,000 total for family, $30,000 total for individual, including tools of trade Athletic equipment, bicycles, sporting equipment Burial plots (excluded from total exemption amount) Clothing & food Domestic animals & pets plus their food; 12 head of cattle, 2 donkeys, horses, or mules plus tack, 60 head of other livestock, 120 fowl 2 firearms Health aids (excluded from total exemption amount) Home furnishings, family heirlooms Jewelry, limited to 25% of total exemption amount 1 2-, 3-, or 4-wheeled motor vehicle per family member or adult who holds driver's license or relies on another to operate vehicle
Tools of Trade	Farming or ranching implements & vehicles Books, equipment, & tools, including boats & motor vehicles used in trade

Wild Card	None
Wages	Earned, unpaid wages Unpaid commissions, not to exceed 25% of total personal property exemption
Pensions	County & district employees Elected officials, municipal, & state employees Emergency medical personnel, firefighters, & law enforcement officers survivors benefits ERISA government or church benefits, including IRAs & Keoghs Firefighters Judges Police officers Retirement benefits to extent tax-deferred Teachers
Public Benefits	Crime victim's compensation Medical assistance Public assistance Unemployment compensation Worker's compensation
Insurance	Accident, annuity, health or life insurance benefits, cash values, monies, & policy proceeds due or paid to beneficiary or insured Church benefit plan benefits Fraternal benefit society benefits Texas employee uniform group insurance Texas public school employee group insurance Texas state college or university employee benefits
Miscellaneous	Alimony & child support Higher education savings plan trust account Liquor licenses & permits Prepaid tuition plans Property of business partnership
Federal Exemptions	Allowed
Notes	

Utah

Asset Type	Exemption
Homestead	$20,000 in real property, mobile home, or water rights, if primary residence; $5000 in not primary residence; joint owners may double Must file homestead declaration before attempted sale of home Sale proceeds exempt for 1 year
Personal Property	$500 in animals, books, & musical instruments Artwork created by or depicting a family member Bed, bedding, carpets, clothing, except furs & jewelry, 1 year food supply, freezer, microwave, refrigerator, sewing machine, stove, washer, & dryer

Burial plot
$500 in dining & kitchen tables & chairs
Health aids
$500 in heirlooms
$2500 in motor vehicle
Personal injury or wrongful death recoveries for debtor or
    person debtor depended on
Proceeds for damaged, lost, or stolen exempt property
$500 in sofas, chairs, & related furnishings

Tools of Trade	$3500 in books, implements, & tools of trade Military property of National Guard member
Wild Card	None
Wages	75% of disposable weekly earnings or 30 times the federal hourly minimum wage, whichever is greater
Pensions	ERISA benefits, IRAs, Keoghs; benefits accrued & contributions made at least 1 year prior to filing Public employees Other pensions & annuities needed for support
Public Benefits	Crime victim's compensation General assistance Occupational disease disability benefits Unemployment compensation Veterans' benefits Worker's compensation
Insurance	Disability, hospital, illness, or medical benefits Fraternal benefit society benefits $5000 in life insurance policy cash surrender value Life insurance proceeds, if beneficiary is insured's spouse or dependent, as needed for support Medical, hospital, & surgical benefits
Miscellaneous	Alimony needed for support Child support Property of business partnership
Federal Exemptions	Not allowed
Notes	Bankruptcy judge may authorize higher wage exemption for low-income debtors

Vermont

Asset Type	Exemption
Homestead	$75,000 in real property or mobile home; may also claim rents, issues, profits, & out-buildings; spouses may double Spouse of deceased owner may claim homestead exemption
Personal Property	$2500 in animals, appliances, books, clothing, crops, furnishings, goods, & musical instruments $700 in bank deposits

	10 chickens, 1 cow, 2 goats, 10 sheep & feed to last one winter; 3 swarms of bees plus honey; 5 tons of coal or 500 gallons of heating oil, 10 cords of firewood; 500 gallons of bottled gas; $5000 in growing crops; yoke of oxen or steers, plow, & ox yoke; 2 horses with harnesses, halters, & chains
	Freezer, heating unit, refrigerator, sewing machines, & water heater
	Health aids
	$500 in jewelry, unlimited for wedding ring
	Lost future earnings, personal injury, wrongful death recoveries for debtor or person debtor depended on
	$2500 in motor vehicles
Tools of Trade	$5000 in books & tools of trade
Wild Card	$400 plus up to $7000 in unused exemptions for appliances, clothing, crops, household furniture, jewelry, motor vehicle & tools of trade, in any property
Wages	75% of weekly disposable earnings or 30 times the federal minimum hourly wage, whichever is greater; all wages if debtor received welfare during 2 months prior to filing
Pensions	Municipal employees
	Self-directed accounts, such as IRAs & Keoghs, if contributions made 1 year prior to filing
	State employees
	Teachers
	Other pensions
Public Benefits	Aid to aged, blind, disabled; general assistance
	Crime victim's compensation needed for support
	Social Security needed for support
	Unemployment compensation
	Veterans' benefits needed for support
	Worker's compensation
Insurance	$350 per month in annuity contract benefits
	Disability benefits that supplement life insurance or annuity contract
	Disability or illness benefits needed for support
	Fraternal benefit society benefits
	Group life or health benefits
	$200 per month in health benefits
	Life insurance proceeds, if beneficiary is not the insured
	Life insurance proceeds for person debtor depended on
	Life insurance proceeds, if clause prohibits use for beneficiary's creditors
	Unmatured life insurance contract other than credit
Miscellaneous	Alimony & child support
Federal Exemptions	Allowed
Notes	Per *In re McQueen*, 21 B.R. 736 (D. Ver. 1982), property held as tenancy in the entirety may be exempt against debts owed by only one spouse
	Bankruptcy judge may authorize higher wage exemption for low-income debtors

Virginia

Asset Type	Exemption
Homestead	$5000 plus $500 per dependent; rents & profits; $5000 in sale proceeds; spouses may double May include mobile home $15,000 for surviving spouse; if no surviving spouse, children may claim exemption Must file homestead declaration before filing
Personal Property	Bible Burial plot $1000 in clothing $5000 in family portraits & heirlooms Health aids $5000 in household furnishings $2000 in motor vehicles Personal injury causes of action & recoveries Pets Prepaid tuition contracts Wedding & engagement rings
Tools of Trade	Arms, equipment, & uniforms of military member For farmer, $1000 in fertilizer; 2 horses or mules with gear; 2 plows & wedges; one drag, harvest cradle, pitchfork, rake; $3000 in one tractor; one wagon or cart $10,000 in books, instruments, & tools of trade needed in debtor's occupation or education, including motor vehicles
Wild Card	Unused portion of homestead or personal property exemption $2000 in any property for disabled veterans
Wages	75% of weekly disposable earnings or 30 times the federal minimum hourly wage, whichever is greater
Pensions	City, county, & town employees $17,500 in ERISA benefits Judges State employees State police officers
Public Benefits	Aid to aged, blind, disabled; general relief Crime victim's compensation, unless seeking to discharge debt from injury incurred during crime Payments to tobacco farmers Unemployment compensation Worker's compensation
Insurance	Accident or sickness benefits Burial society benefits Cooperative life insurance benefits Fraternal benefit society benefits Group life insurance policy or proceeds Industrial sick benefits Life insurance proceeds
Miscellaneous	Property of business partnership
Federal Exemptions	Not allowed

Notes	Per *In re Bunker*, 312 F.3d 145 (4th Cir., 2002), property held as tenancy in the entirety may be exempt against debts owed by only one spouse Bankruptcy judge may authorize higher wage exemption for low-income debtors

Washington

Asset Type	Exemption
Homestead	$40,000 in real property or mobile home; $15,000 in unimproved property intended for residence; spouses may not double Must record homestead declaration before sale of home, if property unimproved or home unoccupied
Personal Property	$2700 in appliances, furniture, household goods, home & yard equipment; community may double $1500 in books Burial ground Burial plots sold by nonprofit cemetery association Clothing, limited to $1000 in furs, jewelry, & ornaments Food & fuel for comfortable maintenance Insurance proceeds for destroyed, lost, or stolen exempt property Keepsakes & family pictures Prescribed health aids $2500 in motor vehicle; community may double $16,150 in personal injury recoveries
Tools of Trade	Commercial fishing license $5000 in farmer's equipment, seed, stock, supplies, tools, & truck $5000 in library, office equipment, office furniture & supplies of attorney, clergy, physician, surgeon, or other professional $5000 in materials & tools used in any other trade
Wild Card	$2000 of any personal property; no more than $200 in bank deposits, bonds, cash, securities & stocks
Wages	75% of weekly disposable earnings or 30 times the federal minimum hourly wage, whichever is greater
Pensions	City employees ERISA benefits, IRAs & Keoghs Firefighters & law enforcement officials Judges Police officers Public & state employees State patrol officers Teachers Volunteer firefighters
Public Benefits	Child welfare Crime victim's compensation

	General assistance
	Industrial insurance (worker's compensation)
	Old-age assistance
	Unemployment compensation
Insurance	$250 per month in annuity contract proceeds
	Disability avails, benefits, or proceeds
	Group life insurance proceeds or policy
	Life insurance proceeds or avails, if beneficiary is not the insured
Miscellaneous	Child support payments
Federal Exemptions	Allowed
Notes	Bankruptcy judge may authorize higher wage exemption for low-income debtors

West Virginia

Asset Type	Exemption
Homestead	$25,000 in real or personal property used as residence; spouses may double
Personal Property	$8000, $400 per item in appliances, animals, books, clothing, crops, furnishings, household goods, & musical instruments
	$25,000 in burial plot, in lieu of homestead
	Health aids
	$1000 in jewelry
	Lost earnings payments needed for support
	$2400 in motor vehicle
	$15,000 in personal injury recoveries
	Prepaid higher education tuition trust fund & savings plan payments
	Wrongful death recoveries for person debtor depended on or needed for support
Tools of Trade	$1500 in books, implements, & tools of trade
Wild Card	$800 plus unused portion of homestead or burial exemption in any property
Wages	30 times the federal minimum hourly wage per week
Pensions	ERISA benefits, IRAs needed for support
	Public employees
	Teachers
Public Benefits	Aid to aged, blind, disabled; general assistance
	Crime victim's compensation
	Social Security & unemployment compensation
	Veterans' benefits
	Worker's compensation
Insurance	Fraternal benefit society benefits
	Group life insurance policy or proceeds

	Health or disability benefits Life insurance payments from policy for person debtor depended on or needed for support Unmatured life insurance contract, except credit insurance policy $8000 in unmatured life insurance contract's accrued dividend, interest, or loan value, if debtor owns contract & insured is either debtor or a person debtor is dependent on
Miscellaneous	Alimony & child support needed for support Property of business partnership
Federal Exemptions	Not allowed
Notes	Bankruptcy judge may authorize higher wage exemption for low-income debtors

Wisconsin

Asset Type	Exemption
Homestead	$40,000 in property debtor occupies or intends to occupy; sale proceeds exempt for 2 years if debtor intends to purchase another home; spouses may not double
Personal Property	Burial plot, coffin, & tombstone; spouses may double College savings account or tuition trust fund $1000 in deposit account Fire & casualty insurance proceeds for destroyed exempt property for 2 years after receipt $5000 in appliances, animals, books, clothing, firearms, household goods, & furnishings, keepsakes, jewelry, musical instruments, sporting goods, & other tangible property; spouses may double Lost future earnings recoveries, if needed for support $1200 for motor vehicle; spouses may double; unused portion of $5000 personal property exemption may be added $25,000 in personal injury recoveries Tenant's lease or stock interest in housing co-op, to homestead exemption amount Wages used to purchase savings bonds Wrongful death recoveries, if needed for support
Tools of Trade	$7500 in books, equipment, farm products, inventory, & tools of trade
Wild Card	None
Wages	75% of weekly net income or 30 times the federal or state minimum wage, whichever is greatest Wages of inmates under work-release plan Wages of county jail prisoners Wages of county work camp prisoners
Pensions	Firefighters, police officers who worked in city of over 100,000 Military pensions

	Private or public retirement benefits Public employees
Public Benefits	Crime victim's compensation Social services payments Unemployment compensation Veterans' benefits Worker's compensation
Insurance	Federal disability insurance benefits Fraternal benefit society benefits Life insurance proceeds held in trust by insurer, if clause prohibits use for beneficiary's creditors Life insurance proceeds for someone debtor depended on or needed for support Unmatured life insurance contract, except credit insurance contract and $4000 in unmatured life insurance contract's accrued dividends, interest or loan value if debtor owns contract & insured is debtor or dependents, or someone debtor is dependent on
Miscellaneous	Alimony & child support needed for support Property of business partnership
Federal Exemptions	Allowed
Notes	Bankruptcy judge may authorize higher wage exemption for low-income debtors

Wyoming

Asset Type	Exemption
Homestead	$10,000 in real property or $6000 in house trailer debtor occupies; joint owners may double Spouse or child of deceased owner may claim homestead exemption
Personal Property	$2000 per person in home in bedding, food, furniture, & household articles Bible, pictures, & schoolbooks Burial plot $1000 in clothing & wedding rings $2400 in motor vehicle Medical savings account contributions Prepaid funeral contracts
Tools of Trade	$2000 in library & implements of profession or implements, motor vehicle, team, & stock in trade & tools
Wild Card	None
Wages	75% of disposable weekly earnings or 30 times the federal minimum hourly wage, whichever is greater Wages of inmates in adult community corrections program Wages of inmates in correctional industries program Wages of inmates on work release Earnings of National Guard members

Pensions	Criminal investigators & highway officers Firefighters' death benefits Game & fish wardens Police officers Private or public retirement accounts & funds Public employees
Public Benefits	Crime victim's compensation General assistance Unemployment compensation Worker's compensation
Insurance	$350 per month in annuity contract proceeds Disability benefits, if clause prohibits use of proceeds for beneficiary's creditors Fraternal benefit society benefits Group life or disability policy or proceeds, cash surrender & loan values, premiums waived, & dividends Individual life or disability policy or proceeds, cash surrender & loan values, premiums waived & dividends Life insurance proceeds held by insurer, if clause prohibits use of proceeds for beneficiary's creditors
Miscellaneous	Liquor licenses & malt beverage permits
Federal Exemptions	Not allowed
Notes	Per *In re Anselmi*, 52 B.R. 479 (D. Wy. 1985), property held as tenancy in the entirety may be exempt against debts owed by only one spouse

Glossary

Bankruptcy has its own language. This Glossary contains brief definitions of some of the legal terms used in this book and in the Bankruptcy Code, as well as in bankruptcy law and practice in general.

acceleration   The termination of the debtor's right to pay a debt in installments or at a future maturity date, so that the debt becomes immediately due and payable. Many contracts have *acceleration clauses*, entitling the creditor to allow for acceleration of payments upon the happening of specific events, usually the debtor's default.

account receivable   A right to payment for goods sold or services rendered.

adequate protection   If the bankruptcy estate retains property in which a creditor has an interest, that interest is entitled to "adequate protection." This just means that the value of the creditor's interest must be maintained during the period the asset is retained, so that when the creditor is reimbursed for that interest, the amount will be no less than the creditor would have received had the property been surrendered or liquidated immediately.

We have provided you with this Glossary to help you read our book. Naturally, the concepts defined here have been highly simplified to aid your reading. You must not rely on these definitions as legal advice, but should instead consult an attorney about the details of your own case.

adversary proceeding   A lawsuit filed in the bankruptcy court that is related to the debtor's bankruptcy case. Examples are complaints to determine the dischargeability of a debt and complaints to determine the extent and validity of liens.

amortization   The payment of a loan by monthly payments of principal and interest, resulting in a declining principal balance and eventual repayment in full. Because a Chapter 13 plan is not a loan, but a statement as to how each type of debt (unsecured, priority, secured, co-signed, etc.) will be paid back, what percentage will be paid back and at what interest rate, you can start to see the complexity of calculating the right plan payment that will completely fulfill the terms of the plan during its duration. If your attorney fails to take into account all aspects, your payment may be too high or too low, both of which will cause problems.

arrears   The amount that is unpaid and overdue as of the date the bankruptcy case is filed. The word *arrears* is usually used when referring to past-due child support, back alimony owed, or the amount that is past due on mortgage payments including interest and penalties.

assets   Assets are every form of property that a person owns or has any interest in. They include such intangible things as business goodwill, the right to sue someone, and stock options. The debtor must disclose all of his assets in the bankruptcy schedules. Exemptions take assets away from property of the estate.

automatic stay   The injunction issued automatically upon the filing of a bankruptcy case, which prohibits collection actions against the debtor, the debtor's property, or the property of the estate.

avoid   To undo. To make void, cancel, or annul.

avoidance of liens   The Bankruptcy Code permits the debtor to eliminate (avoid) some kinds of liens that impair or interfere with an exemption claimed in the bankruptcy. Most judgment liens that have attached to the debtor's home can be avoided if the total of the liens (mortgages, judgment liens, and statutory liens) is greater than the value of the property in which the exemption is claimed.

avoidance power   The trustee's power to overturn certain transfers or obligations improperly made or incurred by the debtor prior to the bankruptcy, as well as certain post-petition dispositions of estate property. Also, the debtor's right to set aside specific interests to the extent they impair qualified exemptions in property.

Bankruptcy Code   The federal law that governs bankruptcy proceedings. Because bankruptcy is a matter of federal law, with the exception of exemptions, the law is the same in every state. When federal bankruptcy law conflicts with state law, federal law controls.

bankruptcy estate The estate is all of the legal and equitable interests of the debtor as of the commencement of the case. From the estate, an individual debtor can claim certain property as exempt. The balance of the estate is liquidated in a Chapter 7, to pay the administrative costs of the proceeding and the claims of creditors according to their priority.

Chapter 7 The most common form of bankruptcy, a Chapter 7 case is a liquidation proceeding, available to individuals, partnerships, and corporations. It gives the debtor a fresh start by eliminating most of the debtor's unsecured debts. It works best for someone with no assets over and above the exemptions.

Chapter 11 A reorganization proceeding in which the debtor may continue in business or in possession of its property as a fiduciary. This type of bankruptcy is mostly used by corporations and partnerships but is also available to individuals. A confirmed Chapter 11 plan provides for the amount and manner in which the debtor will pay the creditors' claims.

Chapter 12 A simplified reorganization plan for family farmers whose debts fall within certain limits.

Chapter 13 A repayment plan for individuals with debts falling below statutory levels, which provides for repayment of some or all of the debts out of future income for three to five years. Chapter 13 is often used to save a house from foreclosure or to save a car from repossession, because it can be used to repay past due secured claims over time.

collateral The property that is subject to a lien securing payment of a debt or performance of a contract. A creditor with rights in collateral is a secured creditor and has additional protections in the Bankruptcy Code for the claim secured by collateral. The measure of the secured claim is sometimes the value of the collateral available to secure the claim and sometimes the amount of the loan.

confirmation The process a debtor goes through to get his or her plan approved by the bankruptcy court. The bankruptcy court will enter an order, making the terms of the plan for repayment of debts in a Chapter 11, 12, or 13 binding. The terms of the confirmed plan replace the debtor's and creditors' pre-bankruptcy rights.

consumer debt A debt incurred by an individual primarily for personal, family, or household purposes.

contingent claim A claim in which the debtor's potential liability has been created by contract or wrongful or negligent act, but actual liability will arise only upon the happening of a future event that may not occur.

conversion A change in the form of bankruptcy relief sought; for example changing from a Chapter 13 to a Chapter 7.

creditor   Any entity that has a claim against the debtor that arose at the time of or before the filing of the bankruptcy petition. In certain circumstances as set forth in the Bankruptcy Code, a creditor's claim may arise after the filing of the debtor's bankruptcy petition.

credit report   A report outlining an individual's credit history, public records, and creditworthiness.

creditors' committee   A committee of creditors appointed by the U.S. Trustee in Chapter 11 cases, to represent the interests of the unsecured creditors.

creditors' meeting (First Meeting of Creditors, 341 Hearing)   The statutory meeting of creditors required in all bankruptcy cases by Section 341 of the Bankruptcy Code. The meeting must be convened by the U.S. Trustee within a prescribed time following the filing of the bankruptcy petition. The meeting's primary purpose is to examine the debtor about the assets and liabilities and the causes of the bankruptcy.

cure of default   The payment of arrears or the rectification of any other breach of contractual obligation, so that the party's performance is brought into compliance with the terms of the contract.

debt   An obligation to pay money. A liability on a claim or a right to payment.

debtor   The entity (person, partnership, or corporation) who is liable for debts and is the subject of a bankruptcy case.

debtor in possession   In a Chapter 11 case, the debtor usually remains in possession of its assets and assumes the duties of a trustee. The debtor in possession is a fiduciary for the creditors of the estate and owes them the highest duty of care and loyalty.

debtor's equity   The debtor's unencumbered ownership interest in property, the part not covered by any liens.

default   The debtor's material breach of contract, such as the failure to pay a debt on the due date. Some contracts provide that the insolvency or bankruptcy of the debtor constitutes an automatic default. Such a provision is not enforceable in bankruptcy.

deficiency   The shortfall that results when a debt is undersecured, that is, when the collateral securing the debt is worth less than the amount owed, so that sale of the collateral does not fully satisfy the debt.

delinquency   Failure to make payments on a debt when it is due. Even though the creditor may not charge a *late fee* for a number of days, the payment is still considered to be late and the loan delinquent. When a loan payment is more than 30 days late, most lenders report the late payment to one or more of the credit bureaus, and the late payment appears on the debtor's credit report.

denial of discharge   The penalty for debtor misconduct with respect to the bankruptcy case or creditors. The grounds on which the debtor's discharge may be denied are found in 11 U.S.C. 727. Denial of a discharge means the entire case has been a waste. The debtor gets no benefit from the bankruptcy case at all.

discharge   The debtor's release from liability for the unpaid balance of all debts that are provable in bankruptcy and that are not excluded from discharge under the Code. This is the legal elimination of debt through a bankruptcy case. When a debt is discharged, it is no longer legally enforceable against the debtor, though any lien that secures the debt may survive the bankruptcy case.

dischargeable   Debts that can be eliminated in bankruptcy. Certain debts are not dischargeable. That is, they may not be dischargeable through bankruptcy at all or may be discharged only through Chapter 13. Child support and criminal restitution are examples of debts that cannot be discharged.

dismissal   The termination of the case with neither the entry of a discharge nor a denial of discharge. After a case is dismissed, the debtor and the creditors have the same rights as they had before the bankruptcy case was commenced. If a bankruptcy is dismissed, the case is unsuccessful.

disposable income   The portion of the debtor's income not reasonably necessary for the maintenance and support of the debtor or the debtor's dependents and not necessary for the operation and preservation of any business in which the debtor is engaged.

equity   An owner's unencumbered interest in property.

equity cushion   The amount of surplus equity held by the debtor in collateral beyond the amount of the secured debt plus any senior claims. This excess value in the collateral is called an *equity cushion* because it provides a margin of safety for the lienholder to cover any adverse change in the collateral to debt ratio caused by further depreciation of the property or the accumulation of interest or costs.

estate   The total property held by a person. In bankruptcy, the debtor's estate is all of the debtor's legal and equitable interests at the commencement of the case. The debtor can remove certain property from the estate by using the exemptions.

exception to discharge   A debt that is excluded from the debtor's discharge on one of the grounds enumerated in the Bankruptcy Code.

executory contract   A contractual relationship in which neither party has fulfilled all of the requirements of the contract. Failure of either party to complete the requirements would be a material breach of contract. Upon the bankruptcy of one of the parties to such a contract, the trustee or debtor in possession can elect to either reject or assume the contract.

exempt Property that is exempt is removed from the bankruptcy estate and is not available to pay the claims of creditors. The debtor selects the property to be exempted from the statutory lists of exemptions available under the law of the state. The debtor gets to keep exempt property to get a fresh start after bankruptcy.

exemptions Types and values of property that are legally beyond the reach of creditors and the bankruptcy trustee. The debtor in bankruptcy keeps the exempt property. What property may be exempted is determined by state and federal statutes, and varies from state to state.

fair market value The highest price that a willing buyer, who is not compelled to buy, would pay, and the lowest a willing seller, who is not compelled to sell, would accept.

family farmer A person or entity whose income and debts primarily arise from a family owned and operated farm and who meets other eligibility requirements for relief under Chapter 12.

feasible A reasonable likelihood that the debtor will be able to make the payments and meet the rehabilitative goals set out in a Chapter 13, Chapter 12, or Chapter 11 plan.

fiduciary One who is entrusted with duties to act in the best interest of another. The law requires the highest level of good faith, loyalty, and diligence of a fiduciary, higher than the common duty of care that all people owe one another. The debtor in possession in a Chapter 11 is a fiduciary for the creditors, owing loyalty to the creditors, not the shareholders.

foreclosure The legal process by which a borrower in default under a mortgage is deprived of his or her interest in the mortgaged property. This usually involves a forced sale of the property at public auction with the proceeds of the sale being applied to the mortgage debt.

fraudulent transfer/conveyance A disposition of property by a debtor with the actual or constructive intent to defraud creditors or to delay or hinder their collection efforts.

fresh start The rehabilitation of a debtor through the process of bankruptcy, achieved by the resolution and discharge of pre-petition debt.

garnishment A court-ordered method of debt collection in which a portion of a person's salary is paid to a creditor by a third party, such as a bank or employer.

general unsecured claim Claim without a priority for payment or lien against the debtor's property. If the available funds in the estate extend to payment of unsecured claims, the claims are paid pro rata, which means in proportion to the size of the claim relative to the total of claims in the class of unsecured claims.

homestead exemption An exemption in an individual debtor's interest in property in which the debtor or his dependent resides, granted under state law or federal bankruptcy law.

individual A natural person, as distinct from a corporate entity.

insider A person who has such a close relationship with the debtor that he or she has special access to information and opportunities for favorable treatment. An insider includes relatives of an individual debtor, partners in a partnership, and persons in control of a corporate debtor.

insolvency Inability to pay debts, determined by one of two methods: inability to pay debts as they become due (the "equity" test) or liabilities greater than assets (the "balance sheet" or "bankruptcy" test).

judgment lien A lien imposed on a debtor's property after a court judgment against the debtor. If the judgment is filed with the county clerk, a lien is created against all of the debtor's real property within the county. In some states this also creates a lien on personal property.

lien A creditor's interest in real or personal property that secures a debt. A lien may be voluntary, such as a mortgage in real property, or involuntary, such as a judgment lien or tax lien. If the debt is not paid, the creditor may have the recourse of taking the property to satisfy the debt.

lienholder/lienor The holder or owner of a lien.

lien stripping or strip-down The practice of capping a creditor's secured claim at the value of the collateral, as determined by the bankruptcy court.

liquidated debt A debt in an amount that can be calculated. An unliquidated debt is one where the debtor has liability, but the exact monetary amount of that liability is unknown. Tort claims are usually unliquidated until a trial fixes the amount of the liability.

liquidation The conversion of the debtor's nonexempt assets to cash for the payment of debts.

meeting of creditors The debtor must appear at a meeting with the trustee to be questioned under oath about his or her assets and liabilities. Creditors are invited to the meeting, but seldom attend. Sometimes the meeting is called the *341 meeting*, named after the section of the Bankruptcy Code that requires it.

no-asset case A Chapter 7 case in which there are insufficient assets to allow for a distribution to creditors.

nondischargeable debt A debt that is not released by the bankruptcy discharge. Nondischargeable debts remain legally enforceable despite the bankruptcy discharge.

objection A written response that challenges assertions by another party, such as a claim of exemption, a proposed plan, or the discharge of a debt.

perfection When a secured creditor has possession of the collateral, or has filed a statement in the appropriate public office, the lien is senior to any liens that arise after perfection. A mortgage is perfected by recording it with the county recorder. A lien in personal property is perfected by filing a financing statement with the Secretary of State. An unperfected lien is valid between the debtor and the secured creditor, but a perfected lienholder has a stronger claim to the collateral. The trustee in bankruptcy can avoid an unperfected lien.

personal property Property that is not real property or affixed to real property. Personal property includes cars, stock, furniture, and so on.

petition The document that starts a bankruptcy case. The filing of the petition constitutes an order for relief and causes the automatic stay to kick in. Events are often described as *pre-petition*, occurring before the bankruptcy petition was filed or *post-petition*, occurring after the bankruptcy.

preference Priority of payment given to one creditor by a debtor. If a debtor pays a creditor for a past-due debt within 90 days (or sometimes a year) before the commencement of the case, the payment may be recovered by the trustee for the benefit of all creditors of the estate.

pre-petition Claims or events arising before the commencement of the bankruptcy case, that is, before the filing of the bankruptcy petition. Generally, only pre-petition debts may be discharged in a bankruptcy proceeding.

priority A creditor's right to have a claim paid before other creditors receive payment. The Bankruptcy Code establishes the order in which claims are paid from the bankruptcy estate. All claims in a higher priority must be paid in full before claims with a lower priority receive anything. All claims with the same priority share pro rata (in equal percentages of the debt). Claims are paid in this order: (1) costs of administration; (2) priority claims; and (3) general unsecured claims. Secured claims are paid from the proceeds of liquidating the collateral that secured the claim.

priority claims Certain debts, such as unpaid wages, alimony, child support, and taxes that are elevated in the payment hierarchy under the Bankruptcy Code. Priority claims must be paid in full before general unsecured claims are paid.

proceeds Any property or money received in exchange for an asset.

proof of claim The form filed with the court establishing the basis and amount of the creditor's claim against the debtor.

property of the estate   The debtor's property that is not exempt and that belongs to the bankruptcy estate. Property of the estate is usually sold by the trustee, and the claims of creditors are paid from the proceeds.

reach-back period   The time frame immediately before the filing of a bankruptcy petition within which certain of the debtor's transfers can be avoided.

reaffirm   An agreement between the debtor and a creditor to repay a prepetition debt that would otherwise be discharged by the bankruptcy. Generally, when a debt is reaffirmed, the parties have the same rights and liabilities that each had prior to the bankruptcy filing. The debtor is obligated to pay, and the creditor can sue or repossess the property if the debtor doesn't pay.

relief from stay   A creditor can ask the judge to lift the automatic stay and permit some action against the debtor or the property of the estate. If the motion is granted, the moving party (but no one else) is free to take whatever action the court permits.

repossession   Taking collateral upon default, as defined by the creditor in the security agreement. The creditor can: (1) repossess the collateral with or without the aid of a court order, (2) dispose of the collateral by public or private foreclosure sale, (3) keep the collateral, (4) terminate the debtor's right of redemption, (5) add the costs of repossession and foreclosure to the unpaid balance of the debt, and (6) pursue the debtor for any debt remaining after the collateral has been sold. None of this can be done once a bankruptcy case is filed.

schedules   The lists of assets and liabilities that must be filed by the debtor in a bankruptcy case, collectively called *the schedules*.

secured debt   A debt backed by a lien in the debtor's property, which helps ensure the creditor's financial confidence. The lien can be created as an involuntary lien such as a judgment or tax lien or by agreement with the debtor. The creditor's claim sometimes can be divided into a secured claim to the value of the collateral, and an unsecured claim equal to the remainder of the total debt. Generally a secured claim must be perfected under applicable state law to be treated as a secured claim in the bankruptcy.

trustee   The court appoints a trustee in every Chapter 7 and Chapter 13 case to review the schedules filed by the debtor and represent the interests of the creditors in the bankruptcy case. The role of the trustee is different under the different chapters.

unsecured   A claim or debt with no collateral as security for the debt. Most consumer debts are unsecured.

References

Books

Bartiromo, Maria. *Use the News* (New York: Harper Collins, 2001).

Bridgforth, Glinda, and Gail Perry-Mason. *Girl, Make Your Money Grow: A Sister's Guide to Protecting Your Future and Enriching Your Life* (New York: Broadway Books, 2003).

Bridgforth, Glinda, and Gail Perry-Mason. *Girl, Make Your Money Straight: A Sister's Guide to Healing Your Bank Account and Finding Your Dreams in 7 Simple Steps* (New York: Broadway Books, 2000).

Cunningham, L. A. *The Essays of Warren Buffett* (New York: Wiley, 2002).

Fisher, Phillip A., and Kenneth L. Fisher. *Common Stocks and Uncommon Profits and Other Writings* (New York: Wiley Investment Classics, 2003).

Fridson, Martin S. *How to Be a Billionaire* (New York: Wiley, 2000).

Graham, Benjamin, and Jason Zweig. *The Intelligent Investor* (New York: HarperBusiness Essentials, 2003).

Lynch, Peter. *One Up on Wall Street* (New York: Simon & Schuster, 2000).

Orman, Suze. *9 Steps to Financial Freedom* (New York: Crown, 1997).

Schilit, Howard. *Financial Shenanigans: How to Detect Accounting Gimmicks and Fraud* (New York: HarperCollins, 2001).

Thomsett, Michael C. *Support and Resistance Simplified* (New York: Wiley Marketplace Books, 2003).

Web Sites

Consumer Action web site: Federal Citizen Information Center, Investing—
General Tips, www.consumeraction.gov/caw_investing_general_tips.shtml,
visited on August 1, 2005.

U.S. Securities and Exchange Commission web page, Tips for Online Investing: What You Need to Know about Trading in Fast-Moving Markets,
www.sec.gov/investor/pubs/onlinetips.htm, visited on August 1, 2005.

Index

Abuse test, Chapter 7 dismissal under
   new law, 120–125
Actual fraud, 81, 109
Adequate protection payments, 131
Alabama, 151–152
Alaska, 84, 91, 152–153
Alimony, *see* Marital property settlements
All Your Worth (Warren and Warren), 41
Alternatives to bankruptcy, 42–50, 52
Antimodification clause, 133
Appraisal, *see* Valuation
Arizona, 84, 91, 153–154
Arkansas, 73, 154–155
Assets, *see also* Full disclosure of assets;
      Transfers
   debtor's estate and, 67–69
   exempt from bankruptcy, 45
   legal protection of, 30–31
   schedules of, 85–87
Attorneys:
   fees and, 58–59, 134–136
   new law and, 51–52, 76, 126
   required for reaffirmation, 117–118
   tips for choosing, 53

Audits, random under new law, 98–99
Automatic stay, 62–67
   creditors and, 65–67
   exceptions to, 63–64
   marital obligations and, 105
   new law and, 64–65
Automobiles, *see also* Secured creditors
   federal bankruptcy exemptions, 74
   loans for, as secured credit, 27–29
   loans for, new law and, 53–54
   saving money on, 17–18
   valuation and, 76
Avoiding powers, 78–81

Banking, saving money on, 17
Bankruptcy, *see also specific*
      bankruptcies
   alternatives to, 42–50, 52
   assessing need for, 38–42
   Bankruptcy Code, 70
   basic procedures in, 69–71, 85–100
   entrepreneurs, 146–147
   filing for, 51–61
   good candidates for, 42

Bankruptcy (*Continued*)
  laws common to all, 62–81
  poor candidates for, 45–50
  timing your filing, 60–61
  types of, 31–35
Bankruptcy trustee, 68, 70–71
  Chapter 13 commission for, 128
  at 341 meeting, 71, 93–97
Best efforts test, Chapter 13, 136–139
Best interests of creditors test, Chapter
      13, 142–143
Bifurcated claim, 130–131
Businesses:
  bankruptcy law and, 146–147
  statement of affairs and, 92

California, 84, 91
  option 1, 155–157
  option 2, 157–159
Cash advances, 60, 108–110
Chapter 7 bankruptcy:
  discharge in, 32–33, 36, 101–114,
      141–142
  dismissal of, 48–49, 119–125
  filed before Chapter 13, 48–49, 140–141
  in general, 32–33, 71
  loan cosigners and, 48
  new law and, 34, 54–55, 97–100
  post-petition assets and, 68–69
  preferential transfers and, 80
  priority claims in, 78, 88
  refiling under, 46–47, 114
  secured creditors and, 28, 66–67,
      83–84, 88, 92, 115–118, 124
  341 creditor's meeting and, 93–96
  trustee and, 70–71
  valuation and, 76–77
Chapter 11 bankruptcy:
  discharge in, 102
  in general, 35
Chapter 12 bankruptcy:
  discharge in, 101
  in general, 34–35
Chapter 13 bankruptcy:
  Chapter 7 dismissed to, 48–49
  discharge in, 37, 102–103
  in general, 33–34, 71, 96–97

information required under new law,
      97–100
  payment plan cases, 126–145
  post-petition assets and, 69
  preferential transfers and, 80
  priority claims in, 78
  refiling under, 46–47, 114
  secured creditors and, 28, 49, 53–54,
      66–67, 84, 128–134
  trustee and, 70–71
  used to address business problems,
      146–147
  valuation and, 76
Charitable contributions, 18, 91, 124,
      137
Child support, nondischargeable, 104,
      134–136
Claim, defined, 102–103
Clothing, saving money on, 16–17
Collateral, *see* Secured creditors
Community property states, 84, 91
Compound interest, 19–20
Confirmation hearing, 128–129
Connecticut, 73, 159–160
Constructive fraud, 81
Consumer credit:
  economics of, 21–25
  history of, 1–6
Consumer credit counseling services,
      43–44, 56, 99
Courts, 70
Credit cards, 4–6
  applying for new, with lower interest,
      43
  higher spending due to use of, 25
  nondischargeable charges close to
      bankruptcy, 107–111
  paying off balances, 23–24
  shopping without, 11, 12–13
Credit counseling services, 43–44, 56, 99
Creditors, *see also* Debtor-creditor law;
      Secured creditors
  automatic stay and, 65, 66–67
  defined, 26–27
  negotiating with, to avoid bankruptcy,
      42–43
  at 341 meeting, 71

Credit report, correcting errors in, 44
Cruz, Humberto, 19–20

Debt:
   avoiding in future, 44
   consolidation loans for, 43
   demographics of debtors, 7
   full disclosure of, 59
   making payments on current, 44
   reported in statement of affairs,
      90–92
   schedule of liabilities, 87–90
   ways of avoiding, 9–11
   ways of getting into, 1–8
Debtor, defined, 26–27
Debtor-creditor law:
   bankruptcy discharge, 35–37
   bankruptcy types, 31–35
   debtors and creditors defined, 26–27
   liens types, 27–30
   state collection law and exemptions,
      30–31
Debtor's estate, 67–69. *See also* Assets
Deficiency claim, 29
Deficiency judgment, 83
Delaware, 160–161
Diary, of spending, 16, 38–42
Discharge, of Chapter 7 bankruptcy,
      101–114
   exceptions to, 103–111
   in general, 32–33, 36, 96, 101–103
   objections to global discharge,
      111–114
Discharge, of Chapter 13 bankruptcy, 37,
      96
Disclosure, *see* Full disclosure of assets
Dismissal, of Chapter 7 bankruptcy,
      119–125
   for abuse, 120–125
   for failure to cooperate, 119
   within past 180 days, 47
Dismissal, of Chapter 13 bankruptcy, 71,
      144, 145
Disposable income test, 97, 136–139
District of Columbia, 73, 161–162
Divorce, bankruptcy and, 8. *See also*
      Marital property settlements

Donations to charity, *see* Charitable
      contributions
DWI (driving while intoxicated) debts,
      nondischargeable, 106

Education retirement account, 69
Embezzlement, 110
Entertainment, saving money on, 18
Entrepreneurs and bankruptcy,
      146–147
Equity, in property, 30–31
Estate, property of, 67–69
Eviction proceedings, 64–65
Exemptions, 72–78
   avoiding liens that interfere with,
      78
   schedules for, 87
   under federal law, 73–76
   under state law, 72–73
   valuation and, 76–77
Expenses:
   means test and, 48–49, 122–124
   schedules of, 89–90
   tracking of, 38–42

False financial statement, fraud and,
      107–108
False oath, 112
Family, *see* Friends and relatives
Farmers, *see* Chapter 12 bankruptcy
Feasibility requirement, Chapter 13,
      143–144
Federal exemptions, 73–76
Fees:
   of attorneys, 128
   of trustees, 58–59
Filing, *see also* Paperwork
   new law and, 60–61
   timing of, 51–56
   tips on, 57–61
Financial management course, required,
      99–100
Fishermen, *see* Chapter 12 bankruptcy
Florida, 73–74, 162–163
401(k) plans, 137–138
Fraud, 46, 55, 81, 107–111
Fraudulent transfers, 80–81, 113–114

Friends and relatives:
    payback of money borrowed from, 60
    preferential transfers and, 46, 49,
      79–80, 90
Full disclosure of assets, 46, 57–58. *See*
    also Paperwork
Furniture loans, new law and, 53–54

Garage sales, 18
Georgia, 163–164
Good faith test, Chapter 13, 139–142

Happiness and money, 10–11
Hawaii, 73, 164–165
Health-care costs, bankruptcy and, 7–8
Home equity loans, 3–5, 43
Homestead, federal exemptions and, 74.
    See also Mortgages

Idaho, 84, 91, 165–166
Illegal substances, renters and, 65
Illinois, 166–167
Illness, avoiding filing during, 49
Income:
    in new Chapter 7 means test, 122
    reported in statement of affairs, 90
    schedules of, 89
    statement of current monthly, 98
    timing filing with paycheck, 60–61
Indiana, 167–168
Inheritance, 68
Insiders, *see* Preferential transfers
Intentional torts, nondischargeable, 55, 106
Interest, *see also* Present value interest
    rate
    compounding of, 19–20
    rates on credit cards, 4–5, 23–24
Investing, after bankruptcy, 148–149
Involuntary liens, 30, 78, 82
Iowa, 168–170
IRA, Roth, 19–20
IRS collection standards, 122. *See also*
    Taxes; Tax refunds

Jewelry, federal bankruptcy exemptions, 74
Job market volatility, bankruptcy and, 7
Judgment-proof individuals, 45

Kansas, 170–171
Keep and pay option, in Chapter 7, 116, 118
Kentucky, 171–172

Larceny, 110
Late fees, 22–23
Lawyers, *see* Attorneys
Liabilities, *see* Debt; Expenses
Liens, *see also* Strip-down
    exemptions and, 78
    types of, 27–30
Loans, *see also* Secured creditors
    cosigners of, 48
    new Chapter 13 treatment of, 130–133
Local Loan v. Hunt, 36
Losses, recent, 46
Louisiana, 84, 91, 172–173
Low-income individuals, 45
Luxury goods, 60, 108–110

Maine, 173–174
Marital property settlements, 69, 104–105,
    134–135
Maryland, 174–175
Massachusetts, 73, 175–176
Means test:
    Chapter 7 and, 120–125
    Chapter 13 and, 48–49, 128
    new law and, 51, 54–55, 120–125
Median income, means test and, 122
Michigan, 73, 176–177
Minnesota, 73, 177–178
Mississippi, 179–180
Missouri, 180–181
Money, inexplicable loss of, 112
Montana, 181–182
Monthly income, current defined, 98
Mortgages, 2–5, 43
    Chapter 13 and, 128, 133–134
    new law and filing date, 53–54
Motor vehicles, *see* Automobiles
Multiple filings, *see* Refiling

National Consumer Law Center, 25
Nebraska, 182–183
Nevada, 84, 91, 183–184
New Hampshire, 184–185

New Jersey, 73, 185–186
New Mexico, 73, 84, 91, 186–187
New York, 187–188
Nifto, John C., II, 25
No-load mutual funds, 14, 148–149
Nondisclosure, *see* Full disclosure of assets
North Carolina, 188–189
North Dakota, 189–190

Objections to discharge, 111–114
Objections to dischargeability, 111
Ohio, 190–191
Oklahoma, 191–192
Oregon, 192–194

Paperwork, 85–86. *See also* Full
    disclosure of assets
  creditor forgotten in, 110–111
  falsification, destruction, failure to
    keep records, 112–113
  mistakes in and new law, 47, 53, 56,
    102–103
  organization of, 59
  random audits of, 98–99
  schedules of assets and liabilities, 85–90
  statement of affairs, 90–92
Paycheck, *see* Income
Payment plans, Chapter 7, 124–125
Payment plans, Chapter 13, 126–145
  best interest of creditors test and,
    142–143
  discharge under new law, 145
  disposable income test and, 136–139
  eligibility for, 129
  feasibility of plan and, 143–144
  good faith test and, 139–142
  modification or dismissal of plan and,
    144
  overview, 126–129
  priority claim treatment under,
    134–136
  secured creditor treatment under,
    129–134
"Pay-out cases," *see* Chapter 13
    bankruptcy
Penalty of perjury, 92, 94
Pennsylvania, 73, 194–195

Pension plans, 137–138
Perjury, 92, 94
Personal property:
  disclosure of, 86–87
  federal bankruptcy exemptions, 74
  valuation and, 76–77
Post-filing debt, 102
Post-petition assets, 68–69, 127–128
Post-petition financial management
    course, 99–100
Pre-bankruptcy debtor counseling, 99
Pre-bankruptcy planning, 113–114
Preferential transfers, 46, 49, 79–80, 90
Present value interest rate, 132–133
Presumptive fraud, 108–110
Priority claims, 32, 78, 88, 134–136
Property of estate, 67–69
Property settlements, discharge and,
    104–105
Puerto Rico, 84, 91

Qualified state tuition programs, 69

Reaffirmation, of secured property in
    Chapter 7, 115–118
Records, *see* Paperwork
Redemption, of secured property in
    Chapter 7, 115–116
Refiling:
  allowable frequency, 114
  automatic stay and, 64
  Chapter 13 and, 14, 46–47, 140–141
  waiting period for, 46–47
Relatives, *see* Friends and relatives
Renters:
  automatic stay and, 64–65
  means test and, 49
Repossession, 28, 83
Residency requirements, for federal
    exemptions, 74–75
Residential real estate leases, automatic
    stay exceptions for, 64–65
Retirement plans, 137–138
Rhode Island, 73, 195–196
Ride-through, of secured property in
    Chapter 7, 115–116, 118
Roth IRA, 19

Saving, 12–20
  incentives for, 18–20
  by payroll withdrawal, 14–15
  with spending diary, 16
  by spending only cash, 12–13
Schedules of assets and liabilities, 86–92
Sears, 2, 118
Section 707(b), *see* Means test
Secured creditors, 27–32, 81–83
  automatic stay and, 66–67
  Chapter 7 and, 28, 66–67, 83–84, 88, 92,
    115–118, 124
  Chapter 13 and, 28, 49, 53–54, 66–67,
    84, 128–134
  new law and filing date, 53–54
  schedules of, 88
Security interests, unperfected, 81
"Sell out" cases, *see* Chapter 7 bankruptcy
Serial filers, 64
Simester, Duncan, 25
Simplify Your Life (St. James), 19
Small businesses, 146–147
Social Security card, 93
South Carolina, 196–197
South Dakota, 197–198
Spending, ways to control, 9–11. *See also*
    Saving
Spending diary, 16, 38–42
St. James, Elaine, 19
State collection laws and exemptions,
    30–31, 72–73. *See also specific states*
Statement of affairs, 90–92
Statement of monthly net income, 98
Statutory (common law) liens, 30, 82
Straight bankruptcy cases, 32
Strip-down, in Chapter 13, 54, 130–134
Student loans, nondischargeable, 106
Subprime lending, 22
Substantial abuse provisions, 120
Super-discharge, elimination of, 145

Taxes:
  evasion of, 49
  nondischargeable, 104, 134–136

Tax refunds:
  filing timing and, 60–61
  new law and, 98
  post-petition assets and, 69
Tennessee, 198–199
Texas, 73–74, 84, 91, 199–200
341 meeting, 71, 93–96
Totality of circumstances test, 121
Transfers:
  fraudulent, 80–81, 113–114
  preferential, 46, 49, 79–80, 90
  unperfected, 81
Trigg, Tom, 53
Trustee, *see* Bankruptcy trustee

Unemployment, avoiding filing during,
    49
Universal default provisions, 23
Unperfected security interests, 81
Unsecured debts, 29, 32
Utah, 200–201

Valuation:
  exemptions and, 76–77
  for strip-down, 132
Venti, Steven, 14
Vermont, 73, 201–202
Virginia, 203–204
Voluntary liens, 29, 82–83

Warren, Amelia Tyagi, 41
Warren, Elizabeth, 7, 41
Washington (state), 73, 84, 91
West Virginia, 205–206
Wild-card category, of federal exemption,
    73–74
Wisconsin, 73, 84, 91, 206–207
Wise, David, 14
Wrongdoing, *see* Fraud
Wyoming, 207–208

Yingling, Ed, 22

Zero percent plans, in Chapter 13, 141